AIR WAR
KOREA

1950 - 1953

AIR WAR KOREA
1950-1953

ROBERT JACKSON

Motorbooks International
Publishers & Wholesalers ®

Acknowledgement

This is the second book I have written on the Korean air war. The first was over twenty years ago, and a lot has come to light since then through correspondence, archive material and so on, so I have incorporated as much as possible of it in the present work.

It takes an American to write a really good book on what was essentially an American war, and my fellow aviation writer Robert F. Dorr did just that, so I am grateful to him not only for his help and encouragement but also for allowing me to trawl his extensive photo archive for the colour illustrations. Thanks, Bob.

Robert Jackson
Darlington, County Durham, England
1997

This edition first published in 1998 by Motorbooks International, Publishers & Wholesalers, 729 Prospect Avenue, PO Box 1, Osceola, WI 54020, USA.

© Robert Jackson 1998

Previously published by Airlife Publishing Ltd, Shrewsbury, England.

Library of Congress Cataloging-in-Publication Data is available

ISBN 0-7603–0551–X

Printed and bound in Singapore.

Contents

A List of Abbreviations

AAA	Anti-Aircraft Artillery
AACS	Airways and Air Communications Service
AB	Air Base
AFB	Air Force Base
ANG	Air National Guard
AOP	Air Observation Post
ARS	Air Rescue Service (Squadron)
ATG	Air Task Group
AWRS	All-Weather Reconnaissance Squadron
AWS	Air Weather Squadron
Bcn	Beacon
BG	Bombardment Group
BS	Bombardment Squadron
BW	Bombardment Wing
BW(L)	Bombardment Wing (Light)
CAP	Combat Air Patrol
CCF	Chinese Communist Forces
CPAF	Chinese People's Air Force
DZ	Dropping Zone
ECM	Electronic Countermeasures
Eng Avn Battn	Engineer Aviation Battalion
FAA	Fleet Air Arm
FAC	Forward Air Controller
FAWS	Fighter All-Weather Squadron
FBG	Fighter Bomber Group
FBS	Fighter Bomber Squadron
FBW	Fighter Bomber Wing
FEAF	Far East Air Force
FEG	Fighter Escort Group
FES	Fighter Escort Squadron
FEW	Fighter Escort Wing
FIG	Fighter Interceptor Group
FIS	Fighter Interceptor Squadron
FIW	Fighter Interceptor Wing
GCA	Ground Control Approach
GCI	Ground Controlled Interception
GMU	Guided Missile Unit
HVAR	High Velocity Aircraft Rocket
IFF	Identification Friend or Foe
JATO	Jet Assisted Take-off
JCS	Joint Chiefs of Staff
JOC	Joint Operations Centre
KIA	Killed in Action
KIFA	Killed in Flying Accident
MAG	Marine Air Group
MATS	Military Air Transport Service
MAW	Marine Air Wing
MLR	Main Line of Resistance
NKA	North Korean Army
NKAF	North Korean Air Force
PMF	Photo-Mapping Flight
POL	Petroleum, Oil and Lubricants
Post MoH	Posthumous Medal of Honor
PR	Photo Reconnaissance
PSP	Pierced Steel Planking
RAAF	Royal Australian Air Force
RAF	Royal Air Force
RCT	Regimental Combat Team
RN	Royal Navy
ROK	Republic of Korea
SAAF	South African Air Force
SAC	Strategic Air Command
SAP	Semi-Armour Piercing
SRS	Strategic Reconnaissance Squadron
SRW	Strategic Reconnaissance Wing
TAC	Tactical Air Command
Tac Con	Tactical Control
Tac Spt Gp.	Tactical Support Group
TCG	Troop Carrier Group
TCS	Troop Carrier Squadron
TCW	Troop Carrier Wing
TRS	Tactical Reconnaissance Squadron
TRW	Tactical Reconnaissance Wing
USAF	United States Air Force
UNC	United Nations Command
USMC	United States Marine Corps
USN	United States Navy

Introduction

In November 1943, British Prime Minister Winston Churchill, US President Franklin D. Roosevelt, and the Chinese Nationalist leader Generalissimo Chiang Kai-shek met in Cairo to thrash out plans for the re-shaping of the Far East after Japan's defeat. The Soviet Union, which was not then engaged in war against Japan, was not represented; its signature was added later. Among the pledges made at the Cairo Conference was that Korea, annexed by Japan in 1910, should once again become a free and independent state. Thus was laid the foundation of the issues that were to dominate international relations throughout the early 1950s, and which would bring the hitherto obscure name of this Asian peninsula to the front pages of the world's newspapers for three long and bloody years.

After the collapse of Japan in August 1945, the Soviet Union, exploiting the advantages of her belated entry into the war in the Far East, occupied the northern half of Korea. The 25th Army of the 1st Far Eastern Front, commanded by General I.M. Chistyakov and supported by units of the Soviet Pacific Fleet, broke over the border of North Korea on 9 August and quickly captured all strongly fortified points in the North Korean plain. By 15 August the Russians were able to set up a military government, administered from Pyongyang.

United States forces occupied the southern half of the country, and in order to facilitate the surrender of Japanese troops in Korea the United States and Russia agreed, purely for military purposes, that their respective zones of occupation would be separated by the 38th parallel of latitude. This demarcation was to have been a temporary measure until the promise of a unified, independent Korea – a promise underwritten by the Soviet Union on its entry into the Far Eastern war – became reality. But two years of haggling and bargaining achieved nothing; all attempts by the USA and USSR to reach agreement on the Korean independence issue and the withdrawal of their respective forces of occupation ended in failure. In 1947 the talks broke down completely, and in September of that year the US Government laid the whole question of Korea's future before the General Assembly of the United Nations. By this time Korea had become yet another pawn in the growing and worldwide power struggle between Russia and America, and the rift between the two halves of the country was becoming wider rapidly; the 38th Parallel, now far removed from a simple demarcation line running east–west across the waist of Korea, had been turned into a strongly fortified defensive wall.

A majority at the United Nations favoured all-Korean elections to unite the country, but the Russians, using their power of veto, rejected this outright and claimed that the future of Korea was a matter to be decided by the four signatories to the Cairo Agreement. The United Nations nevertheless went ahead and formed a Commission to supervise the elections for a Korean National Assembly; the Russians refused to allow the Commission into the Soviet-occupied zone. The result was that the UN-supervised voting was held only in the South, and in August 1948 it led to the establishment of the Republic of Korea under the presidency of Dr Syngman Rhee.

The Soviet military government of North Korea lasted until 26 December 1948, during which time the Russians were able to create a properly subservient indigenous regime led by Kim Il-sung. A minor guerrilla leader in Manchuria during the 1930s, Kim had disappeared into the USSR in 1941 or 1942, returning to Korea in 1945 as a captain in the Red Army; he was reported to have fought at Stalingrad, and the Russians built him up as a legendary figure who had been a terror to the Japanese during the guerrilla campaign in Manchuria.

The Soviet military government, faced with the task of creating a loyal and efficient North Korean army, held a trump card in Kim. First of all, a Peace Preservation Corps was set up in 1946, a force of 20,000 men equipped with captured Japanese weapons, its task ostensibly to guard the borders and rail communications; in reality it was the nucleus of a future army, and one of its first jobs was to hold in check the so-called Yenan group of Korean exiles who had been trained by Mao Tse-tung's Chinese Communist regime. With the Stalinist faction firmly in control, some 10,000 young men were sent to Siberia and trained as future officers in the Soviet military schools at Khabarovsk and Chita. Finally, on 8 February 1948, the North Korean People's Army, some 60,000 men, was officially activated as a regular army, and in September that year the Democratic People's Republic of Korea came into being at Pyongyang, with Kim Il-sung at the helm.

The majority of the western nations recognised the Republic of Korea in the South, while the Democratic People's Republic had the recognition and support of the Soviet Union and its satellites. The two republics faced each other across the 38th Parallel, each antagonistic towards the other, each claiming jurisdiction over the entire country, and each backed by the political, economic and military power of a giant nation.

North Korea was now almost completely sealed off. The American intelligence network there was virtually non-existent, and consequently neither the Republic of Korea nor the US Government was aware of the extent of the military build-up that was taking place north of the Parallel. Although there was no denying that a real threat to the security of South Korea existed –

skirmishing along the 38th Parallel had become an almost daily occurrence by the winter of 1949–50 – the Americans believed that it would take the form of terrorism, psychological warfare, and guerrilla attacks. The Americans, in fact, were so confident that that there would be no communist invasion of the South, at least for the foreseeable future, that they withdrew their troops in the summer of 1949. In any case, American strategic planning was dictated by the belief that any future conflict would be global, and the US Joint Chiefs of Staff considered Korea to be outside the US defensive perimeter in the Pacific.

They failed to appreciate the fact that Russian military planners were thinking along somewhat different lines. The Russians were well aware that communist domination of South Korea would greatly strengthen their own Pacific defences; moreover, a communist takeover would in all probability lend weight to anti-American factions in Japan at a time when the United States was negotiating a peace treaty with her former enemy. (In fact, this was not ratified until April 1952.)

Such, in brief, was the sequence of events that was to precipitate the Korean War. But if the Americans had made their mistakes, so had the Russians. In the early hours of 25 June 1950, when eight North Korean divisions stood poised for an invasion of the South, the architects of the offensive in Pyongyang and Moscow did not consider it likely that armed communist aggression in South Korea would be resisted by force from outside. They were wrong.

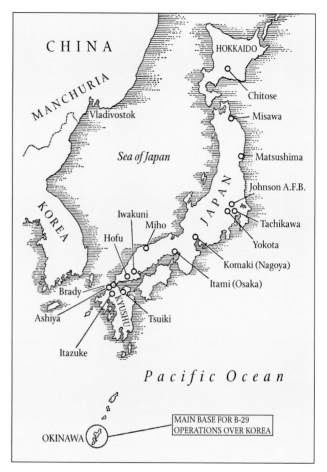

United Nations' air bases in Japan, 1950-53.

CHAPTER 1

Invasion

Crews of the 339th FS (All Weather) in the process of converting from Northrop P-61 Black Widows to North American F-82 Twin Mustangs at Johnson AB, Japan in 1949, some months before the outbreak of the Korean War. (Martin Bambrick)

The North Korean Army launched its attack on the South at dawn on Sunday, 25 June 1950, the infantry assault heralded by a fierce artillery bombardment and led by squadrons of Russian-built T-34 tanks. The breakthrough was achieved quickly, and while the tanks rolled on towards their first objectives, Kaesong and Chunchon, more North Korean troops, including marines, were landed at Kangnung on Korea's east coast in an armada of small craft. By 0900 Kaesong was in North Korean hands and the seaborne columns were pushing steadily inland to link up with the forces that had crossed the 38th Parallel. The North Koreans' choice of a Sunday morning for their invasion of the South was not accidental. Shrewdly, their military commanders had reasoned that any possible American response would be at its lowest level on a Sunday, with many military personnel absent on weekend leave. After all, there had been a precedent – the Japanese attack on Pearl Harbor less than a decade earlier, which had caught the main American base in the Pacific completely off balance.

In 1950, the formation best placed to mount a military response against North Korea was the United States Fifth Air Force which, based on the Japanese Home Islands since 1945, formed the front line of America's air defences in the Far East against the potential air threat from the Soviet Union. The backbone of the Fifth AF's defensive capability was the

Lockheed F-80C Shooting Star fighter-bomber, which equipped the 35th Fighter Interceptor Wing at Yokota, near Tokyo, the 68th Fighter Bomber Wing at Itazuke Air Base on Kyushu, and the 49th Fighter Bomber Wing at Misawa on northern Honshu. The PR version of the Shooting Star, the RF-80A, also equipped the 8th Tactical Reconnaissance Squadron at Yokota. There were also two all-weather fighter units, the 68th Fighter All-Weather Squadron at Itazuke and the 339th Fighter All-Weather Squadron at Yokota, both equipped with North American F-82 Twin Mustangs; two tactical light bomber squadrons of the 3rd Bombardment Wing, equipped with Douglas B-26s and based at Johnson Air Base (AB), north of Tokyo; and a transport echelon in the shape of the 374th Troop Carrier Wing, operating out of Tachikawa AB with two squadrons of Douglas C-54s.

Commanded by Major-General Earle E. Partridge, the Fifth AF was the largest subordinate command of the US Far East Air Forces (FEAF), holding as it did a position of vital importance at the edge of the US defensive shield in the Pacific. In the event of war with the USSR it would be the first to absorb an attack from the mainland of Asia, and as a result its level of readiness was expected to be high. The perceived threat had grown considerably since the summer of 1949, when the Soviet Union had detonated its first atomic device, robbing the United States of the nuclear weapons monopoly it had hitherto enjoyed. The other subordinate commands of FEAF were the Twentieth Air Force, based on Okinawa and the Marianas, and the Thirteenth Air Force in the Philippines. In addition to the fighter interceptor and fighter all-weather units equipped with F-80 and F-82 aircraft, the Twentieth AF also had two squadrons of B-29 Superfortress long-range medium bombers, deployed with the 19th Bombardment Group and based on Andersen Air Base, Guam. Also attached to the Twentieth AF was a USAF Strategic Air Command unit, the 31st Photo-Reconnaissance Squadron, equipped with long-range RB-29s and based on Kadena AB, Okinawa, which it shared with the 51st Fighter Interceptor Wing and the 4th Fighter All-Weather Squadron, the former equipped with F-80s and the latter with F-82s. In the Philippines, the Thirteenth Air Force's assets were the 18th Fighter Bomber Wing at Clark AB, with F-80s, and the C-54s of the 21st Troop Carrier Squadron. The Far East Air Forces were commanded by General George E. Stratemeyer.

On the morning of the North Korean invasion, General Stratemeyer, who had been attending a conference in Washington, was airborne over the Pacific, en route from San Francisco to Hawaii. General Partridge, Stratemeyer's deputy, was on weekend leave in Nagoya with his family. Although first reports of the invasion were received by FEAF HQ at 0945, it was not until 1130 that General Partridge was made aware of the situation, and at this juncture he was powerless to order his combat units to intervene. The Fifth Air Force's operational plan in the event of an outbreak of hostilities in Korea was to evacuate US nationals, and even this plan could only be implemented on the direct request of the US ambassador in Seoul. If the North

Koreans attempted to interfere with the evacuation of US nationals, Partridge would be permitted to release his aircraft for attacks on enemy ground targets, but only when such operations were duly authorised by General Douglas MacArthur, the Supreme Commander Allied Powers in the Pacific Theatre. Detailed plans for the evacuation of American personnel from Korea were already in place, and General Partridge, anticipating an early call from the US ambassador, quickly deployed his forces in readiness to carry them out. Colonel John M. Price, commanding the 8th Fighter Bomber Wing, was appointed officer in charge of the operation. Air cover over the South Korean airfields and ports from which the evacuation would take place was to be provided by F-80s and F-82s, while the sea areas off Korea were to be patrolled by the B-26s of the 3rd Bombardment Wing, operating out of Ashiya AB. By the end of the afternoon, Price had assembled a transport force of twelve C-54s and three C-47s, and informed Fifth AF that these could be in place and ready to begin the airlift by 0330 the next morning, 26 June.

In the meantime, reports from Korea painted a more encouraging picture, suggesting that after the initial shock of the invasion the Republic of Korea (ROK) Army was beginning to rally and fight back, blunting the impetus of the enemy advance. Nevertheless, the appearance of North Korean Yak-9 fighters over Kimpo and Seoul airfields underlined the potential air threat to the planned evacuation; the Republic of Korea Air Force – comprising sixty aircraft, all trainers – had nothing with which to oppose them.

This lamentable state of affairs was a direct result of United States policy. Following repeated pleas by President Syngman Rhee, Major-General Claire L. Chennault, who had commanded the American

A Lockheed F-80C Shooting Star of the USAF's 44th FBS (the 'Vampires') on a flight from Clark Field in the Philippines just before the outbreak of the Korean War. (Duane E. Biteman)

Pilots of No 77 Squadron, RAAF, with F-51D Mustang, pictured at Yonpo airfield in December 1950.

Volunteer Group and later the US Fourteenth Air Force in China during World War Two, had drawn up a plan for a South Korean Air Force comprising ninety-nine aircraft, including twenty-five North American F-51 Mustang fighter bombers, but this had been rejected by General MacArthur, who considered that the build-up of such a force would serve to increase the tension that already existed between North and South Korea and would lend weight to communist claims that the United States was deliberately seeking to promote an arms race in the area. The result was that when the North Koreans invaded the South, they enjoyed complete and overwhelming air superiority. On 25 June 1950 the North Korean Air Force (NKAF) possessed a total of 132 combat aircraft, comprising sixty-two Ilyushin Il-10 ground-attack machines and seventy Yak-3, Yak-7B, Yak-9 and La-7 fighters. There were also twenty-two Yak-18 twin-engined light transports and eight Polikarpov Po-2 trainer aircraft. The majority of the combat types were concentrated on two principal airfields at Pyongyang and Yonpo, but by the time war broke out several flights had been moved forward to advanced airstrips near the 38th Parallel. Unlike the North Korean Army, which was composed largely of conscripts, the pilots of the infant NKAF were all volunteers and, although they lacked operational experience, their eagerness and willingness to fight

were not in doubt. The NKAF's Russian instructors were all carefully selected veterans of World War Two and the North Korean students were given a thorough grounding in the tactical lessons learned by the Soviet Air Forces on the Eastern Front between 1941 and 1945.

It was not long before the North Korean pilots demonstrated their aggressive tendencies. At 1500 on 25 June, following the earlier appearance of two Yak-9s on what was probably a reconnaissance flight, another pair of Yaks made a strafing attack on Kimpo airfield, hitting the control tower and blowing up a fuel dump. A US Military Air Transport Service C-54 was also hit and damaged. While this attack was in progress four more Yaks strafed Seoul, damaging seven training aircraft, and at 1900 a second attack was made on Kimpo. This time the North Korean pilots concentrated on the C-54 damaged in the earlier raid, and completed its destruction.

The US Government, meanwhile, had asked for and obtained an emergency meeting of the United Nations Security Council to consider the implications of the North Korean invasion, and late on the 25th the Council adopted a resolution calling for the cessation of hostilities and the withdrawal of North Korean forces above the 38th Parallel. The Council also called on all member nations to assist the UN in the execution of the resolution. The Soviet delegation was absent from this

North American F-82G Twin Mustang on patrol over Korea, 1950. (via Robert F. Dorr)

crucial meeting, and was therefore unable to exercise its power of veto; the Russians were never to make the same mistake again.

Shortly before midnight, with North Korean tanks only seventeen miles north of Seoul, the United States ambassador, John J. Muccio, ordered the evacuation of all American women and children from the South Korean capital and from Inchon. On his orders several freighters were already standing by in Inchon harbour, ready to embark the evacuees and take them to Japan. In the early hours of 26 June General MacArthur ordered General Partridge to provide fighter cover over Inchon during the embarkation and subsequent withdrawal. The fighters were forbidden to venture over the Korean mainland, and were to engage in combat only if the transport ships were directly threatened. The only

aircraft really suitable for carrying out this patrol task, because of the distances involved, was the F-82 Twin Mustang. Colonel Jack Price had at his disposal twelve serviceable F-82s of the 68th Fighter All-Weather Squadron, but these were too few to carry out effective standing patrols. The only other unit based on Honshu that might have been able to help was No. 77 Squadron, Royal Australian Air Force, which operated F-51 Mustangs out of Iwakuni Air Base. However, the reaction of the British Commonwealth to the events in Korea was not yet known, and although No. 77 Squadron was technically at the disposal of the Supreme Commander Allied Powers, General MacArthur, the idea of asking for Australian assistance at this stage was rejected. In an effort to resolve the problem, General Partridge ordered the 339th All-

Weather Squadron to redeploy its F-82s from Yokota to Itazuke, and also requested the Twentieth Air Force to dispatch eight F-82s of the 4th Squadron to Itazuke from their base on Okinawa.

The evacuation got underway at first light on 26 June, the majority of the refugees embarking on a Norwegian vessel. Overhead the F-82s circled watchfully in flights of four, a few hundred feet below the cloud base. The evacuation proceeded without interference during the morning, but at 1330 there was a sudden alarm when a North Korean La-7 fighter dropped down out of the clouds and attacked a flight of F-82s. The American fighter pilots took evasive action, and after this single pass the enemy fighter climbed steeply back into the clouds and disappeared. This action was taken to present a direct threat to the evacuation, and during the

remainder of the day the F-82s ventured inland to cover evacuation convoys en route from Seoul to Inchon. After dark the fighters continued to accompany the merchantman as it headed out into the Yellow Sea, only breaking contact when the ship was met by an escort of American destroyers. On the 27th, the maritime patrol task off the Korean coast was assumed by Navy Patrol Squadron VP-47, based at Iwakuni and equipped with Martin PBM-5 Mariners.

The airlift of evacuees from Seoul and Kimpo also got underway on 27 June, the day on which US President Harry S. Truman ordered sea and air forces in the Far East to give support and cover to the ROK forces, in effect authorising an armed conflict if necessary. Finding transport aircraft to carry out the airlift had presented something of a problem: the C-54s of the

374th Wing were widely dispersed on routine duties, and only two were immediately available to Colonel Price. The situation was saved by the arrival of eleven C-47s, hastily assembled from various FEAF transport units. The first transports took off from Itazuke before dawn, escorted by F-82s. At daybreak, while the transports landed at Kimpo and Suwon under the protection of the Twin Mustangs, two flights of F-80 Shooting Stars of the 8th Fighter Bomber Wing arrived over the Han river and began a high-level patrol, covering the approaches to the South Korean capital.

The patrolling fighters encountered no enemy opposition until midday, when five Yak-7s appeared over Seoul and initiated an attack on Kimpo. They were intercepted by five F-82s of the 68th and 339th Squadrons, and in a five-minute air battle three Yaks were shot down, the first by Lt William G. Hudson of the 58th Squadron, to whom fell the distinction of destroying the first communist aircraft over Korea. The other American pilots who scored were Major James W. Little and Lt Charles B. Moran. An hour later the North Koreans launched a second attack, this time with eight Il-10 fighter-bombers. The intruders were sighted over Seoul by the pilots of four F-80s of the 35th Fighter Bomber Squadron, who dived down to intercept. Two Il-10s were destroyed by Lt Robert E. Wayne, while Captain Raymond E. Schillereff and Lt Robert H. Dewald shot down one each. The surviving Ilyushins ran for the 38th Parallel and the Americans, with no orders to pursue, broke off the combat and resumed their patrol. There were no more attempts to interfere with the evacuation during the remainder of that day.

Late on 27 June, General MacArthur, acting on President Truman's authority, directed General Partridge to employ the Fifth Air Force's B-26s, F-80s and F-82s against enemy armour, artillery, military convoys, supply dumps, bridges and troop concentrations; in short, the American pilots were given *carte blanche* to operate freely between the front line and the 38th Parallel, seeking out targets of opportunity. The 374th Troop Carrier Wing, now that its primary task of evacuating American non-combatants was completed, was to begin an immediate airlift of ammunition and war materiél to South Korea.

It was soon apparent that implementing this directive would not be easy. For one thing, the 3rd Bombardment Wing's 8th Squadron, which had been assigned the task of night interdiction, had only four B-26s immediately available; the other six were on patrol duty over the Yellow Sea. The four available aircraft did take off to attack enemy armour north of Seoul on the night of 27/28 June, but they failed to find their targets in the darkness and deteriorating weather and returned with their bombs still on board. A second B-26 mission also had to be abandoned for the same reason. However, the weather report for the following morning lent some encouragement: although there would be low cloud and heavy rain over the Fifth Air Force's Japanese bases, reconnaissance by an RF-80A at dawn indicated that the weather over Korea was clearing slightly, and that if the strike aircraft could get airborne there was a good chance they might be able to find and hit their targets.

The first strike on 28 June was launched at 0730, when twelve B-26s took off from Ashiya to attack the rail marshalling yards at Munsan near the 38th Parallel. The target was successfully bombed, the B-26s afterwards attacking enemy troops and motor transport in the area with rockets and machine-guns. The enemy suffered heavily, but almost all the B-26s were damaged. One made an emergency landing at Suwon, another was so badly damaged that it had to be scrapped, and a third crashed on landing at Ashiya, killing its crew. Nine more B-26s which attacked targets north of Seoul later that day returned safely to base.

The Douglas B-26, used extensively in Korea, carried a powerful armament of 0.50 machine-guns, rocket projectiles and up to 4,000lb of bombs.

Pilot and ground crew member alongside an F-80C of the 80th FBS, Korea, 1950. (via Robert F. Dorr)

During the afternoon the programme of strikes was continued by Fifth AF's F-82s and F-80s, the latter doing particularly good work despite the fact that their time in the target area was restricted to only a few minutes. Shortly before dusk four B-29s of the 19th Bombardment Group arrived over Korea from Guam and bombed road and rail communications north of Seoul.

In the afternoon of 28 June the North Korean Air Force again entered the battle when four Yak-9s strafed Suwon airfield at 1330, destroying the 8th Squadron B-26 which had made an emergency landing there earlier and also an F-82 of the 68th Squadron which had been compelled to land with mechanical trouble. At 1830 three pairs of Yaks appeared over the field as a C-54 of the 22nd Troop Carrier Squadron was approaching to land; the transport was damaged but the pilot managed to get away and returned to Ashiya, where he landed safely. A second C-54 on the ground was hit and set on fire.

In the evening of 27 June an Advance Command and Liaison Group (ADCOM) under the command of Brigadier-General John H. Church was set up adjacent to HQ ROK Army at Suwon, its task to co-ordinate and control all US military activities in Korea. Church had practically no information on the situation at the battlefront to act upon; even the C-in-C ROK Army had no real idea where his units were located. He only knew that they had suffered forty per cent casualties in the last two days, and that up to seventy per cent of the army's automatic weapons and artillery pieces had fallen into North Korean hands. Church's first priority was to set up an effective logistics machine to ensure the smooth flow of American aid to Korea, and he appointed a USAF officer, Lt-Col John McGinn, to set up facilities at Suwon for the handling of the airlift from Itazuke. The first transport aircraft arrived the following morning, laden with arms and ammunition.

McGinn also drew up a list of priority front-line targets which he sent back to Itazuke with the transport crews for evaluation. During this time Suwon was virtually cut off from the outside world; it was not until 29 June that a high-frequency radio set with sufficient range to reach Tokyo was flown in. In the meantime, one important step taken by McGinn was to set up a ground–air link with US fighter-bombers using the only two VHF sets available to him.

The first offensive mission of 29 June was carried out on the direct orders of General MacArthur and involved a strike on Kimpo airfield, now in North Korean hands, by nine B-29s of the 19th Group from Kadena armed with 500lb bombs. The attack went in at 3,000 feet and was challenged by three Yak-9s, one of which was shot down and a second damaged. In the afternoon, at the request of General Church, B-26s attacked bridges on the Han river while F-82s bombed and strafed troops in the vicinity, the 68th Squadron using napalm for the first time in Korea. Some ground attack missions were also flown by F-80s, although the main task of the jet fighters was to patrol the Han at 10,000 feet on the lookout for enemy aircraft. The fighters broke up five separate attempts by the NKAF to attack Suwon airfield, shooting down an La-7 and an Il-10, but in a sixth attack three Il-10s broke through to Suwon and destroyed a C-54 on the ground. The biggest fighter effort of the day was mounted in mid-afternoon when F-80s of the 8th FBW, together with a flight of Mustangs which were about to be delivered to the ROK Air Force, orbited in relays over Suwon to cover the arrival of a C-54 carrying General MacArthur, who had decided to fly to Korea to make a first-hand appraisal of the situation. An hour after his arrival, four Yak-9s attempted to attack the airfield and were intercepted by the Mustangs; two were quickly shot down by Lt Orrin R. Fox of the 8th Squadron, a third by Lt Harry T. Sandlin of the same unit, and the fourth by Lt Richard J.

15

Burns of the 35th Squadron.

After touring ROK defences on the Han river, MacArthur contacted General Stratemeyer and authorised FEAF to begin immediate attacks on NKAF airfields north of the 38th Parallel. The first of these was carried out at dusk by eighteen B-26s of the 3rd BG, which attacked the airfield at Pyongyang with fragmentation bombs and destroyed about twenty-five enemy aircraft on the ground. The bombers were attacked by a lone Yak-3, which was shot down. The majority of the NKAF airfields north of the 38th Parallel were photographed by RF-80As of the 8th Tactical Reconnaissance Squadron soon after first light on 30 June, but there was no immediate major offensive against them as the main American air effort throughout the day was devoted to attacks on North Korean military formations massing on the north bank of the Han river. As a result, fifteen B-29s of the 19th BG, originally scheduled for a strike on Wonsan airfield, were diverted to carry out attacks on enemy forces north of the Han with 260lb fragmentation bombs. Meanwhile, eighteen B-26s of the 3rd BG carried out intensive attacks on enemy convoys in the Seoul area; during one sortie, the American crews located a long convoy of armoured and soft-skinned vehicles piled nose to tail along a stretch of roadway leading to a bridge that was under repair, and wiped it out in a five-minute attack using rockets and machine guns.

The Shooting Stars, meanwhile, continued to fly combat air patrols over the battle area. The pilots saw few enemy aircraft, but in the afternoon of 30 June two Yak-9s were shot down by Lts Charles A. Wurster and John B. Thomas of the 36th Squadron. That same afternoon, the 36th Squadron suffered the first American jet casualty of the Korean War when one of its pilots, diving down to attack an enemy target towards the end of his patrol, flew through high-tension cables and lost part of his wing. He was left with just enough control to enable him to reach friendly territory before bailing out.

Generally speaking, the relatively small number of ground attack missions flown in support of the ROK forces on 30 June produced no effective result, and it was clear that there could be no increase in the sortie rate as long as the fighter bombers continued to operate from Japanese bases. In the evening of 30 June, therefore, General Stratemeyer directed the Fifth AF to establish combat units on Korean airfields, with the main concentration on Suwon. In the course of the day President Truman had announced to the world that in keeping with the UN Security Council request for support to the Republic of

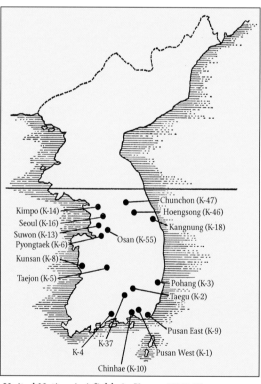

United Nations' airfields in Korea, 1950-53.

Korea, he had authorised the USAF to bomb targets in North Korea, the use of US Army ground troops in action to support ROK forces, and had directed a naval blockade of the entire Korean coast. The conduct of the war was now firmly in the hands of the military commanders.

By the time Stratemeyer's order was received, it was apparent that the Allied position at Suwon was rapidly becoming untenable. The ROK defensive line along the Han river was rapidly crumbling, and the North Koreans had already established bridgeheads on the south bank of the river. At 1800 General Church told the assembled staff of ADCOM that he had no alternative but to order the evacuation of Suwon, and at 2130 the American personnel set off in convoy for Taejon. Only hours later, in darkness and pouring rain, the first North Korean infantry infiltrated Suwon airfield.

Meanwhile, following high-level discussions between the Pentagon and US Headquarters in Tokyo, the decision had been taken to establish a new defensive line in Korea in the event of a massive enemy breakthrough across the Han river. New defences were to be established along the line of the 36th Parallel to the north of Taegu, running east–west across the country. Priority was to be given to the defence of the vital port of Pusan and to the airfields of Pusan and Taegu. To ensure the defence of these positions, President Truman authorised American combat troops to be sent to South Korea from Japan, although he emphasised that such troops were not to be used in direct combat with the enemy. The latter decision ran contrary to the wishes of General MacArthur who, following his tour of the ROK defences on the Han river, was convinced that North Korean forces would soon be in Seoul unless there was a large and immediate injection of US troops into the combat area to assist the beleaguered ROK. He said so in a report to the US Joint Chiefs of Staff, adding that 'to continue to utilise the forces of our Air and Navy without an effective ground element cannot be decisive'.

Once the North Korean advance had been checked in the Suwon area with American help, MacArthur told the Pentagon that plans should be laid for a rapid counter-offensive using two divisions of US infantry from Japan. Truman concurred and authorised the transfer of a regimental combat team to the Suwon area, promising to make an early decision regarding the future commitment of larger numbers of American troops to the conflict. MacArthur, anticipating a positive response from the highest command level, had already ordered units of the 24th Infantry Division to readiness on Kyushu for immediate transfer to Pusan. Fewer than five years after the end of the Pacific war, American troops were once again preparing for action.

CHAPTER 2
The Combat Arena

Douglas AD-4 on a bombing mission over mountainous Korean terrain. (via Robert F. Dorr)

hile General MacArthur strove to plug the widening gaps in South Korea's defences, the naval blockade of the Korean coast was gradually being established. On 30 June, with the British Government's backing for United Nations action in Korea secured, the aircraft carrier HMS *Triumph* arrived in Korean waters from Hong Kong accompanied by two cruisers, two destroyers and three frigates, and on the following day the USS *Valley Forge* and her escorts also took up station in the Yellow Sea, the Allied force operating under the designation Task Force 77.

It was the British force that opened the naval war off Korea when, at dawn on 2 July 1950, the cruiser HMS *Jamaica* and the sloop *Black Swan* engaged six North Korean MTBs that were presenting a threat to the aircraft carriers and sank five of them. At 0545 the next morning, the carrier aircraft flew their first strikes against targets in North Korea. Twelve Fairey Firefly fighter-bombers of No. 827 Squadron and nine rocket-armed Seafire 47s of No. 800 Squadron were launched

by HMS *Triumph* to attack Haeju airfield, with railways and bridges as secondary targets. The aircraft returned safely, although some had minor flak damage. At 0600, the *Valley Forge*'s Air Group 5 (VF-51 and VF-52 with Grumman F9F-3 Panthers, VF-53 and VF-54 with Vought F4U-4 Corsairs, and VA-55 with Douglas AD-4 Skyraiders), thirty-six aircraft in all, struck at rail bridges, railway yards, airfields and roads in the Pyongyang area. Some NKAF Yak-9s tried to intervene, and two were shot down by Panthers of VF-51, sweeping ahead of the strike aircraft, flown by Lt (JG) L.H. Plog, who was credited with the first US Navy kill of the war, and Ensign E.W. Brown. The carriers mounted further air strikes that day and on 4 July, destroying three hangars and some aircraft on the ground at Pyongyang as well as bombing and strafing rolling stock, buildings and various installations in the city. Four Skyraiders were slightly damaged by flak, and one of them caused far more trouble than the enemy when, unable to lower its flaps, it bounced over *Valley Forge*'s crash barriers, landed among the aircraft

Letters from home: US Navy crewmen take a break on the USS Valley Forge.

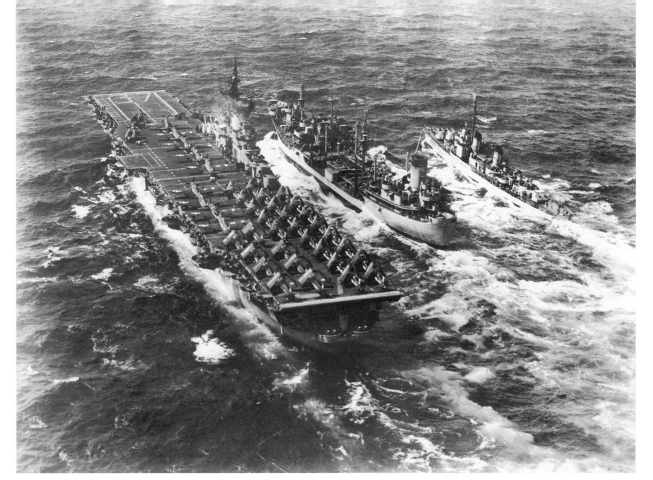

F4U-4 Corsairs aboard the USS Princeton. *The carrier and her destroyer escort are accompanied by an Underway Replenishment Ship.*

parked forward on deck, destroyed a Skyraider and two Corsairs and badly damaged another three Skyraiders, two Panthers and a Corsair. The carriers withdrew from the combat zone for replenishment at sea on 5 July.

Meanwhile, plans for the rapid airlift of the 24th Infantry Division to Korea by the 374th Transport Wing had been frustrated by bad weather, which had clamped down after only six C-54s had flown to Pusan with their loads of troops on 1 July. It was not until the next morning that the airlift began in earnest, and now another problem arose: Pusan's primitive runway was taking such a pounding from the four-engined transports that by the afternoon of 2 July it was virtually unusable. Major-General Edward J. Timberlake, Acting Commander of the Fifth Air Force in the temporary absence of General Partridge, accordingly ordered the 374th Wing to continue the operation with lighter, twin-engined C-46s and C-47s. The runway held, and by nightfall on 4 July the 374th had flown in the two battalions of the 24th Division (which was under strength) as well as the Divisional HQ and a Regimental Combat Team of the 21st Infantry Division.

The commanders in the field were appalled by what they found. For example, there were no firm plans for the all-important support of ground forces by tactical aircraft once the troops entered combat; a formula for effective air–ground co-operation, a lesson learned so well in World War Two and apparently forgotten in the five short years since then, had to be worked out from scratch. In the meantime, the American effort had to be sustained largely as a result of personal initiative on the part of certain commanders. A good example of this was the decision taken by General Hoyt S. Vandenberg, the USAF Chief of Staff, to authorise the immediate move of two medium bombardment groups, the 22nd and 92nd, to the Far East from their bases in the United States. The 22nd went to Kadena Air Base, Okinawa,

and the 92nd to Yokota, Japan. On arrival the two groups joined the 19th Bomb Group to form the FEAF Bomber Command (Provisional), which was manned mainly by Strategic Air Command (SAC) personnel. Its first commander was Major-General Emmett 'Rosie' O'Donnell, who was temporarily pulled out of his job as commander of the Fifteenth Air Force to direct the bombing effort in Korea. SAC's 31st Strategic Reconnaissance Squadron, whose RB-29s were on temporary duty (TDY) at Kadena when the Korean conflict began, was also attached to FEAF Bomber Command.

The lack of co-ordination was particularly apparent in the time it took to get messages from ADCOM in Korea to the Advance HQ of Fifth AF in Japan. Requests for air support of any kind had to follow a tortuous route through GHQ in Tokyo and FEAF before they finally reached Itazuke, and delays of up to four hours, even with urgent messages, were normal. The dangers resulting from this lack of an effective communications system were tragically highlighted when, on 3 July, Fifth AF HQ received a report that a strong North Korean convoy was pushing southwards between Osan and Suwon. Five Mustangs of No. 77 Squadron, Royal Australian Air Force, now released for combat duty by the Australian Government, were detailed to attack the convoy. What the Australian pilots did not know was that it was at least five hours since the original report had been sent out, and that the location they had been given was an estimated one. Arriving over the sector indicated to them by Fifth AF Operations, the Australians sighted a long line of soft-skinned vehicles moving slowly southwards along a road near Suwon, and attacked it. Later they learned that their target had been an ROK convoy filled with retreating troops, who had suffered severe casualties as a result of the air attack. It was only No. 77's second mission in Korea,

and the incident did nothing to improve the morale of the Australians, who had been on the point of going home when hostilities started. One immediate consequence was that General MacArthur ordered the ROK forces to paint large and distinctive white stars on the bonnets of their vehicles so that the latter could be readily identified from the air. No. 77 Squadron's first mission had been to escort B-29s attacking the North Korean airfield of Yongpu on 2 July. The Squadron suffered its first casualty five days later when Sqn Ldr G. Strout in Mustang A68-757 failed to pull out of a dive in an attack on Samchok railway station.

By the end of the first week of July, it was becoming clear that the plan to stiffen the resistance of the ROK forces with the help of the US 24th Infantry Division had failed. Lightly armed American infantry, outnumbered by ten to one, lacking supporting artillery and armour and an effective forward air control system, were no match for the North Koreans' T-34 tanks, and on 6 July they were in full retreat towards Chonan. This location also had to be evacuated fewer than twenty-four hours later, producing an extremely critical situation and threatening the Allies' tenuous hold on the Pusan perimeter. Failing a massive and early injection of suitably equipped ground forces, the only card the Allies had left to play was tactical air power, and even this was restricted by the problem of range. It was an unfortunate handicap, because at this juncture the North Korean People's Army, strung out in long convoys on narrow roads as it pushed southwards, was extremely vulnerable to air attack. The only aircraft able to carry enough fuel to permit a reasonable loiter time in the target area were the B-26s of the 3rd Bombardment Wing, whose crews seldom returned from a mission without reporting some success against enemy ground forces. Most of the unit's aircraft were solid-nosed B-26Bs, which in addition to the usual war load of bombs and rockets carried a powerful punch in the shape of up to fourteen fixed forward-firing guns. These aircraft accounted for a high proportion of the 197 trucks and forty-four tanks knocked out in the area between Pyongtaek and Seoul during the three days between 7 and 9 July.

It was the Fifth Air Force's F-80 Shooting Stars, however, which bore the main burden of the ground attack work during this phase, completing a good two-thirds of all combat sorties flown, and the pilots quickly built up a high level of experience, particularly in the use of the five-inch high-velocity aircraft rocket (HVAR) against enemy armour. Each Shooting Star could carry up to sixteen of these projectiles in addition to its primary armament of eight 0.50 machine-guns; in this configuration, and with a full fuel load on take-off, its combat radius was 225 miles and it had a loiter time over the target of about fifteen minutes. Pilots were unanimous in their praise of the F-80 in the ground attack role. Its high speed gave it an important element of surprise, and because there was no propeller torque to cope with it was a far better gun platform than any conventional propeller-driven machine. The F-80C could also carry a pair of 1,000lb bombs in place of its 165-gallon wingtip fuel tanks, but this reduced its combat radius to about 100 miles. Improvements were clearly necessary, and General Partridge assigned the

Sikorsky HO3S-1 rescue helicopter on a Navy carrier off Korea. (via Robert F. Dorr)

task of working out a solution to the 49th Fighter Bomber Wing, whose engineers soon provided one by fitting the two centre sections of a Fletcher fuel tank into the middle of the standard Lockheed wingtip tank carried by the F-80, creating a new tank with a capacity of 265 gallons. By the end of July about a quarter of the Japan-based F-80 units had received the modified tanks, increasing the loiter time in the target area to forty-five minutes or thereabouts.

A request for an additional 164 F-80Cs was at the top of the list of urgent aircraft requirements sent to Washington by General Stratemeyer at the end of June. The list also included an additional sixty-four F-51 Mustangs and twenty-one F-82s, both of which types were suitable for long-range ground attack work. The Mustangs were to be used to form a new fighter-bomber group based on Iwakuni; meanwhile, General Stratemeyer ordered the Thirteenth Air Force to form an F-51 Squadron at Johnson AB with thirty Mustangs taken from storage. All the other aircraft on Stratemeyer's list were needed for existing FEAF units, some of which were seriously under strength; a second requirements message, dated 1 July, requested the immediate despatch to Korea of one medium bombardment wing, two Mustang wings, two F-82 all-weather squadrons, a B-26 wing and finally two B-26 squadrons to reinforce the 3rd Bombardment Wing. A

that most were needed for the all-weather defence of the continental United States (a role they would continue to fulfil until the deployment of the Northrop F-89 Scorpion from 1950), there was a critical shortage of spares which frustrated any move to make good the combat attrition suffered by the Fifth AF's F-82s in Korea. As far as the F-51 Mustangs were concerned, the position was a little rosier: 764 of these aircraft were in service with Air National Guard (ANG) units, and a further 794 were in storage.

Upon receipt of Stratemeyer's requirements list 145 F-51s were recalled from the ANG and made ready for shipment to Korea on the aircraft carrier USS *Boxer*, together with pilots and ground crews. The plan was to deploy a proportion of these aircraft to the airfields still in South Korean hands at the earliest possible opportunity, but in July 1950 the only such airfield suitable for operations even by piston-engined combat aircraft was Taegu, and even that had little to offer: the runway was made of packed earth and gravel that quickly turned to mud in heavy rain, and the amenities consisted of a few ramshackle buildings. There was only one latrine on the entire base, and the men existed on C-rations and bathed in the nearby river for want of kitchen and shower facilities.

Since 30 June Taegu, known also by the military designation K-2, had been the home of ten worn-out

F-80C of the 51st FIW heading out on a bombing mission, 1950. (via Robert F. Dorr)

few days later the requirement was extended to include an RF-51 tactical reconnaissance squadron, an RB-26 night photographic reconnaissance squadron and a tactical air control squadron.

Meeting these requirements presented a whole set of problems. For one thing, F-80C Shooting Stars were in short supply, priority having been given to the European theatre where the recent blockade of Berlin and the subsequent formation of NATO had led to a major military re-equipment programme, and although there were more than 300 F-80As and F-80Bs that could be brought up to C standard by Lockheeds, this could only be done at the rate of twenty-seven a month. Also, the USAF was unable to meet the requirement for additional F-82 Twin Mustangs: there were only 168 of these aircraft in USAF service and, apart from the fact

Mustangs supplied to the Republic of Korea at the request of President Rhee. This unit, manned by ROK and American personnel under the command of Major Dean Hess (whose story was later to become famous through the book and film *Battle Hymn*), was in action almost continually during the early days of July, although its effectiveness was hampered by the fact that many of the ROK pilots lacked sufficient experience to handle the F-51 properly and also by the lack of a suitable tactical air control system. On 9 July, as a first step towards remedying this situation, three Stinson L-5G observation aircraft and seven officers were deployed to Taejon and began flying forward air control missions. They were followed the next day by a North American T-6C. Assigned to the 35th Fighter Interceptor Group in Japan, this aircraft had been grounded for over

Above: Nose art on an F-80 Shooting Star. (via Robert F. Dorr)
Below: F-51D of the ROK Air Force running up at a forward airstrip near Kongnung.

a year; hastily brought up to airworthy standard, it was fitted with an AN/ARC-3 radio for communication with both ground forces and fighter-bombers. On the first day of operations its crew, Lts James Bryant and Frank Mitchell, sighted a column of forty-two enemy tanks on a road near Chochiwon and called in an F-80 strike, which destroyed seventeen of the AFVs. As more T-6s arrived, they were assigned to the 6132nd Tactical Air Group at Taegu; three weeks later, HQ Fifth AF activated the 6147th Tactical Control Squadron (Airborne), which assumed responsibility for all FAC operations. By the end of July, when the T-6 unit comprised twelve aircraft and twenty-five men, it had flown 269 sorties across the whole breadth of the

and Corsairs. During the remainder of the month, TF 77 struck deep behind enemy lines and flew close support missions as required, the carriers moving around the peninsula from the Sea of Japan to the Yellow Sea. The naval close support missions in these early stages were not particularly successful for a variety of reasons, not least the fact that Air Force and Navy were using two different types of map. Naval pilots also found difficulty in establishing contact with the 'mosquito' airborne controllers, so that in many cases they were reduced to flying around seeking targets of opportunity with no guidance from anyone. The British element of TF 77, meanwhile, was experiencing growing problems with the serviceability and suitability of its aircraft,

Preparing to arm F-80s with rocket projectiles.

battlefront, operating under the callsign 'Mosquito'.

Although the North Korean airfields were beginning to suffer from the attentions of the Allied air forces, the NKAF was still in evidence. On 10 July four Yak-9s attacked elements of the US 19th Regiment near Chongju and inflicted some casualties. The next day more Yaks attacked a flight of F-80s engaged in strafing ground targets in the same area, and the American pilots, short of fuel, were lucky to escape without loss. This incident was repeated on 12 July, near Chochiwon; once again the American pilots were able to get away, but a B-29 of the 19th BG was intercepted by three Yaks and shot down. An L-4 liaison aircraft was also shot down by Yaks towards the end of the day. On 14 July two more Yaks came up to intercept a flight of four B-26s over Seoul and harried the bombers for ten minutes, severely damaging one of them.

Air reconnaissance had revealed that seven or eight Yak-9s were operating out of Kimpo, and in the afternoon of 15 July this airfield was attacked by a flight of F-80s and then bombed by three B-29s. The majority of the NKAF's assets, however, were reported to be concentrated on the airfields of Pyongyang, Onjong-ni, and Yonpo, and on 18 and 19 July these targets were heavily attacked by aircraft of Task Force 77 (USS *Valley Forge* and HMS *Triumph*) which claimed the destruction of thirty-two enemy aircraft on the ground and a further thirteen damaged. The naval aircraft also hit railroads and factories at Hungham, Hamhung, Numpyong, and Wonsan, where particularly heavy damage was inflicted on the oil refinery by Skyraiders

particularly the Seafires which had a very restricted endurance and were prone to deck-landing accidents because of their narrow-track undercarriage. In the end they were assigned to CAP duties over the fleet, leaving the American aircraft to concentrate on ground attack operations.

On 19 July seven F-80s of the 8th FBG hit the NKAF satellite airfield at Pyongyang, destroying fifteen enemy aircraft, and the next day fourteen B-29s bombed the runways of all the airfields clustered around the North Korean capital. During this period – between 17 and 20 July – F-80 pilots of the 8th FBG also destroyed six enemy fighters in air combat. By 21 July, although the NKAF had still not been totally destroyed, it had become almost completely ineffective as a fighting force. Wherever reconnaissance located enemy aircraft, they were immediately neutralised by air strikes. By 10 August Allied pilots had claimed the destruction of 110 enemy aircraft in the air and on the ground, and although there was doubt about the validity of this figure as it was known that some of the aircraft claimed to have been destroyed on the ground were dummies, the absence of the NKAF in combat during the first week of August 1950 indicated that it had, to all intents and purposes, been knocked out of the fight. NKAF aircraft did in fact put in an occasional appearance – on 15 August, for example, a lone Lavochkin La-7 attacked a B-29 of the 307th BG without inflicting any damage – but such incidents were isolated.

There were also clear indications by the end of July that the communist offensive was being blunted by

Lockheed F-80 Shooting Star, the true workhorse of the war in Korea. (via Robert F. Dorr)

tactical air power. The indications, in fact, were there as early as 8 July when enemy forces were compelled to rest and regroup after their capture of Chonan; had they been able to push on immediately they might well have succeeded in rolling up the remnants of the US 24th Division and annihilating them. The elimination of the NKAF meant that FEAF's medium bomber groups could now range freely over the whole of North Korea without fear of interference from hostile aircraft. The first strategic mission of the newly activated FEAF Bomber Command had been flown on 13 July, when fifty B-29s of the 19th, 22nd and 92nd Bombardment Groups bombed the marshalling yards and oil refinery at Wonsan through cloud, with the aid of radar. The number of strategic missions of this kind was stepped up during the remainder of July, as the increasing successes of Fifth AF's fighter bombers enabled more medium bombers to be released from the tactical support role, a task to which they were totally unsuited.

Although the Japan-based fighter bombers were already inflicting great carnage on the advancing North Koreans, the real turning point in the air–ground offensive came in mid-July with the establishment of the Mustang-equipped 51st Fighter Squadron at Taegu. This squadron, which absorbed the battle-weary survivors of Major Dean Hess's composite ROK/American unit, flew its first ground attack mission on 15 July.

Meanwhile, Air Force engineers had been labouring to extend the runway facilities of an old wartime Japanese airfield near the town of Pohang on the east coast of Korea. Their work was completed by 14 July, and two days later the Mustangs of the 40th Fighter Squadron flew in from Ashiya. This squadron was the first Fifth AF unit to exchange its F-80 jets for piston-engined F-51s, and the pilots had completed their conversion to the older type in record time. It was not long before the two squadrons, with their ability to be over the front line within minutes of a call for assistance being received, had begun to take a heavy toll of enemy troops and transport. Beginning on 17 July, the 40th Fighter Squadron, bereft of almost all communications with the outside world, began what almost amounted to a private war against a strong force

of North Korean regular troops advancing down the east coast towards Pohang. Within three days the enemy force had lost all its transport, and the troops, under threat of constant air attack, were restricted to moving under cover of darkness. The North Korean armour suffered particularly heavy losses: the Russian-built T-34 tanks were found to be extremely vulnerable to napalm attacks as the flaming jelly was easily sucked into the tank's engine compartment. Both Mustang squadrons made extensive use of this weapon.

The tactical air onslaught succeeded in slowing down the North Korean offensive, but was unable to stop it. The enemy advance continued along the entire front, with a main drive directed towards Taejon. On the morning of 19 July the communists opened a major assault on the city, which was defended by the battered US 24th Infantry Division. The latter's main task now was to fight a delaying action, buying time for two more divisions – the 25th Infantry Division and the 21st Cavalry Division, which had landed in Korea on 15 and 18 July respectively – to deploy their forces to the south and east. In the early hours of 20 July, however, the T-34 spearheads broke through and entered the city, and although fifteen were destroyed in the course of the day by the new 3.5" bazookas which had just been flown in from the USA, and which were now being used in action for the first time, the odds proved too great for the Divisional Commander, Major-General William F. Dean, to hold the city with the 4,000 men at his disposal. By nightfall the remnants of the 24th Division were withdrawn from the shattered town, leaving only a small rearguard, commanded by Dean himself, to fight on. When the city fell Dean, along with the other survivors, took to the neighbouring hills, where he spent more than a month before being captured. He spent the rest of the war in PoW camp, resisting determined efforts by the enemy to brainwash him.

With the US and ROK forces being driven back towards the Pusan perimeter, the need for close support aircraft operating from Korean airfields was now imperative. On 23 July, two days after the fall of Taejon, the aircraft carrier USS *Boxer* arrived at Tokyo and offloaded the 145 Mustangs drawn from Air National Guard units. These aircraft were assembled by the Far

East Air Materiel Command in record time and flown to Tachikawa for collection by their pilots, who had been undergoing a conversion course at Johnson AB. The first batch of combat-ready Mustangs was delivered to the 40th and 51st Squadrons in Korea on 30 July, bringing the strength of each unit up to twenty-five aircraft, and preparations were made to move another Mustang unit, the 67th Squadron of the 18th FBG, to Taegu from Ashiya. This move was in fact delayed for a while because Air Force engineers were still working on the refurbishment of Taegu and the airfield was not yet ready to receive a second Mustang squadron. In the event, the third Mustang squadron to arrive in Korea was the 39th, which exchanged its F-80 jets for Mustangs during the first week of August and moved to Pohang on the 7th of the month. Four days later the 8th Group's 35th and 36th Squadrons also converted to Mustangs, although for the time being both units continued to operate from Japanese bases. By 11 August, six Fifth Air Force fighter bomber squadrons had converted to Mustangs, and these, together with No. 77 Squadron RAAF, were to bear the brunt of close support operations during the critical days to come, with both sides engaged in the sternest test so far. The prize was Pusan, and with it the whole of Korea.

The communist offensive in Korea, June–July 1950.

F4U-5 Corsairs of Composite Squadron VC-3 on the USS Boxer.

CHAPTER 3
The Battle for Pusan

F4U-5N Corsair night fighters on a carrier in Yokosuka Bay, Japan, during the Korean War.

By the beginning of August 1950, air reconnaissance and other intelligence sources had confirmed that the main threat to Pusan was the North Korean 6th Division, which a few days earlier had crossed the Kum estuary at Kunsan before moving on to capture Chonju in what appeared to be the preliminary to a drive on Pusan from the west, outflanking the UN forces. The division was forging ahead at an average speed of two miles per hour by day and night, easily rolling up the feeble resistance it encountered.

Only the rapid deployment of reinforcements could stabilise the situation, and these were at last beginning to appear in numbers. The last day of July saw the arrival of the 2nd Infantry Division, the first ground troops to reach Korea from the continental United States, and they were followed on 2 August by the 1st Provisional Marine Brigade, also from the USA. The 5th Regimental Combat Team was also deployed to Korea from Hawaii and was attached to the 24th Infantry Division. With the Marines came air support: first of all Marine Air Group 33, which arrived at Kobe, Japan on 31 July and proceeded to Itami to begin working up. MAG 33 was the vanguard of the 1st Marine Air Wing, which was the air component of the 1st Marine Division. The Group's two tactical support squadrons, VMF-214 and VMF-323, both equipped with F4U-4B

Corsairs, were immediately tasked with the support of the 1st Provisional Marine Brigade, and on 3 August VMF-214 (the 'Blacksheep') deployed aboard the escort carrier USS *Sicily*, which had transported them to the theatre, to begin operations. Two days later VMF-323 (the 'Deathrattlers') also deployed to the escort carrier USS *Badoeng Strait*, and the two carriers – designated Task Element 96.8 – stationed themselves off the south coast of Korea to begin offensive operations. The remainder of the Marine Air Group, with no possibility of deployment to Korea for the time being, was placed under the temporary control of the Fifth Air Force in Japan; VMF(N)-513, equipped with F4U-5N Corsair night fighters, was attached to the the 8th FBW at Itazuke and began night intruder operations over Korea as directed by Fifth AF, while Marine Observation Squadron VMO-6 remained at Itami.

The first Marine air strike of the Korean War was flown by VMF-214 on 3 August, the Corsairs attacking supply dumps, bridges and railways at Chinju and Sinban-ni, and by the end of the first week of of the month the Marine pilots were flying an average of forty-five sorties a day. On the 7th they were heavily committed to a counter-attack against Chinju by the Marine Brigade, two regiments of the 25th Infantry Division, and the 5th RCT, supported by some of the 500 American tanks which had just reached Korea. The

Fine view of an F9F Panther at altitude over warships of Task Force 77.

19th Group B-29s approaching the Korean coast.

Corsairs wiped out a large enemy motorised column at Kaesong for the loss of two aircraft, one pilot being rescued by helicopter. Observation Squadron VMO-6's Sikorsky H03S-1 helicopters were now operating in Korea, and during this period they flew many casualty evacuation sorties, as well as rescuing downed pilots. The Squadron's fixed-wing Consolidated OY-1 aircraft also carried out water drops to Marines in forward positions – not a particularly successful operation, as the five-gallon drums usually burst when they hit the ground.

On 5 August 1950 the carrier USS *Philippine Sea* joined Task Force 77, replacing the *Valley Forge*, which had completed her first combat tour. Her Air Group 11 (CVG-11) consisted of VF-111 and VF-112 with F9F-2 Panthers, VF-113 and VF-114 with F4U-4 Corsairs, and VA-115 with AD-4 Skyraiders. Also assigned were detachments of Composite Squadron 3 (VC-3) with F4U-5s and AD-4s, VC-11 with AD-4s, and VC-61 with F4U-4s. The carrier arrived just in time to take part in the UN counter-offensive of 7 August, which was unsuccessful despite the weight of Allied air power. The North Koreans resisted fiercely and the American units involved failed to reach their primary objectives. By 12 August they were pulling back towards Masan, with men dropping like flies from heat exhaustion (it was over 100°F), and by the 14th they were back on their start line. Nevertheless, the counter-offensive had succeeded in bringing the NKA 6th Division to a standstill, and for the remainder of August this dangerous enemy spearhead made no further serious advance.

28

In the meantime, however, another serious threat had developed in the area defended by the 24th Infantry Division on the Naktong. If the enemy succeeded in breaking through here, they would be in a position to cut the vital road and rail link between Pusan and Taegu, ten miles to the east, cutting the perimeter in two and causing the collapse of the whole Allied defence. On the night of 6 August the North Korean 4th Division began crossing the Naktong near Yongsan, where the line was thinly defended, and occupied strategic high ground to the east of the river. While the 1st Marine Brigade rushed to the aid of the 24th Division, flare-dropping B-26s of the 3rd Bombardment Wing made night attacks on enemy transport and artillery crossing the river; bombing operations were also carried out by Lockheed P2V-2 Neptunes of Navy Patrol Squadron VP-6, diverted from their more usual role of maritime reconnaissance. On 17 August the Allies launched a counter-offensive, and by the next morning, after hard fighting, the Marines and elements of the 24th Division had retaken most of the high ground overlooking the enemy bridgehead. At first light on 19 August the bridgehead itself was heavily attacked, and the NKA 4th Division was thrown back across the river with severe casualties.

The focus of the battle now switched to the Taegu sector, where five NKA divisions were massing at Waegwan, twenty miles from the town of Taegu itself. On 15 August Fifth Air Force launched heavy attacks against the enemy forces in this area, the fighter bombers destroying a number of T-34 tanks and killing an estimated 300 troops. It was not enough, and General MacArthur held urgent consultations with General Stratemeyer on the possibility of using the whole B-29 force to make a tactical strike on the enemy. General Emmett O'Donnell, commanding FEAF Bomber Command, had mixed feelings about the use of strategic bombers in this way, but agreed that they might make the necessary impact if the enemy troop concentrations were sufficiently dense, and indications were that such was the case: there were intelligence reports that an estimated 40,000 communist troops were assembled in an area three and a half miles wide by seven and a half miles long extending along the Naktong to the north-west of Waegwan.

On the morning of 16 August ninety-eight B-29s attacked this area from altitudes of between 5,000 and 10,000 feet with 500lb HE bombs. Fragmentation bombs would have been better, but the mission had been planned at such short notice that stocks of these were not readily available. The attack lasted less than half an hour, and when the dust and smoke cleared the area

A Marine Air Wing Corsair climbs away after an attack on an enemy position in Korea, late 1950.

Skyraiders and Corsairs ranged on the flight deck of a carrier off Korea. (via Robert F. Dorr)

was photographed by RF-80s. The photographs they brought back served only to confirm that 'Rosie' O'Donnell had been right in his misgivings: they revealed no troops or vehicles at all, and no evidence was ever produced that this mission – the biggest use of air power in direct support of ground troops since the Normandy invasion of 1944 – had killed a single North Korean soldier. It certainly produced no easing of the relentless communist pressure on the Allied defences.

At the north-western end of the Pusan perimeter the

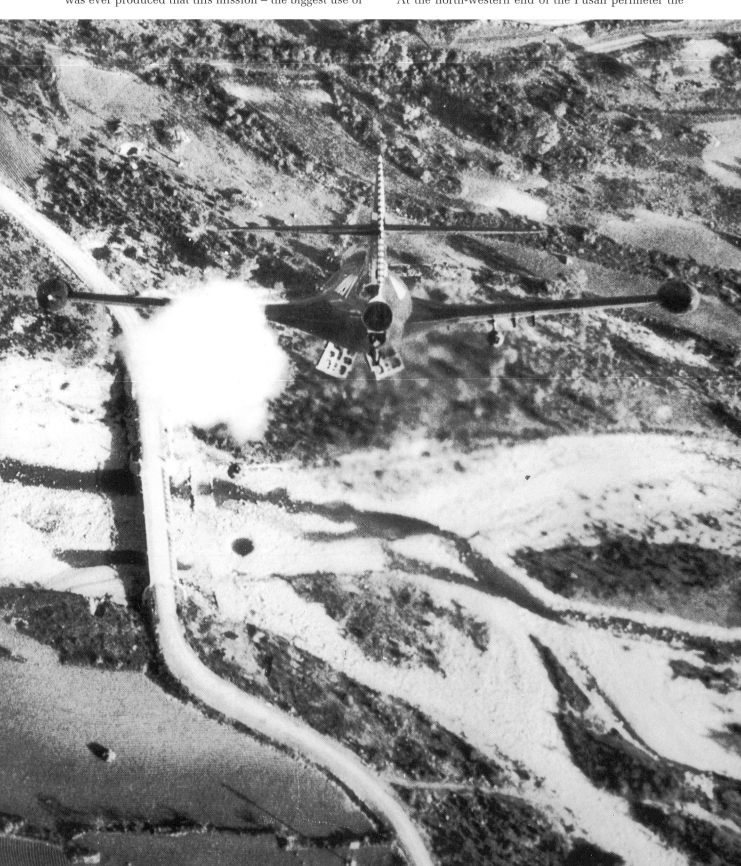

An F9F Panther from the carrier USS Bon Homme Richard *attacking a road target in North Korea. A bomb has just been dropped from its cradle, with a second bomb, still in its cradle under the starboard wing, about to follow. The puff of white smoke is the result of the aircraft firing its six-inch rockets.*

A General Motors TBM-3R Avenger carrier onboard delivery (COD) transport conversion on a US carrier off Korea. (via Robert F. Dorr)

main threat came from the NKA 5th Division, which had pushed down the coast and driven the ROK 3rd Division from the Yongdok area. Suddenly a new threat developed when elements of the NKA 12th Division were detected moving through a mountain corridor that ran all the way to Pusan. Pohang-based Mustangs of the 35th Fighter Interceptor Group (39th and 40th Squadrons) struck hard at this column, but on 12 August the NKA entered the port of Pohang and later in the day the 35th's ground crews found themselves skirmishing with communist irregular forces on the airfield perimeter. The Americans had no choice but to destroy all the equipment that could not be moved and fly their Mustangs out to Japan. This sudden removal of its air support meant that the ROK 3rd Division, penned against the coast, had no chance of holding on, and it was evacuated by sea to new positions within the Pusan perimeter. On 20 August the Allies counter-attacked and succeeded in dislodging the NKA from Pohang, removing the immediate threat to the perimeter in this sector.

The anticipated communist assault in the Taegu sector began on 18 August, the NKA driving a wedge between the ROK 1st and 6th Divisions and penetrating to within twelve miles of the town. The Fifth AF's Mustangs were very active during this critical period; the initial strikes were made from Japan, the fighter bombers carrying maximum fuel and weapons load and afterwards landing at Taegu to refuel and rearm for a new series of strikes. The Mustang pilots, ready to drop from exhaustion and suffering from extreme heat in the cockpits, operated virtually non-stop for forty-eight hours while daylight lasted, taking an enormous toll of the enemy. The air attacks reduced the pressure on the ROK until the arrival of a regiment of the US 25th Division, with whose help the NKA forces were pushed steadily back. By 21 August the Allies had recaptured most of the ground that had been lost during the enemy offensive, and as they advanced the Allied troops found plenty of evidence of the key role played by the Mustangs; on one stretch of road they counted the bodies of 700 NKA dead, the result of a Mustang attack with rockets, napalm and machine guns.

While the battle for Pusan raged, the Allied air forces had been conducting a mounting offensive against targets far to the north. Known as Interdiction Campaign No. 1, it had begun on 4 August with a two-day series of attacks on the marshalling yards at Seoul

by B-29s of the 19th, 22nd and 92nd Bombardment Groups. Two days later, marshalling yards and ammunition factories at Pyongyang were also attacked by aircraft of the 22nd, 92nd and 98th Groups, and on 8 August these targets were bombed by B-29s of the 307th Group. The 98th and 307th Groups, released by Strategic Air Command for duty in the Far East, had just arrived in the theatre and were operating respectively from Yokota and Kadena.

After these initial strikes, which culminated in an attack on marshalling yards and an oil refinery at Wonsan by the 22nd, 92nd and 98th Groups on 10 August, the emphasis of the interdiction campaign switched to bridge targets, and in an eight-day offensive starting on 12 August three B-29 Groups attacked forty-four bridges north of the 37th Parallel, destroying thirty-seven of them and damaging the other seven so badly that they were unusable for some considerable time. It was no mean achievement, for most of the bridges were strong steel and concrete structures built by the Japanese during the occupation and it required very precise bombing to ensure their destruction. Moreover, the B-29 crews achieved their task with 500 and 1,000lb bombs, far from ideal weapons for use against this kind of objective. One bridge, however, persistently refused to be destroyed. This was the big steel railway bridge west of Seoul, which had withstood many attacks since the start of the air campaign. It became the object of what amounted to a personal vendetta on the part of the 19th Group's crews, who dropped 2,000 and 4,000lb bombs on it almost every day for three weeks. On one occasion they dropped fifty-four tons of bombs around it, and yet it still stood. In desperation, General Stratemeyer promised a case of best Scotch to the crew who succeeded in knocking it down. The word spread and suddenly the bridge became a priority target for the navy pilots of TF 77 too. On 19 August thirty-seven Corsairs and Skyraiders from the *Philippine Sea* and *Valley Forge*, the latter on station again after replenishment, scored eight direct hits on it. Much to the 19th Group's delight, post-strike reconnaissance showed that the structure did not appear even to have been buckled, and the B-29 crews set off again the next day determined to finish the job and claim their prize. On arrival over the target, much to their chagrin, they found that two spans of the bridge had collapsed during the night, obviously having been weakened by the Navy's bombing. Determined to make the best of things, they dropped their bombs on what remained and destroyed a third span. General Stratemeyer decided to do the decent thing and gave a case of Scotch to both the 19th Group and the Navy.

Bridge targets and other communications links between the 37th and 38th Parallels were also heavily attacked during this phase by Fifth AF fighter bombers, which claimed the destruction of ninety-three bridges by the end of August, with forty-seven more severely damaged and unusable. The problem was that as fast as the Air Force or Navy knocked a bridge down NKA engineers threw up pontoons alongside it, so that the flow of men and materiel to the battlefront continued virtually unchecked. These pontoon-building operations were conducted under cover of darkness, and although constant attempts were made to disrupt them by flare-dropping B-26s of the 3rd Bombardment Wing, assisted from time to time by F-82s of the 68th Fighter (All-Weather) Squadron and by F4U-5N Corsairs of VMF(N)-513, very little success was achieved.

On the night of 31 August 1950 the North Koreans unleashed their do-or-die offensive against the Pusan perimeter and enjoyed initial success, driving on to capture Haman through crumbling UN resistance. At the same time, two NKA divisions with armoured support crossed the Naktong and occupied Yongsan the next day,

The Allied breakout and drive towards the Yalu, October–November 1950.

splitting the US 2nd Infantry Division in half. Another heavy attack developed in the Waegwan sector, which was held by the 1st Cavalry, and by 6 September the NKA had advanced to within eight miles of Taegu, cutting the lateral Taegu road in two places. At this juncture elements of the British 27th Brigade – a battalion each of the Middlesex Regiment and the Argyll and Sutherland Highlanders, newly arrived in the theatre – were sent into the line on the Naktong in the hills north of Taegu. While attempts were made to stabilise the battlefront here, General Walker deployed his Marines to Yongsan, and they succeeded in driving the NKA out of the area.

The Air Force and Navy fighter-bomber pilots made an unprecedented effort in support of the ground forces. On 1 September, Fifth AF made over 160 ground attack sorties in support of the US 2nd and 25th Divisions, the Mustangs again proving particularly effective: on several occasions they enabled pockets of Allied infantry encircled by the North Koreans to break out by dropping clusters of napalm on the enemy. Other groups of soldiers, surrounded in their positions, clung on thanks to the efforts of the 21st Troop Carrier Squadron, which air-dropped rations and ammunition to them. During the afternoon, Allied air support

intensified with the arrival of Task Force 77 whose carriers, in response to the urgency of the situation, had raced down the coast at top speed from the positions from which they had been launching interdiction sorties against targets in the north. The Navy pilots flew eighty-five sorties before dusk, mostly in support of the 2nd Division.

Support of the 2nd and 25th Divisions was again given priority on 2 September, the Air Force and Marine pilots flying 200 missions and TF 77 127. In addition, twenty-five B-29s of the 307th BG attacked NKA supply dumps at Kumchon, Kochang and Chinju. On 3 September, before withdrawing for replenishment at sea, the carriers of TF 77 launched a further twenty-eight sorties in support of ground forces in the Yongsan sector; after replenishment, they moved north again to continue their task of interdiction. With the departure of TF 77 the Fifth Air Force fighter bombers redoubled their efforts; on 3 September they flew 249 close support and eighty-nine interdiction missions, while B-29s struck at troop concentrations and supplies in selected areas near the battlefront. The overall result was an appreciable easing of communist pressure by the end of the day, and on the 4th, when most of the tanks supporting the two NKA divisions in the Yongsan sector were knocked out by air attack, the tide at last began to turn. In the early hours of the following morning, in the face of determined counter-attacks by the 2nd Division, the North Koreans began to fall back.

The Fifth AF now switched its attention to the support of the ROK divisions in action east of Taegu; on 4 September it flew 160 sorties in this sector, fifty-one on the 5th, and 183 on the 6th. Here, too, the communist offensive was blunted by the weight of air attack, and with the help of the US 24th Division the ROK forces were able to mount a counter-offensive. By the end of the first week of September the North Koreans were being held all along the battlefront, and on the 11th, when the Fifth Air Force, Marines and Bomber Command launched 683 sorties against them, they began to show signs of breaking. In the 2nd Division's sector alone, 1,500 enemy soldiers were killed by air attack, and on the following day the Allied situation had improved to such an extent that General MacArthur was able to order a general counter-offensive.

The North Koreans' gamble had failed, and the immediate threat to Pusan was over. The stage was now set for a brilliant Allied counter-stroke which had been in the making since the dark days of July. Its objective was to hurl the North Korean People's Army, in its entirety, back across the 38th Parallel.

CHAPTER 4

INCHON:
MacArthur's Gamble

The idea of a bold counter-stroke aimed at removing the North Koreans from the south once and for all was not something that was conceived overnight. As early as 7 July, General MacArthur had appealed to the Joint Chiefs of Staff for reinforcement by no fewer than five divisions and three tank battalions to enable him to strike behind the North Korean forces 'by amphibious manoeuvre'. Such reinforcements that did arrive over the next few weeks, however, were assigned to the defence of the Pusan perimeter. On 29 July, after the 1st Cavalry Division, the 2nd Division, and the 1st Marine Brigade had been allotted to Pusan, he informed the Joint Chiefs that he proposed to use his only remaining force – the 7th Division – 'along a separate axis in mid-September'.

MacArthur's mind was firmly set on an amphibious landing at Inchon, south of the 38th Parallel on the west coast of Korea. His experiences as Allied Commander in the Pacific during World War Two had taught him that a rapid advance by an enemy was almost always accompanied by a dangerous overstretching of his supply lines and communications. It was this factor – coupled with the surprise achieved by an amphibious landing on the Admiralty Islands in February 1944 that had enabled his forces to bypass an entire Japanese army by leapfrogging 500 miles along the coast of New Guinea, a move that shortened the war by a month – which determined his preferred course of action. This 1944 manoeuvre, on a smaller scale, was the strategy MacArthur planned to use to ensure an early communist defeat in Korea. A seaborne force of United States Marines, taking advantage of the full element of surprise, would land at Inchon far behind the battlefront, at one blow slicing the North Koreans' vital supply lines in the Inchon–Seoul area in two and opening up a second front. The scheme was named Operation 'Chromite' and MacArthur planned to launch it on 15 September 1950, by which time it was hoped that the whole of the 1st Marine Division would have arrived in Korea. There were four major objectives: the elimination of North Korean artillery batteries on Wolmi-do, an island which controlled the approaches to Inchon harbour; a landing in the town of Inchon itself; the seizure of Kimpo airfield; and the recapture of Seoul. As MacArthur had envisaged from the start, the main thrust would be carried out by the Marines while the 7th Infantry Division, which had been held in reserve in Japan, covered the right flank and then pushed south towards Suwon; the Eighth Army would advance from the Pusan perimeter to link up with it.

Although the Joint Chiefs agreed in principle to an amphibious landing, they did not agree with MacArthur's choice of objective. A landing at Inchon involved plenty of risk, as MacArthur himself was well aware. Only on two days, 15 September and

11 October, would the water be deep enough to allow the big landing craft to scrape through into the harbour, and even then the safety margin would be only three hours. At low tide the inner harbour was a mud flat with a twisting channel about twelve feet deep, and assuming the landing craft got into the inner harbour, the Marines would then have to scale twelve-foot-high sea walls using ladders before they could get to grips with the enemy. The whole issue was debated at a high-level conference on 23 July, and MacArthur's rhetoric won the day. He compared Inchon with the assault on Quebec by General Wolfe nearly two centuries earlier. Wolfe's forces had scaled the Heights of Abraham, taking the very route that General Montcalm, the French commander, claimed was impossible. The result was that the British had achieved complete surprise and Canada had been won for Britain in the subsequent battle. 'It is plainly apparent,' MacArthur told the Joint Chiefs' representatives, 'that here in Asia is where the communist conspirators have elected to make their play for global conquest. The test is not in Berlin or Vienna, London, Paris or Washington. It is here and now. It is along the Naktong river in South Korea . . . I can almost hear the ticking of the second hand of destiny. We must act now or we will die. Inchon will succeed and it will save 100,000 lives. We shall land at Inchon and I shall crush them.'

Although this meeting was crucial to MacArthur's scheme, it was not until 28 August that the Joint Chiefs formally approved the plans for Chromite, enabling the final details to be worked out. MacArthur himself knew that the operation would be in the nature of a terrible gamble, yet he was conscious of the fact that the United Nations forces in Korea too were racing against time and that it was a race that amply justified the gamble, no matter how great the odds might be against it. One additional worry was that for several weeks there had been intelligence reports, substantiated by RB-29 overflights, that Chinese Communist forces were massing in Manchuria north of the Yalu river. There had already been several serious border incidents. On 27 August, for example, two Fifth Air Force Mustang pilots had crossed the border as a result of a navigational error and strafed a Chinese Communist airstrip near Antung. The Americans also claimed that RB-29s over North Korea had been fired on by Chinese AA batteries sited across the border, which was true; what the Americans did not say was that some of the RB-29s had been well inside Communist China at the time. MacArthur's concern was to roll up the North Koreans as quickly as possible and win the war before the Chinese intervened, as seemed increasingly likely. The alternative would be a long and costly war of attrition.

For two weeks prior to the scheduled date of the

F-80C Shooting Star in Korea; legend on nose reads Guns for Hire. (via Robert F. Dorr)

invasion the Inchon–Seoul area was repeatedly photographed by RF-80s of the 8th TRS, providing accurate and up-to-the-minute intelligence on enemy troop movements and defences. Meanwhile, Bomber Command continued to attack communications in the Seoul area to prevent the North Koreans from rushing reinforcements to Inchon; between 9 and 13 September the B-29s cut forty-six rail links, the biggest raid taking place on the 13th when sixty B-29s from four groups bombed marshalling yards and railway lines running southwards from Anju and Hungnam.

That evening, fewer than thirty-six hours before the Marines were due to go in, a sudden crisis developed when a typhoon swept over the Japanese Home Islands and threatened to ground the entire Fifth Air Force. Fortunately, there had been adequate warning and two Mustang groups, the 8th and 18th, were deployed to Taegu and the primitive K-9 airstrip near Pusan to continue operations in support of the Eighth Army's breakout. The typhoon made life difficult for the invasion forces, whose various components, comprising 260 ships carrying nearly 70,000 men, were assembling off Sasebo. Despite all the problems, however, the transports managed to keep station and after a few hours the typhoon wandered away. In the early hours of the 13th, shepherded by its warship escorts, the armada set course for Inchon.

The backbone of tactical air support for Chromite was to be provided by the US Navy and Marine Corps, and the order of battle was as follows:

Task Force 77 Carrier Division 1 aboard USS *Philippine Sea* (CV-47), Air Group 11 embarked. Carrier Division 3 aboard USS *Valley Forge* (CV-45), Air Group 5 embarked. Carrier Division 5 aboard USS *Boxer* (CV-21), Air Group 2 embarked.

Task Group 90.5 Air Support Group; TG 90.51 CVE Element USS *Badoeng Strait* (CVE-116), VMF-323 embarked. USS *Sicily* (CVE-118), VMF-214 embarked.

Task Force 91, Blockade and Covering Force HMS *Triumph* with No. 800 Squadron (Seafires) and No. 827 Squadron (Fireflies).

Task Force 99, Patrol and Reconnaissance Force TG 99.1 Search and Recce Group; VP-6 with P2V-2 Neptunes. Nos. 88 and 209 Squadrons RAF with Short Sunderlands.

Task Group 99.2, Patrol and Escort Group Patrol Squadrons 42 (VP-42) and 47 (VP-47) with Martin PBM-5 Mariners.

On 10 September, Marine Corsairs from USS *Sicily* and *Badoeng Strait* began a preliminary series of attacks on targets in the Inchon area, the first being directed against Wolmi-do island and its neighbour, Solmi-do. On the 13th the pre-invasion sea bombardment began, four cruisers – the USS *Toledo* and *Rochester*, HMS *Kenya* and *Jamaica* – and six US destroyers closing in to shell the offshore islands.

At 0633 on 15 September the 5th Marines went ashore on Wolmi-do, meeting with only scattered resistance, and within half an hour the island was in Allied hands and the way to Inchon harbour was open. Early in the afternoon the warships, joined by Navy and Marine fighter-bombers, turned the full weight of their firepower on the buildings along the Inchon waterfront, softening up the area in readiness for the main landing, which was to be made with the high tide at 1730. The assault went ahead on schedule after a final intense forty-five-minute bombardment by rocket ships, destroyers, cruisers and aircraft. The approaches were not mined, although it later transpired that if the

This F4U-5 Corsair landed on the wrong carrier and was the subject of some graffiti before returning to its rightful one, the USS Boxer.

operation had been delayed a few more weeks, they would have been. The Marines went ashore at two separate points and by midnight they had taken all their primary objectives at the cost of 196 casualties, including twenty killed. MacArthur's gamble had paid off, but it might have been otherwise. The North Korean defences were strong, but they were badly undermanned.

At dawn the following morning, while ROK Marines and No. 5 Regimental Combat Team completed the mopping-up operations at Inchon, the main forces began a two-pronged drive towards Seoul: 1st Marines advancing direct to the Han and the industrial suburbs of the city while 5th Marines headed for Kimpo with the object of capturing the airfield and striking into Seoul from the north-west. The North Koreans hastily assembled a scratch force designated the 1st Air Force Division to defend Kimpo, but after a confused night action the airfield fell to the Americans on 17

Damaged and beached Short Sunderland of the RAF's Far East Flying Boat Wing at Oppama, Japan during the Korean War. (via Robert F. Dorr)

Dakota of No. 30 Squadron RAAF unloading casualties at Iwakuni, Japan.

September. The North Koreans appeared to have made very little use of Kimpo airfield: only two Il-10s and a Yak-9 were found intact there. It seemed that the enemy had withdrawn most of their serviceable aircraft out of the area as soon as the carrier aircraft had begun their air strikes prior to the Inchon landing. Only on one occasion, at dawn on 17 September, did enemy aircraft put in an appearance when two Yak-9s dropped down out of the clouds and released a few light bombs at the cruisers USS *Rochester* and HMS *Jamaica.* One of the fighters got away but the other was shot down by the British warship.

On the following day, an advance party of Marine Air Group 33 personnel flew into Kimpo, which had

sustained very little damage, to prepare the airfield for the arrival of Marine fighter bomber units. The first American aircraft to arrive after the base was made secure was a HO3S-1 helicopter of VMO-6 flown by Marine Captain Victor A. Armstrong and carrying Lt-Gen. Lemuel C. Shepherd Jr, Commandant of the US Marine Corps.

On 19 September Corsairs of VMF-212 and Grumman F7F-3N Tigercats of VMF(N)-542 arrived from Japan, and on the night of the 20th/21st the latter flew their first operational mission from Kimpo, an interdiction sortie against enemy supply lines. The Tigercats had deployed to Yokosuka from the USS *Cape Esperance* on 11 September. After daybreak on the 21st, Corsairs of

The Grumman F7F Tigercat performed useful service as a night intruder before being replaced by the Skynight.

VMF-323, operating from the carriers offshore, attacked NKA troops in the Yongdung-po area as they attempted to dislodge men of the 1st Marines from a feature known as Hill 118. By this time an airlift of considerable size was under way, with a constant stream of C-54s and C-119s flying into Kimpo with supplies for the ground forces and spare parts, fuel and ammunition for the aircraft. The airlift brought a daily average of 226 tons of supplies into the airfield, and on the return trip the C-54s carried casualties for hospital treatment in Japan. On 21 September several C-54s were diverted to the newly captured airfield at Suwon, where they offloaded sixty-five tons of rations and ammunitions while nine C-119s air-dropped more food and ammunition to troops in the front line.

Preparations for the Eighth Army's breakout from the Pusan pocket, meanwhile, had been completed by 16 September, but bad weather delayed the start of the ground offensive until the next day, and it was not until the afternoon that the Fifth Air Force's fighter bombers were able to operate. When they did eventually get airborne, however, the Mustangs and F-80s dealt out considerable punishment to the enemy, attacking with napalm at low level, just under the cloud base. In the sector covered by the advance of the US 2nd Division alone, napalm attacks killed over 1,000 enemy soldiers as they were attempting to retreat across the Naktong river.

At dawn on 18 September, as the weather cleared, forty-two B-29s of the 92nd and 98th BG, once again called upon to operate in the tactical role in support of the ground forces, laid sixteen hundred 500lb bombs with great precision on a strip of land a mile long by 500 yards wide as the North Koreans were attempting to cross the Naktong by means of two bridges. Unlike the B-29 tactical bombing missions of 16 August, this one was very successful and the approaches to the bridges

were completely pulverised, effectively bottling up the retreating North Korean infantry and what remained of their motor transport.

It was time for the Fifth AF to turn its fighter-bombers loose. On 18 September they carried out 286 ground attack sorties, a figure that was stepped up to 361 on the following day when the Eighth Army, led by troops of the 24th Division, began to cross the Naktong in force near Waegwan. Spearheaded by armour, the leading columns plunged on into enemy territory, sweeping aside crumbling NKA resistance. Where resistance was encountered, tactical air controllers quickly called in the fighter-bombers to deal with it; on 21 September, for example, TAC pilots sighted a force of thirty enemy tanks attempting to make a flank attack on the leading elements of the 24th Division and summoned flights of F-80s and F-51s, which destroyed fifteen T-34s. By 24 September, Fifth AF Intelligence estimated that its aircraft had killed some 8,000 enemy soldiers since the breakout began, and as the NKA forces broke up and scattered, United Nations pilots reported that they were finding it increasingly difficult to find worthwhile targets. Rather than risk hitting friendly forces, many pilots returned to base with their weapons still on board; the danger had been highlighted on 23 September, when Mustangs mistakenly attacked a company of the Argyll and Sutherland Highlanders (27th Brigade). As a result, General Stratemeyer decreed that all targets must be positively identified.

As North Korean resistance continued to crumble the UN drive northwards gathered momentum and on 26 September the 1st Cavalry joined up with 7th Infantry at Osan, cutting off large numbers of NKA troops. Meanwhile, supported by Corsairs, US Marines were fighting their way into Seoul from the north, south and west, and by nightfall on the 27th they had driven

Top: Lockheed F-80C Shooting Stars. While the Sabre got the glamour, the F-80 was the true workhorse of the Korean air war. (Martin Bambrick)
Above: F-80 of the 18th FBG mounted on jacks for gun testing. (via Robert F. Dorr)

enemy forces from the battered South Korean capital.

On 25 September Fifth AF re-established its headquarters in Taegu city, while engineers worked to refurbish the runways at Taegu airfield in readiness to receive jet aircraft. By the end of the month the F-80 Shooting Stars of the 49th Fighter Bomber Group were in position, followed a few days later by the RF-80As of the 8th TRS and the RB-26s of the 12th TRS. Air Force engineers were also improving the facilities at K-3, Pohang, and by 12 October this was the home of the Mustangs of the 39th and 40th Squadrons (35th Fighter Interceptor Group) and No. 77 Squadron RAAF. The F-51s of the 18th Fighter Bomber Group were based further south on K-9, Pusan East airfield. Refurbishing the airstrip at Suwon, which was badly churned up by Allied bombing and tank tracks, presented more of a problem. Mustangs of the 35th Squadron of the 8th FBG began operating from this base on 7 October, but only half the runway was usable and at the end of the month the 35th moved to Kimpo, where it was joined by the 36th Squadron. By this time the 51st Fighter Interceptor

Group was also established at Kimpo with its three squadrons, the 16th and 25th Fighter Interceptor and the 80th Fighter Bomber.

Squadron personnel at the Korean airstrips soon discovered that the problems were only just beginning. At Taegu, for example, the steel plank runway subsided in places and became irregular, with the result that the 49th Group's F-80s frequently burst their tyres on landing. On one occasion an RB-26 burst a tyre and slewed off the runway into a line of parked F-80s, writing off four of them. Excessive dust blown up by taxying jets and sucked into air intakes was another hazard, reducing engine life and making frequent overhauls imperative. Nevertheless, the Shooting Star performed well under these difficult conditions, earning the praise of air and ground crews alike.

The question that now faced the United Nations was whether the retreating enemy should be pursued across the 38th Parallel, and if so where the pursuit should stop. After some hesitation – there was a very real fear of Chinese or Russian intervention – the United States

Firefly being loaded on board HMS Theseus *at Iwakuni.*

As an AD Skyraider (upper right) pulls away from its bombing run, three bombs fall from the shackles of the Skyraider in the foreground towards targets at Wonsan.

Government authorised the Eighth Army to continue its offensive into North Korea. On 27 September, General MacArthur was ordered to achieve the total destruction of the North Korean Army and to form a united Korea under President Rhee. However, extreme caution was to be exercised: only ROK forces were to be used in the vicinity of the Chinese and Soviet borders. The directive did not appeal to MacArthur who wanted all the forces under his command to have complete freedom to advance as far as necessary to ensure the

surrender of the enemy. A surrender demand had already been issued to the NKA commander-in-chief, provoking threatening murmurs from Communist China, and on 3 October 1950 Premier Chou En-lai warned the United Nations that China would come to the aid of the North Koreans if the latter's territory were invaded. The Americans did not believe the threat to be valid, regarding it as a form of political blackmail and, when North Korean Premier Kim Il-sung rejected the surrender demand outright on 10 October, the plan to occupy the whole of the north was implemented.

Once again it was a race against time. Chinese forces were massing in Manchuria and Allied Intelligence indicated that if the Chinese did come to North Korea's aid, a possibility that was still considered unlikely, they would have the ability to send nine field armies into action by the middle of November. MacArthur did not believe this either: at a high-level conference on Wake Island, at which he met President Truman, representatives of the Joint Chiefs and other dignitaries, he gave the opinion that, 'with our largely unopposed air forces, with their potential capability of destroying at will bases of attack and lines of supply north as well as south of the Yalu, no Chinese military commander would hazard the commitment of large forces upon the devastated Korean peninsula'. Questioned as to how many troops he thought the Chinese could maintain in Korea, MacArthur said 50,000 to 60,000, about half the number the UN could deploy for battle. He was devastatingly wrong. What MacArthur, and presumably Allied Intelligence, did not know was that by 14 October, only a fortnight after the first ROK troops had crossed the 38th Parallel, Chinese forces had already begun to cross the Yalu river into North Korean territory. The crossings were made at night over two large bridges at Antung and Manpojin, undetected by Allied air reconnaissance.

General MacArthur's plan for the rapid conquest of North Korea involved a second amphibious landing, this time at Wonsan on the east coast, by the Marine units which had carried out the Inchon operation. The landing was to take place in conjunction with a drive by the Eighth Army towards Pyongyang, the North Korean capital. The scheme was opposed by General Walker and Admiral Turner Joy, both of whom felt it would be quicker to capture Wonsan by means of an overland march rather than a cumbersome amphibious operation. Besides, ROK forces were pushing rapidly along the east coast and would probably be in a position to capture the city first. These objections, however, were overruled, and on 7 October the Marines re-embarked in their ships and sailed around the peninsula in readiness for the landing, which was scheduled to take place on the 20th.

Prior to the operation, the carriers of Task Force 77 – the USS *Boxer*, USS *Leyte*, USS *Philippine Sea*, and USS *Valley Forge* – were directed to concentrate fifty per cent of their strike missions against the local defences at Wonsan, and on 8 October additional striking power was added to TF 77 in the shape of HMS *Theseus*, which relieved HMS *Triumph* in Korean waters. She had been in port in the UK when she was alerted for Korean duty in late August; the two squadrons of her 17th Carrier Air Group, No. 807 with Hawker Sea Furies and No. 810 with Fairey Fireflies, immediately embarked on a period of intensive training that lasted six weeks, both in the UK and while the carrier was en route to the Far East. *Theseus* went on active duty in the Yellow Sea on 9 October, launching her first sorties that same day. With its armament of four 20mm cannon and provision for up to 2,000lb of external stores, the Sea Fury was to provide a useful asset to Allied naval air power in Korea for the duration of hostilities.

On 10 October, as the critics of the Wonsan operation had predicted, ROK forces penetrated the town and the Marines found themselves in the embarrassing position of being unable to go ashore because the harbour and its approaches were sown with uncharted minefields. PBM Mariners of Fleet Air Wing 6, supported by RAF Sunderlands, flew over the area and their crews attempted to destroy as many mines as possible with gunfire, but it was a hopelessly ineffective method and there was a considerable delay while surface sweeping units were called in. The 1st Marine Division eventually went ashore on 24 October, supported by the Corsairs of VMF-214, VMF-323 and VMF(N)-513, operating from Wonsan airfield. The Corsair night fighters flew daylight missions until runway lighting was installed at Wonsan, after which they resumed

Troops of the 187th Airborne RCT embarking on a C-119. The C-119 was plagued with problems and the fleet was often barely airworthy, but it continued flying throughout the Korean War.

F-51D Mustangs of the 18th FBG at Chinhae. (via Robert F. Dorr)

their usual night intruder operations.

Meanwhile, on 9 October the Eighth Army had captured Kaesong and pushed on across the 38th Parallel, supported by Fifth AF fighter-bombers. On the 15th, armoured columns of the 1st Cavalry began a drive to Pyongyang. The only serious opposition was encountered some ten miles south of the city when the Americans ran into a North Korean force supported by thirty-five tanks and some self-propelled guns. The enemy force was smashed by air attacks and artillery fire and on 19 October the 1st Cavalry Division, supported by advance elements of the 27th Commonwealth Brigade, entered the outskirts of the North Korean capital.

It was at this juncture that General MacArthur put another phase of his strategic plan into operation. For two weeks the 187th Airborne Regimental Combat Team had been standing by to carry out an air drop behind the enemy lines wherever it would be most effective, and it was now decided that the 187th should be dropped near the towns of Sukchon and Sunchon, about thirty miles north of Pyongyang astride an important road and rail complex leading to the city. At noon on 20 October seventy-five Mustangs, sixty-two F-80s and five B-26s of the Fifth AF began a series of intensive air attacks on targets in and around the dropping zone, and in the course of the afternoon, after a short delay caused by bad weather, seventy-one C-119s and forty C-47s dropped 2,860 paratroops and over 300 tons of equipment on the DZ. The paratroops suffered thirty-seven casualties, including one fatality. They quickly secured the high ground overlooking the DZ, and during the next three days fourteen C-119s dropped an additional 1,000 paratroops and 190 tons of supplies. On 23 October, by which time the 187th RCT had killed an estimated 2,700 enemy troops and taken 3,000 prisoners, the 1st Cavalry joined up with the paratroops after pushing on from Pyongyang.

At sea, HMS *Theseus* withdrew to Iwakuni for replenishment on 22 October, her Sea Furies and Fireflies having completed 264 and 120 sorties respectively against targets at Chinnampo, Heiju in Hwanghai Province, Pakchong and Chongju. She returned to her war station early in November to cover minesweeping operations in the Chinnampo estuary, then went to Hong Kong to take part in an exercise having temporarily disembarked six of her Fireflies to carry out bombardment spotting duties.

On 29 October the US 7th Infantry Division went ashore at Iwon, about ninety miles to the north-east of Wonsan. Meanwhile, supported mainly by Marine Corsairs, ROK forces had been pushing steadily up the coast towards the Yalu river and the Manchurian border, and on 25 October they reported that enemy resistance was stiffening. The reason became clear within the next forty-eight hours: the South Koreans were facing elements of two Chinese Communist divisions, and by the end of the month it was apparent that the Chinese were already intervening in North Korea on a massive scale.

There were signs, too, that the Chinese were about to enter the air war. On 18 October an RB-29 of the 31st Strategic Reconnaissance Squadron returned with photographic evidence that seventy-five Chinese fighters, including MiG-15 jets, were assembled on the airfield at Antung, just across the river. Then, on the morning of 1 November a B-26 of the 730th Bombardment Squadron (part of the 452nd Wing, which had just arrived in the theatre) and a T-6 'Mosquito' tactical control aircraft were attacked by Yak-9 fighters bearing Chinese markings. One of the Yaks was shot down by the B-26's gunners, and the other two were destroyed by a pair of 18th Group Mustangs which made a timely arrival on the scene. The action took place near Yangsi, fifteen miles south of Sinuiju. At noon an RF-80 reported that fifteen Yaks were parked in revetments on Sinuiju airfield, and Fifth AF ordered a strike by three flights of Shooting Stars. The F-80s strafed the airfield, destroying one Yak and damaging six more, but one American aircraft was shot down by flak from across the Yalu. A second F-80 strike was laid on, but the pilots found that the surviving Yaks had departed. At 1345 that day, six swept-wing jets crossed the Yalu and opened fire on a T-6 TAC aircraft and four Mustangs of the 18th Group that formed its escort. They made one firing pass without doing any damage, then flew back across the river. The T-6 pilot returned to Pyongyang to report that he had had a good look at one of the enemy aircraft. It was a MiG-15. The Communist challenge to UN air superiority was beginning.

CHAPTER 5

The Strategic Air Offensive – July-November 1950

Although FEAF Bomber Command's operational task in Korea was clearly defined from 11 July, when General Stratemeyer directed that it was to be responsible for interdiction and attacks on strategic targets north of the 38th Parallel, within a few days – as we have already seen – the situation in South Korea had become so critical that Bomber Command was ordered to apply its main effort to the battle area. Problems soon became apparent, caused mostly by faulty target selection. Most of the targets were too close to the battle zone, they were too numerous to be attacked by the B-29s then available, many of them were so obscure that they could not be visually identified by the bombardiers even under the best conditions, and some simply did not exist. For example, the first batch of targets included railway bridges in towns where no railway existed. The main problem was that obsolete Japanese maps were being used by the Target Group, and these often showed railways which had been projected but never built.

The rapid deployment of SAC B-29 groups to the Far East in July was an excellent demonstration of the Command's mobility. In the words of the official history of the USAF in Korea:

During most of July 1950 the B-29s of the 19th, 22nd and 92nd Groups carried out a diversified and often wasteful bombing effort against targets that included North Korean troop concentrations, marshalling yards and airfields. There were sporadic interception attempts by NKAF Yak-9 fighters: on 19 July air gunners of the 19th Group drove off two Yaks over Seoul before the latter could inflict more than light damage on one of the bombers. On 28 July B-29s of the 22nd Group attacked the Seoul marshalling yards, and since this area was the scene of most enemy fighter interceptions the group commander, Colonel James V. Edmundson, instructed his gunners to open fire on any unidentified fighter that came within range. When four strange aircraft broke cloud astern of a B-29, they came under fire from two gun positions and one of them was shot down. The gunners claimed a Yak, but in fact the aircraft was a Seafire from the carrier HMS *Triumph*. The pilot, luckily, bailed out and was rescued.

On 30 July, Bomber Command launched its biggest B-29 strike to date when forty-seven aircraft of the 22nd and 92nd Groups attacked the Chosen nitrogen explosives factory at Hungnam. All forty-seven bombers passed through the target area in four minutes, the lead squadrons bombing blind through the cloud with their

---

The swiftness of the medium bomber deployment to combat was possible only because of well-established Strategic Air Command mobility plans which had been designed for just such an emergency. In conjunction with the execution of its primary mission, the Strategic Air Command held the responsibility of maintaining air force units in readiness 'for employment against objectives of air attack in any part of the globe'. All units assigned to the Strategic Air Command were required to be 'highly mobile organizations, capable of being dispatched without delay to distant bases'. Command letters, directives and manuals gave, in complete detail, the various requirements for implementing the mobility plan. Emphasis had been placed upon the equipment of all units for thirty days' operations with a minimum amount of support from operating bases. Flyaway kits contained spare parts and served as a kind of airborne base supply. Bomb-bay bins carried other essential supplies. Each wing commander maintained a reserve of spare engines, engine quick-change packups, and power packups. The wing mobility plans and operations had been tested in overseas movements. The 22nd and 92nd Groups had been in the Far East and the United Kingdom; the 98th Group had been in the Far East, the United Kingdom, and at Goose Bay; and the 307th Group had served temporary duty in the United Kingdom and Germany.

The warning alert, followed by appropriate operations orders, went out to the 22nd and 92nd Groups on or soon after 1 July. Officers and airmen who had been planning Fourth-of-July holidays found themselves packing crates, loading cargo planes, or standing in line before the boarding ramps of planes bound for the Far East. After hurried hours of packing and preparation, the deployment airlift got under way. The two groups scheduled flights of ten B-29s each day, departing their home bases on 5 through 7 July. The 22nd left March Air Force Base, California, stopped off at Hickam for a rest period, then flew on to Kadena, with stops at Kwajalein and Guam. The 92nd Group took off from Spokane Air Force Base, Washington, and followed a similar flight plan, with a final destination of Yokota Air Base. The 92nd and 307th Groups were equally well prepared for short-notice departures. The 98th departed Spokane Air Force Base for Yokota between 2 and 4 August, and the 307th left McDill Air Force Base, Florida, between 1 and 3 August, headed for Kadena.

Nose art of a FEAF Bomber Command B-29. (via Robert F. Dorr)

APQ-13 radar. The explosions and fires burned some of the cloud away so that the trailing squadrons were able to bomb visually. The attack, codenamed 'Nannie Able', was highly successful: thirty per cent of the factory was completely destroyed and forty per cent heavily damaged. The second phase of the operation, 'Nannie Baker', was directed against the Chosen nitrogen fertiliser factory and took place on 1 August, when forty-six B-29s from the same two groups attacked the target visually with 500lb bombs from 16,000 feet. The crews reported observing large explosions with intensive smoke and flames in the target area; the shock waves were fierce enough to rock the aircraft, even at an altitude of three miles. The third phase, 'Nannie Charlie', was carried out on 3 August when thirty-nine B-29s attacked the Bogun chemical plant with good results. All three raids had involved precision attacks with high explosives, for authority to use incendiaries had not yet been received by General O'Donnell. Nevertheless, in the space of three days Bomber Command had inflicted appalling damage on the biggest explosives and chemical centre in Asia.

The chemical complex at Hungnam was one of five priority targets selected by Strategic Air Command Intelligence. The others were Pyongyang, which in addition to being the centre of the North Korean aircraft and armaments industry possessed extensive marshalling yards and railway repair shops; Wonsan, with its modern seaport and acres of oil refineries; the harbour town of Chongjin, with its iron foundries and railway yards; and the naval base, oil storage tanks and rail complex at Rashin, which lay only sixty miles from the Russian port of Vladivostok. All these targets, with

the exception of Pyongyang, lay on the north-east coast of Korea. Other targets of secondary strategic importance were the harbour of Chinnampo at the mouth of the Taedong river on the west coast, whose factories produced aluminium, magnesium, copper and zinc, and five east coast hydroelectric power complexes originally built by the Japanese during World War Two at Fusen, Chosin, Kyosen, Funei and Kongosan.

After its initial strategic attacks, Bomber Command switched the weight of its offensive against marshalling yards, bridge targets and troop concentrations, as described in chapter three. The last strategic target to be attacked in this phase was Rashin, which was bombed by radar on 12 August. However, most of the bombs fell in open country because of an azimuth error and no damage was inflicted on the target itself. A second attempt to bomb this target on 27 August was frustrated by bad weather and sixty-four B-29s bombed secondary targets at Chongjin. The fact that the bombers had failed to hit Rashin at all on their first attack, coupled with the target's close proximity to the Soviet border, had given rise to serious anxieties in the US State Department, where there were fears that the B-29s might infringe Soviet airspace – or, worse, bomb Soviet territory by mistake – and so provoke a major international incident. The Joint Chiefs of Staff, on the other hand, reasoned that since large quantities of war supplies were flowing into North Korea through Rashin, Bomber Command was justified in attacking the port, no matter how close it lay to Soviet territory. However, the politicians won the argument and on 1 September 1950 the Joint Chiefs instructed General Stratemeyer to cancel any plans for future attacks on this objective.

At the beginning of September FEAF strategists found themselves in a dilemma. Plans were well advanced for the amphibious landing at Inchon, coupled with a breakout from the Pusan perimeter, but it had not yet been decided whether UN forces would subsequently push on beyond the 38th Parallel or come to a halt when the North Koreans had been cleared from the South. In the latter case FEAF's planners were determined to complete the destruction of a wide cross-section of North Korea's industrial potential, including the hydroelectric plants which were supplying power to the Chinese People's Republic. The problem was that despite repeated requests to Washington for approval to attack the hydroelectric complexes, no advice at all was forthcoming from that quarter. In the end the Far East Command Target Selection Committee, with General MacArthur's approval, directed Bomber Command to carry out attacks on North Korea's hydroelectric power sources as planned, and on 26 September B-29s of the 92nd Group destroyed the Fusen hydroelectric plant near Hungnam. It was the last attack in this phase of the strategic bombing campaign; even as the target was under attack, a signal reached General MacArthur from Washington informing him that his troops were authorised to cross the 38th Parallel.

So far, the strategic bombing campaign in Korea had been characterised by great accuracy; the sole exception was the abortive attack on Rashin. Although industrial targets in the selected North Korean cities had been almost completely wiped out, the urban areas surrounding them had emerged virtually unscathed. Also, in the majority of cases, loss of life among the North Korean workers had been relatively small, for each raid had been preceded by a leaflet-dropping mission stating the time and place selected for the attack. However, there was no escaping the fact that the B-29s had been able to roam at will over North Korea because of a complete lack of opposition; fighter bomber interdiction had taken out the North Korean Air Force on its airfields, and the North Koreans lacked adequate anti-aircraft artillery.

During the last week of September, Bomber Command's B-29s struck hard at North Korean barracks and troop training centres at Pyongyang, Hamhung, Nanam and Hungnam. The Command was now running short of targets, and operations were complicated by the rapid advance of United Nations forces. On 6 October, for example, FEAF sent Bomber Command a list of thirty-three bridges to be attacked, but ROK troops advanced so rapidly up the east coast that ten of these targets were deleted within a week. Because of the shortage of targets, General O.P. Weyland, commanding FEAF, ordered Bomber Command to reduce its sorties to twenty-five per day after 10 October, and this was further reduced to fifteen sorties per day on 22 October. On this day, the 22nd and 92nd Bombardment Groups were released back to Strategic Air Command, the B-29s beginning their departure on 27 October. The whole of Bomber Command was now stood down; the UN forces that were moving forward to occupy the whole of North Korea were more than adequately supported by the fighter bombers of the Fifth AF and Task Force 77.

At a very early stage in the strategic bombing campaign General O'Donnell had stated that he did not intend to allow adverse weather conditions to interfere with the bombing effort. He told FEAF that he intended to drop more than 5,500 tons of bombs per month, more than the peak achievement of the B-29 force that had operated against Japan from the Marianas six years earlier. It was no idle promise: between 31 July and 31 October 1950 Bomber Command dropped over 30,000 tons of bombs on targets in Korea. Although formation attacks were desirable against targets like industrial complexes, which required a heavy bombing concentration, when these were precluded by bad weather the bombers made their run across the target area in a long stream, each aircraft bombing singly with the aid of its AN/APQ-13 bombing radar. (The 19th Group did not have this equipment, which was installed only in the SAC aircraft.) Every effort was made to maintain a high degree of efficiency in ground-controlled approach techniques at the bomber bases, and the fact that there were no major bad weather landing accidents was ample testimony to the skill of the GCA controllers.

The respite for the three remaining Bomber Command groups in the Korean theatre was to be short-lived. In the light of intelligence on Chinese troop movements early in November, General O'Donnell was authorised to send his B-29s to attack four North Korean cities which were key centres of munitions and communications. The B-29s were to carry full loads of incendiaries, and their task was to burn the selected cities from end to end. This decision was ratified on 5 November when General MacArthur issued a directive calling for a maximum air effort lasting two weeks. It was the signal for the beginning of an unrestricted bombing campaign against North Korea.

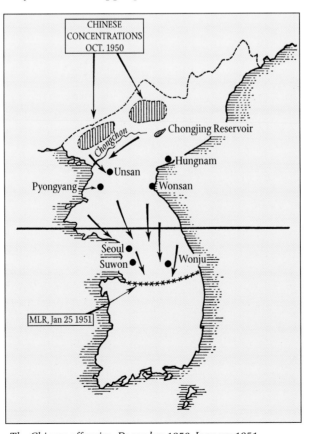

The Chinese offensive, December 1950–January 1951.

CHAPTER 6
Battle Over The Yalu

A3D Skyraider on the elevator of a US carrier off Korea. (via Robert F. Dorr)

Although the extent of the Chinese involvement in Korea had still not been fully assessed in the first week of November 1950, the prospect of massive attacks by Chinese forces presented General Walker, commanding the US Eighth Army, with a serious problem. Because of their rapid drive northwards his forces were badly overstretched, with supplies of food and ammunition for only two or three days, and on 3 November, erring on the side of caution, he ordered the Eighth Army to fall back to the line of the Chongchon river, where it could regroup and build up its resources in readiness for a new offensive. The withdrawal, which was effectively covered by the Fifth AF, was completed by 7 November.

Meanwhile, FEAF Bomber Command was standing by to attack the Korean ends of several strategic bridges over the Yalu river, with particular reference to the twin 3,098-foot bridges which linked Antung in Manchuria with Sinuiju in North Korea, and over which a steady flow of supplies was reaching Chinese troops fighting in the north. Not everyone in US political circles agreed with the plan to attack the bridges, even though there was agreement among the military that if Allied air power was to be exploited to its fullest effect there would have to be a change in the policy that until now had vetoed air attacks on targets that lay close to the Manchurian and Soviet borders.

On 3 November, representatives of the Far East Air

Forces and the US Seventh Fleet met in Tokyo to work out a formula for waging a new and stepped-up air war. Repeated requests by General Partridge for his pilots to be authorised to attack and destroy enemy aircraft on their airfields just over the Manchurian border met with equally repeated refusals, but General Stratemeyer did give authority for the Fifth AF's fighter bombers to range over the whole of North Korea up to the banks of the Yalu river with the proviso that such missions were

Grumman F9F Panther, arrester hook extended, about to touch down on a US carrier off Korea. (via Robert F. Dorr)

49

to be flown only by experienced pilots with accurate details of the targets they were briefed to attack.

By the time a copy of General MacArthur's directive reached Washington in the evening of 5 November, the first of Bomber Command's planned incendiary raids had already taken place. Earlier in the day, B-29s of the 19th BG had dropped 170 tons of fire bombs on the North Korean town of Kanggye. The news of the raid, together with the decision to attack the Yalu bridges, caused a storm in Congress, and a response was not long in coming. Before midnight, President Truman, through the Joint Chiefs of Staff, had sent a signal forbidding MacArthur to employ his bombers within five miles of the Manchurian border. MacArthur immediately countered with another signal in which he informed the Joint Chiefs that vast quantities of Chinese troops and materiel were pouring across the bridges. In fact, most of the damage had been done by now: the majority of the Chinese combat troops, together with their support equipment, had already made the crossing under cover of darkness during the preceding two weeks. Nevertheless, this explanation was enough to convince the Joint Chiefs that MacArthur was right. On

climbed back across the Yalu, but the sixth entered a shallow dive and one of the F-80 pilots, Lt Russell J. Brown, seized his opportunity. The F-80 was heavier than the MiG and Brown rapidly overhauled his target, putting a five-second burst into it as it pulled up into a climb. Burning fiercely, the MiG went down to crash on the banks of the river. It was the first hostile jet-versus-jet combat in history.

On 9 November, the Yalu bridges between Sinuiju and Hyesanjin, some 200 miles upstream, were attacked by aircraft of Task Force 77 operating from the carriers *Valley Forge*, *Philippine Sea* and *Leyte*. The strikes, by Skyraiders carrying 1,000lb bombs and by Corsairs armed with either bombs or rockets, were covered by F9F Panthers. The MiGs came up to challenge the US Navy aircraft, and in the ensuing engagement one of the enemy jets was shot down by Lt-Cdr W.T. Amen, officer commanding VF-111 aboard the USS *Philippine Sea*, who became the first US Navy pilot to score a jet kill. The naval air strikes lasted for nine days, and on 18 November a Panther from *Leyte* and a pair from *Valley Forge* shot down two more MiGs. No US Navy aircraft were lost. In all, the Navy pilots flew 593 sorties and

Ground crew prepare a 49th FBW Thunderjet for a sortie.

6 November attacks on the bridges were authorised, though every precaution was to be taken to ensure that no UN aircraft strayed over the border into Manchuria. The Joint Chiefs also made it clear that the territory in the vicinity of the Soviet border was to remain strictly prohibited and that no attacks were to be made on targets in this area, no matter how promising they might appear.

Bad weather delayed the start of the bombing campaign against the Yalu bridges by twenty-four hours, but at dawn on 8 November seventy B-29s dropped 580 tons of incendiary bombs on Sinuiju, while F-51s and F-80s suppressed flak around the town. Top cover for the mission was provided by two flights of Shooting Stars of the 51st FIW, whose pilots knew what frustration felt like as, powerless to intervene, they watched MiG-15s taking off from Antung airfield just across the river. Six MiGs climbed to 30,000 feet and dived in pairs towards the F-80s, whose pilots turned to meet the attack head-on. Five of the MiGs, after a few bursts of inaccurate fire, broke away and

dropped 232 tons of bombs, an effort that was rewarded with the destruction of only three bridges.

The bridges were proving extremely difficult targets for the B-29s. To avoid the heavy AAA the aircraft had to bomb from altitudes above 18,000 feet, with a resulting drop in accuracy, and to avoid border violations they frequently had to bomb through crosswinds that reached speeds of over 120 knots at high level. In addition, the B-29s began to encounter increasingly determined opposition from enemy jet fighters. On 10 November the 307th Group suffered its first combat loss when a MiG-15 shot down one of its B-29s over Uiju, and on the 12th a 98th Group B-29 just managed to limp in to an emergency landing at Kimpo after being badly mauled by MiGs several miles south of the river. Other 98th Group B-29s which attacked the bridges at Sinuiju two days later sighted no enemy interceptors, but the next day two bombers of the 19th and 307th Groups were badly damaged by MiGs while attacking the same target. Further medium bomber operations were curtailed for a week because of bad weather, but on 25 and 26 November B-29s of the 19th and 307th Groups destroyed two more bridges across the river, one at Manpojin and the other at Chongsonjin.

When the MiG-15 first made its appearance over Korea it soon became clear that the Fifth Air Force's standard jet fighter, the F-80C, was inferior to the Russian jet fighter on every count except diving speed and, perhaps, manoeuvrability. Accordingly, on 8 November 1950 General Vandenberg offered to deploy two more fighter wings to Korea: the 4th, equipped with North American F-86A Sabres, and the 27th Fighter Escort Wing, equipped with Republic F-84E Thunderjets. The latter unit was assigned to Strategic Air Command, its role to escort SAC's B-29s on short-range tactical bombing operations. The 27th Wing was based at Bergstrom AFB near Austin, Texas, while the 4th Fighter Interceptor Wing was at New Castle County airport, Wilmington, Delaware, where it was assigned to the Eastern Air Defence Force. From their respective bases the Thunderjets and Sabres were flown to San Diego, California, where in the two weeks after 14 November they were deck-loaded aboard two aircraft

carriers and a fast tanker. The urgency that accompanied the move to Korea created its own crop of problems, not least of which was that the aircraft were loaded on to the ships without adequate waterproofing. As a result most of them – especially those in passage on the tanker – suffered substantial corrosion damage from salt spray during the journey across the Pacific. As Colonel Ashley B. Packard, commanding the 27th Wing, wrote later, 'Two or three days allowed in properly preparing the aircraft for shipment would probably have saved another week at this [the Korean] end.'

Although the deployment of the two fighter wings to the Korean theatre was accomplished in record time, the situation in Korea had deteriorated rapidly while they were en route. General Partridge had planned to position the 4th Wing at Pyongyang and the 27th Wing at Kimpo, but in early December, with the two wings assembled and combat-ready, such a deployment was no longer possible. The 27th Wing accordingly established a rear echelon at Itazuke, Japan, and deployed its Thunderjets to Taegu airfield to begin armed reconnaissance and close support missions,

F-86 Sabre of the 4th FIW high over Korea. (via Robert F. Dorr)

while Colonel George F. Smith, commanding the 4th Wing, established a large rear echelon at Johnson Air Base, Honshu, and deployed pilots and aircraft to Kimpo. This deployment, known as 'Detachment A', mainly comprised the Sabres and pilots of the 336th FIS. Kimpo was the only Korean airfield suitable for Sabre operation, and was already badly overcrowded.

By the last week of November 1950 the Allied air offensive had destroyed or damaged some sixty-five per cent of North Korea's strategic bridges. The flow of Chinese troops and equipment into Korea, however, continued virtually unabated over pontoon bridges erected by Chinese engineers, and increased dramatically when the Yalu began to freeze and the ice became thick enough to support heavy equipment. Attacks by B-29s and by B-26s of the 3rd and 452nd Bombardment Groups on nine major supply and communications centres in North Korea, although they inflicted considerable damage, did little to hinder the steady Chinese build-up. American Intelligence sources had in fact gravely underestimated the actual number of Chinese troops already in Korea at the beginning of November. Eighth Army G-2, Far East Command Intelligence, and the Central Intelligence Agency all agreed that the number of Chinese Communist Forces (CCF) in North Korea at the beginning of November did not exceed 60,000, but by that time more than 180,000 Chinese troops had already crossed the Yalu. It was only when Allied troops in the front line began to suffer heavy and repeated setbacks at the hands of vastly superior communist forces that the serious nature of the error was appreciated. There were two reasons for this lack of intelligence. The first was that the CCF were adept at moving across country in small groups at night to reach their assembly areas, and in the almost complete absence of an Allied spy network in North Korea these movements went undetected. The second was a critical shortage of air reconnaissance assets, a problem compounded by the fact that the Allies had no detailed and accurate maps of the North – a serious shortcoming when it came to interpreting aerial photographs.

On the outbreak of hostilities in Korea, FEAF did not possess an effective air reconnaissance system. Its sole reconnaissance capability, discounting the two RB-17s of the 6204th Photo-Mapping Flight at Clark AFB, lay with the RB-29s of the 31st Strategic Reconnaissance Squadron at Kadena and the RF-80As of the 8th Tactical Reconnaissance Squadron at Yokota, but no real plans existed for their operational use in the event of war, and their effectiveness suffered as a consequence. This meant that FEAF had to build up a reconnaissance system from scratch, which was a slow process. A third reconnaissance unit, the 167th TRS (Night Photography) with RB-26s, arrived at Itazuke towards the end of August 1950, but the next unit to arrive, the 45th TRS operating RF-51s, was not able to begin operations from Itazuke until November because of a shortage of aircraft. The 45th TRS's role was visual reconnaissance, and until it began operations this task was carried out on behalf of the Eighth Army almost entirely by T-6 Texans, their crews running incredible risks.

An RF-51D Mustang of the 45th Tactical Reconnaissance Squadron taking off from Kimpo.
(Martin Bambrick)

F9F Panthers of VMF-311 on a pierced steel planking hardstand at a Korean airfield.

The first really effective step towards organising an air reconnaissance capability came in September when the 543rd Tactical Support Group was activated at Itazuke to provide a headquarters for the FEAF reconnaissance force. This led to the formation, in February 1951, of the 67th Tactical Reconnaissance Wing, which grouped all existing FEAF reconnaissance units under its command. The designations of some of these were changed: the 543rd Group became the 67th, while the 8th and 162nd Tactical Reconnaissance Squadrons became the 15th and 12th respectively. Only the 45th TRS retained its original designation. Meanwhile, on 16 November 1950, the 31st SRS was redesignated the 91st SRS, which continued to operate RB-29s from Okinawa. Since July 1950 the 91st SRS, based at Barksdale AFB in Louisiana, had been re-equipping with the Boeing RB-50, a much improved variant of the RB-29, but in this paper transaction the more modern aircraft remained in the USA. By this time the Japan-based RB-29s had begun to suffer so heavily from flak and hostile fighters over the Yalu that their task in this sector was assigned to the RF-80As of the 8th TRS, which were ill-equipped to provide the necessary coverage.

Despite the lack of accurate intelligence, and despite continuing reports of growing numbers of Chinese troops assembling south of the Yalu, hopes for a final and successful Allied drive to the Manchurian border remained high in November 1950. Combat patrols pushed out along the front by the Eighth Army and the ROK reported only weak enemy resistance. What the Allied commanders failed to realise, until it was too late, was that the Chinese were faithfully obeying the tactics formulated by Mao Tse-tung's guerrillas in the mountains of China twenty years earlier. The tactics were simple enough: the enemy would be allowed to advance, the communists falling back before him and offering only minimal resistance; then, when the enemy's supply lines were overstretched, the full fury of the communist armies would be unleashed against him. The United Nations forces in Korea, like Chiang Kai-shek's Kuomintang army before them, were soon to learn this elementary military lesson the hard way.

Across the border, China's leaders were under no illusions. They knew that the coming offensive by their armies in Korea would bring with it the possibility of an all-out war with the United States. It was a risk they were prepared to accept, including the awesome threat of an atomic strike against Chinese targets by Strategic Air Command. By the beginning of November 1950, in preparation for such an eventuality, the whole of north-east China was placed on a war footing. Air-raid drill was carried out in every town and village, and deep air-raid shelters were being built in and around major targets. These activities were accompanied by a rapid expansion of the Chinese communist air defence system, which was being brought up to date with Soviet help.

The United Nations Command still had no clear picture of Chinese dispositions and intentions on 23 November, when plans for the big push to the Yalu were finalised. The operational plan envisaged an advance to the Sinuiju–Suiho area by the 24th Division and the ROK 1st Division, with the Commonwealth Brigade in reserve on the Eighth Army's left flank. Simultaneously, in the centre, the 2nd and 25th Divisions would advance north and north-east along the Kuryong and Chingchon valleys to the border, while on the right, covering the mountains around Tokchon, was the ROK II Corps, with the US 1st Cavalry Division in reserve at Sunchon. Two US Marine formations, the 5th and 7th Regiments of the 1st Marine Division, had already advanced as far as Yudam-ni at the eastern end of the Chosin reservoir. Their orders were to remain there for four days before advancing to join up with the Eighth Army at Mupyong, after which the combined force was to press on to Manpojin on the Manchurian border. From the eastern side of the reservoir three battalions of the 7th Division were to drive northwards to the frontier, while the remainder of the division was eventually to join up with the ROK I Corps, advancing towards Chongjin and from there to the Soviet border. The whole offensive plan gave the United Nations a front-line fighting strength of 100,000 troops, facing an as yet indeterminate number of Chinese and North Koreans. In fact, the UN combat troops were already outnumbered by something like two to one.

The renewed Allied offensive began at 1000 on 24 November, and by nightfall the leading echelons had advanced eight miles into enemy territory, meeting almost no opposition. There was little work for the Fifth Air Force, and few calls were made on its fighter bombers. Then, shortly after dawn on 25 November, a company of the 9th Infantry Regiment, 2nd Infantry Division, came under heavy mortar and machine gun fire from Hill 219, overlooking the east bank of the Chongchon. The Americans went to ground and exchanged fire with the enemy. Two hours later, wave after wave of Chinese infantry made a suicidal attack across the river from the north-west, only to be beaten off with terrible losses by Allied artillery fire. That afternoon, however, a second charge smashed through the 2nd Division's line two miles upriver, forcing an American withdrawal. By the evening of 26 November the Division had been forced back another two miles, while on the left in the Kuryong valley the 25th Division was desperately withstanding Chinese attacks.

Then came the big punch; the springing of the trap so carefully laid during the preceding weeks by the Chinese C-in-C, General Lin Piao. At dusk on 26 November the Fourth Chinese Field Army advanced down the central mountain passes and came into violent contact with the ROK II Corps at Tokchon. Within twenty-four hours ROK II Corps had been shattered and dislocated by the onslaught, and with it crumbled the Eighth Army's right flank. The Turkish Brigade, hurrying to the assistance of the South Koreans, met the remnants of the ROK infantry streaming southwards in disorderly retreat, utterly demoralised. Fifth AF fighter bombers flew 345 sorties in two days, but there was nothing they could do to stem the Chinese tide.

By daybreak on 27 November the United Nations commanders had at last begun to realise the full terrifying extent of the Chinese involvement. Ranged against the Allied forces were no fewer than six Chinese armies, comprising eighteen divisions of the Thirteenth Army Group. On the 28th, General MacArthur informed the United Nations in a special communiqué that, 'Enemy reactions developed in the course of our assault operations of the past four days disclose that a major segment of the Chinese continental forces in Army, Corps and Divisional organisation in an aggregate strength of over 200,000 men is now arrayed against the United Nations forces in North Korea. Consequently, we face an entirely new war.'

By the time the communiqué was being read in Washington, Allied forces were in full retreat from the Chongchon in conditions of appalling chaos. Everywhere the Chinese had infiltrated in strength behind the Allied lines. On 30 November the 2nd Division, retreating southwards along the Kunuri-Sunchon road and already reeling from earlier attacks, was ambushed by an entire Chinese division, dug in along a six-mile stretch of the river.

In two hours the Division suffered some 3,000 casualties, adding to the 1,000 it had already sustained in earlier fighting, and lost most of its heavy equipment.

F4U Corsair running-up prior to launch on a combat sortie over Korea. (via Robert F. Dorr)

Crewmen arming a Corsair on the USS Valley Forge *(CV-45).*

Some of the men were victims of friendly fire, as Allied fighter bombers strafed Chinese positions only yards away from the American column. The survivors managed to fight their way out in small groups during the night, eventually staggering exhausted and broken into the lines of the 27th Commonwealth Brigade and the 1st Cavalry to the south. The Division had ceased to exist as a cohesive fighting force, and on MacArthur's orders it was withdrawn to rest and reorganise. In the Chosin area, General Oliver Smith's 1st Marine Division was trapped in some of the most rugged terrain in the whole of Korea. The Marines' only escape route lay along a narrow dirt and gravel road running through the mountain passes. One stretch, known as the Funchilin Pass, was a ten-mile section of winding track that climbed 2,500 feet along a narrow shelf, flanked by a cliff on the one hand and a sheer drop on the other. Another pass was at an altitude of 4,000 feet, where temperatures fell to 32° below zero. Under the circumstances General Smith would have been justified in abandoning his heavy equipment, and in fact was authorised to do so, but he refused and the Marines began their fighting retreat in good order on 1 December, supplied by C-46s, C-47s and C-119s of Combat Cargo Command.

It was now that tactical air power came into its own. From day one, air support was provided by aircraft from the carriers *Leyte*, *Philippine Sea* and *Badoeng Strait*, which were then on station, and as the withdrawal proceeded other carriers added their weight: USS *Princeton* on 5 December, USS *Sicily* on 7 December, USS *Bataan* on 16 December, and USS *Valley Forge* on the 23rd. Operating from Yonpo airfield to the south-west, Marine fighter-bombers of VMF-214, VMF-323 and VMF(N)-513, reinforced by VMF-212 and VMF(N)-542, kept aircraft over the battlefield virtually round the clock. From 6 December tactical air operations were controlled by a modified R5D (C-54) aircraft of Marine Transport Squadron 152 (VMR-152),

fitted with communications equipment.

By 7 December over 14,000 men had reached Koto-ri at the end of the first stage of the breakout. A small landing strip there was lengthened, enabling transports to fly in supplies and evacuate wounded. TBM-3E Avengers were also used in the casualty evacuation role, joining the OY-1, OY-2 and H03S-1 helicopters of VMO-6. There were many acts of bravery during the breakout, both in the air and on the ground. One of the most outstanding occurred on 4 December when an F4U Corsair of VF-32 from the USS *Leyte*, flown by Ensign Jesse L. Brown, was shot down by ground fire. Brown's wingman, Lt (JG) Thomas J. Hudner, crash-landed his own Corsair in the snow beside the wreck and made a vain attempt to save Brown from the burning aircraft while awaiting the arrival of a rescue helicopter. Unfortunately, Brown died before help arrived, but Hudner's gallant action brought him the award of the Medal of Honor. Ensign Brown, who came from Hattiesburg, Mississippi, was the first black US Navy officer to lose his life in combat.

The final stage of the breakout began on 8 December, the Marines crossing a mountain gorge by means of bridge sections dropped by C-119s; the originals had been destroyed by Chinese infiltrators. Three days later the Marines began arriving in the Hungnam assembly area, from where they were to be evacuated by sea behind the security of a strong defensive perimeter. A naval force of about 100 ships, designated Task Force 90, had been assembled for the purpose, and by 24 December 1950 the vessels had embarked 100,000 troops, all their heavy equipment, and some 90,000 North Korean civilians. During the evacuation phase, carrier aircraft (including the Marine fighter-bombers, which had redeployed to their ships from Yonpo) flew 1,700 sorties in support of the perimeter defence, while gunfire support ships fired 22,000 rounds, from sixteen-inch down to 40mm, together with 1,500 rocket projectiles.

CHAPTER 7
Holding On

On 15 December 1950 the 4th FIW's newly arrived F-86A Sabres carried out their first familiarisation flight from Kimpo, and on the 17th the Wing mounted its first offensive sweep of the war when four Sabres of the 336th FIS, each carrying two 120-gallon drop tanks to increase combat radius to 490 nautical miles, headed north towards the Yalu. The American pilots, all of whom were highly experienced – some had already achieved the status of 'aces' by destroying five or more enemy aircraft in World War Two – had given considerable thought to the tactics they would employ. They used the basic and well-tried 'finger four' battle formation which broke down into elements of two upon engaging in combat; the idea was to enter the patrol area at altitudes between 27,000 and 33,000 feet, just below contrail level, so that the pilots could easily spot hostile aircraft above them by their vapour trails. On this first combat mission, however, the Sabre pilots made a mistake that might have cost them dearly had they encountered skilled adversaries.

As the distance between Kimpo and the Yalu was 430 miles and the pilots wanted to extend their patrol time, they entered the combat area at a leisurely, fuel-conserving speed of 0.62M, so that when the Sabre flight, led by Lt-Col Bruce H. Hinton, sighted a battle formation of four MiG-15s the F-86s were flying too slowly to achieve maximum effectiveness. Fortunately, the MiGs were below and climbing; their pilots doubtless believed that the American fighters were F-80s, otherwise they would almost certainly have climbed for altitude on the other side of the Yalu. They realised their mistake only when the Sabres came diving down on them, rapidly gaining speed, whereupon the MiGs broke away and dived for the sanctuary of Manchuria. They were too late. Colonel Hinton's element clung to the tail of the number two MiG and Hinton fired three four-second bursts from his six 0.50-inch machine guns. The enemy aircraft burst into flames and went into a slow spin. It was the first of 792 MiGs which were to be claimed by Sabre pilots during the two and a half years of air combat that followed.

Main Picture: The fighter that trounced the MiGs: an F-86 Sabre lands after a sortie over Korea. Note the extended speed brakes.
Insets: This sequence of four shots from a gun camera film clearly shows the initial strikes on a MiG-15's fuselage, followed by a burst of smoke from the engine.

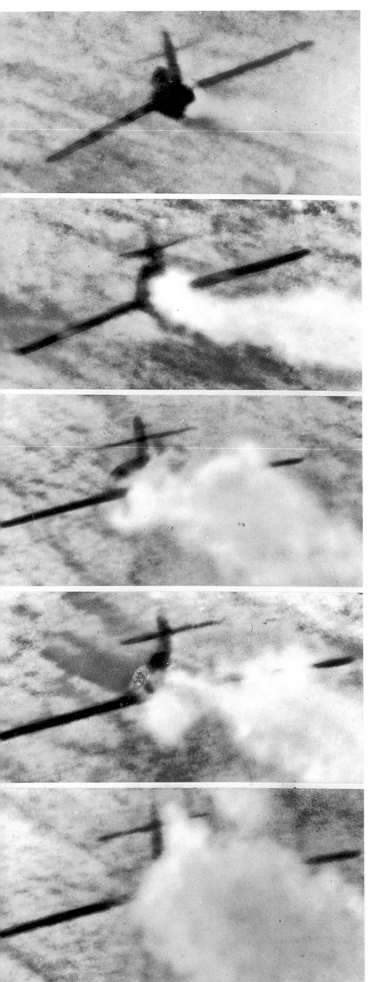

There were several more encounters between MiGs and Sabres during the next few days, but these were inconclusive and no casualties were suffered by either side. By this time both sides were quickly catching on to the other's tactics and rapidly taking steps to counter them. The Sabre's main drawback was its lack of endurance. Patrolling at speeds of 0.85M and higher, the Sabre pilots could afford to spend only twenty minutes in the vicinity of the Yalu before being compelled to return home with a safe margin of fuel. The MiG pilots quickly realised this limitation and exploited it to the fullest advantage, climbing to altitude north of the Yalu and then diving across at high speed to make their attack as the Sabres were withdrawing towards the end of their patrol. The Americans in turn began to mount patrols of sixteen aircraft, operating in four flights of four, which arrived in the combat area at various altitudes at intervals of five minutes. In this way the withdrawal of all but the last Sabre flight was adequately covered.

On 22 December eight Sabres led by Lt-Col John C. Meyer – one of the USAF's leading fighter pilots with twenty-four victories in World War Two – were on an offensive patrol at 30,000 feet south of the Yalu when they were engaged by fifteen-plus MiG-15s. In an engagement lasting twenty minutes and ranging from high altitude to treetop level, the Sabre pilots destroyed six MiGs for the loss of one of their own number, Captain L.V. Bach. After this mauling the MiGs were absent from the sky for a week, and the next time they appeared, on 30 December, their pilots showed extreme caution in joining combat. On this occasion thirty-six MiGs crossed the Yalu and engaged sixteen Sabres, but the enemy quickly broke off the action and headed for home. The Sabre pilots claimed two MiG-15s damaged.

In all, the 4th Wing's Sabres carried out 234 offensive sorties during December 1950, claiming the destruction of eight MiGs, together with two more probably destroyed and seven damaged for the loss of one of their own number. These early encounters left the Sabre pilots with the conviction that the two fighter types were more or less evenly matched; the slight advantages enjoyed by one over the other in various respects could almost be dismissed. What counted was the comparative skill of the pilots, and it was quickly apparent that in this respect the Americans enjoyed an overwhelming advantage. Time and again, superior tactics combined with superior training were to pay dividends for the United Nations in the air war over Korea, and the UN pilots would have been even more encouraged had they known that the majority of their adversaries were not Chinese but Russian, as we shall see later.

The Sabre pilots were almost always at a tactical disadvantage. The MiG pilots, operating from their main base at Antung across the Yalu, could select the time and position for their attacks. Moreover, the combination of high subsonic speeds and G forces permitted hardly any deflection shooting; the way to achieve a sure kill was from astern, but few pilots ever found themselves in this ideal situation more than once in an engagement. The Mk 18 gunsight mounted in the Sabre was found to be too erratic for accurate deflection shooting at indicated airspeeds of more than 500 knots,

A MiG tries to escape from its pursuer by diving away, but is hit and burns.

and the F-86's armament of .50 calibre machine guns was allowing too many damaged MiGs to get away. With heavier-calibre, equally fast-firing guns and a radar-ranging gunsight the Sabres might have achieved more kills than was the case.

While the Sabres took their first steps towards establishing air superiority, the UN ground forces strove desperately to halt the CCF offensive and form a new defensive line, a task in which the only hope of success lay with the expert use of tactical air power. During the first week of December the emphasis was on air strikes in the vicinity of the front line, but after that General Partridge ordered the Fifth Air Force to devote its main effort to interdiction and armed reconnaissance sorties in the enemy rear. On 15 December, FEAF launched Interdiction Campaign No. 4, which called for sustained attacks by Fifth AF and FEAF Bomber Command on targets in eleven separate zones north of the 37th Parallel. Once again the aim was to devastate the enemy's communications, forty-five railway bridges, twelve highway bridges, thirteen tunnels, thirty-nine marshalling yards and sixty-three supply centres being slated for attack. Three of the interdiction zones, on the east coast running from Wonsan to the Siberian border, were to be the responsibility of Naval Forces Far East.

Just as the North Koreans had done in the early days of the war, the Chinese, in their headlong pursuit of the retreating UN forces, cast aside all pretence of stealth and began to move across country in large concentrations in daylight, which made them particularly vulnerable to air attack. The main roads leading south were packed with masses of troops and equipment, and Fifth AF's fighter-bombers inflicted fearful casualties on the enemy with concentrated machine gun, rocket and napalm attacks. By 16 December FEAF Intelligence estimated that air attack had caused 33,000 enemy casualties. This figure was probably grossly exaggerated, but the fact that the Chinese were suffering heavily became apparent when, on 17 December, the Chinese armies suddenly went to ground again, either moving at night or in small camouflaged groups by daytime. Meanwhile, Bomber

Command's B-29s had been active in carrying out the tasks allotted to them under Interdiction Campaign No. 4. On 21 and 22 December, following sporadic attacks on supply centres and troop concentrations in various North Korean towns, the Command launched a maximum effort operation against four principal North Korean bridges, but then the interdiction order was changed and during the remainder of the month most of the bombing effort was once more directed against towns and villages where there were reported to be enemy troop concentrations.

At this critical stage of the battle, serious thought was given by the US Joint Chiefs of Staff to the possibility of using nuclear weapons against the massed Chinese ground forces. Later estimates indicated that a forty-kiloton airburst weapon exploded over a dense enemy concentration at Taechon on the night of 24/25 November would have destroyed about 15,000 of the 22,000 Chinese troops assembled there; six forty-kiloton airbursts over the Chinese troop assembly area in the Pyongyang–Chorwon–Kumhwa triangle between 27 and 29 December 1950 would have destroyed half of an estimated force of 95,000 men, while six thirty-kiloton airbursts laid along enemy lines north of the Imjin river on the night of 31 December 1950 would have wiped out between 28,000 and 40,000 of an enemy force numbering 70,000 to 100,000. The idea, however, was politically untenable, and in any case there were major technical obstacles. At the end of 1950 only a small part of SAC's bomber force was nuclear-capable, and that was based in the United States; it would have taken time to deploy the aircraft (which would have been drawn from the 509th Bomb Group) and their special weapons to the Far East, and by that time the enemy troop concentrations would have long since dispersed. Temporary deployments (TDY) of SAC's nuclear strike force were made to the Far East later in the war, but although the aircraft brought the bomb cases and HE elements with them, nuclear capsules were not fitted and would have had to have been flown out at short notice. Up to the end of 1950 the US stockpile of atomic weapons was small and was wholly assigned to

Laden with two 500lb bombs, an F-80 of the 49th FBW is helped off the runway by JATO (Jet Assisted Take-Off).

This Panther, flown by Lt (JG) Robert E. Rostine of Henderson, Nevada, had a fuel line shot away by AA fire. The fuel ignited as it touched down for an emergency landing.

strategic use. Also, the use of nuclear weapons in a tactical situation in Korea, close to the front line, would have inflicted casualties on friendly forces as well as on the enemy.

The Chinese onslaught in North Korea, unprecedented as it was in size and fury, had made necessary the hasty reorganisation of some of the Fifth Air Force's combat units deployed on forward airfields. The Mustangs of the 8th and 18th Fighter Bomber Wings, for example, had just four days in which to evacuate Pyongyang and pull back to new bases at Seoul and Suwon, and it was to the credit of pilots and ground crews alike that during the withdrawal the Mustangs continued to operate at maximum effort. However, much of the two Wings' supporting equipment and considerable quantities of supplies had to be abandoned. The 35th Fighter Interceptor Wing, which had been operating from Yonpo on the east coast in support of the Marines, had a much more orderly withdrawal, the Mustangs pulling back to Pusan East airfield without incident and the ground personnel being evacuated by sea. It was joined there by VMF-311, the first Marine air squadron to operate jets in combat, whose Grumman F9F Panthers had been carrying out interdiction missions from Yonpo since 10 December.

The Eighth Army's plan was to hold on for as long as possible at its defensive line around Seoul before withdrawing further south to the old Pusan perimeter. It

could therefore only be a matter of time before the United Nations airfields at Seoul, Kimpo and Suwon were also taken by the enemy, and in the middle of December the 18th Fighter Bomber Wing underwent a further move, this time to the old Japanese airfield at Chinhae on the southern coast of Korea. With it went No. 2 'Cheetah' Squadron, South African Air Force, whose Mustangs had been operating in Korea since October as part of the British Commonwealth commitment. The main echelon of the 51st Fighter Interceptor Wing, meanwhile, pulled out to Itazuke, leaving behind only a detachment at Kimpo. The 8th Wing also moved back to Itazuke to re-equip with F-80C Shooting Stars, its serviceable Mustangs re-allocated to other units.

These redeployments imposed an additional strain on the already overtaxed resources of Combat Cargo Command, more than a third of whose effort was directed in support of the Fifth Air Force, and the arrival of reinforcements in the shape of two squadrons of the 61st Troop Carrier Group at Ashiya in mid-December was greeted with considerable relief. The 61st Group's first operation in Korea was a mission of mercy: on 20 December twelve of its C-54s flew to Kimpo in a snowstorm and airlifted nearly 1,000 Korean orphan children – a tiny fraction of the pitiful stream of refugees struggling southwards before the terror of the Chinese invasion – to a safe refuge on

Cheju-do Island off the southern coast of Korea. The mission, known as Operation 'Christmas Kidlift', was flown at the request of two Fifth Air Force chaplains, Colonel Wallace I. Wolverton and Lt-Col Russell E. Blaisdell, who had been preoccupied with the terrible hardships endured by the refugee children since the Chinese offensive began.

By the middle of December morale among the American ground forces, and to a certain extent the air

way, the Chinese armies would have been prevented from crossing the Yalu.

Within twenty-four hours General Ridgway was stepping out of a transport aircraft on to the frozen earth of Taegu airstrip, still clad in the uniform he had been wearing in the Pentagon two days earlier. He was appalled at what he found. The Americans were in low spirits and there was a dearth of good leadership. Moreover, there was an almost complete lack of

The F-80C and some of its extensive weapons load.

forces, was at a low ebb. Then, on 23 December, came another blow: General Walton Walker, the Eighth Army's well-liked commander, was killed when his jeep was hit by a ROK Army truck and overturned in a paddy field. With the United Nations Command already in a state of confusion and another massive Chinese offensive expected at any moment, Walker's death could not have come at a worse time. It was fortunate that General MacArthur had had the foresight to name his successor some time before, should one be needed. The chosen successor was General Matthew B. Ridgway, then the Deputy Chief of Staff. Ridgway arrived in Tokyo on Christmas Day, and on 26 December he was in conference with MacArthur. The Commander-in-Chief told him that all proposals for an attack on China had been rejected by Washington and the objective was now to fight a war of containment in South Korea. Ridgway also noted that, surprisingly, MacArthur appeared to have become disillusioned with the effectiveness of tactical air power. His main objection was that tactical air power had not so far been able to isolate the battlefield or stop the flow of hostile troops and supplies, nor did there seem to be any prospect of its doing so with any degree of success in the future. The principal cause of the C-in-C's main disillusionment, however, lay in the fact that he had advocated the use of Strategic Air Command to attack key targets in Manchuria with conventional weapons; his opinion was that, had SAC been unleashed in this

accurate intelligence. 'All Intelligence could show me,' he wrote later, 'was a big red goose egg out in front of us with 174,000 scrawled in the middle of it.' He quickly realised that his first task was to carry out a lightning tour of the battlefield, telling his troops that they were going to stay in Korea and fight, and, most important of all, why they were going to do it. Only when the rot had been stopped could he hope to draw up a successful plan of action to repel the next Chinese offensive.

The basis of such an action had already been laid by the late General Walker, who had drawn four defensive lines designed to hold up the enemy for as long as possible in their drive south. The first of these lines – 'Able', to the north of Pyongyang – had been pierced by the Chinese before Walker's troops had been able to take up their positions, and when Ridgway assumed command the Eighth Army was establishing itself on the 135-mile-long second line of defence, 'Baker', which ran along the Imjin river and the 38th Parallel. The third line of defence was 'Charlie', stretching around Seoul in a crescent-shaped bridgehead and from there via Hongchon to the east coast, and the fourth line, 'Dog', cut across the Korean peninsula through Pyongtaek, Wonju and Samchok. In theory, Ridgway had at his disposal some 350,000 men to defend these lines, but it was soon apparent that this was nothing more than a paper figure, for on Christmas Day 1950 fewer than half these troops were combat-ready. It must have been one of the gloomiest situations ever to

Douglas B-26 Invader undergoing servicing. (via Robert F. Dorr)

confront a commander in the field, yet Ridgway was undeterred by it. His priorities were simple: first of all to check the Chinese advance, and then to launch an early counter-offensive designed to secure all of Korea south of the 38th Parallel from the threat of communist aggression.

In a bid to fill the intelligence gap Ridgway ordered the Eighth Army to step up its patrol activities by 100 per cent. This had the desired result, and within a few days Far East Command Intelligence officers were able to form a fairly accurate picture of the size and composition of the enemy forces poised for a renewal of their offensive. The main threat came from the Chinese Fourth Field Army which, numbering some 177,000 men, stood directly opposed to the US Eighth Army. Also confronting the United Nations forces were units of the North Korean Army, which had been reorganised and re-equipped by the Chinese. The NKA I Corps with

about 15,000 men lay on the left flank of the Chinese Fourth Field Army, while the NKA II and V Corps with just over 24,000 men between them confronted the ROK forces in the central highlands.

On 27 December, the NKA II Corps made a serious mistake when it launched a series of probing attacks on the ROK positions. From these activities it did not take UN Intelligence officers long to work out that the enemy plan involved a drive southwards from central Korea by the NKA, with the object of diverting a large proportion of the Eighth Army preparatory to a large-scale assault on Seoul by the Chinese Fourth Field Army. In addition, UN Intelligence indicated the possibility that the Chinese Third Field Army, then held in reserve at Hungnam with 100,000 men, might also be committed to the battle early in January soon after the enemy offensive began.

Although the employment of the enemy's ground

forces in the immediate future was now more or less clear, there still remained one big question mark. In Manchuria and China the communists had around 700 combat aircraft, and another 500 Russian first-line types based on airfields around Vladivostok just across the border might conceivably be added to this total. What Allied Intelligence desperately needed to know was whether the communists intended to use a substantial proportion of this air strength in support of the coming offensive. If they did, it would mean not only that the Allied air forces would be diverted from their all-important role of battlefield support, but also that there would be a continual air threat to the air and sea supply routes to North Korea. Looking towards even gloomier horizons, there was also the possibility that the Russians might step in with attacks on strategic ports and airfields in Japan, possibly with atomic weapons. In fact, although Allied Intelligence had no way of

knowing it at the time, both fears were groundless. In the first place, the majority of the communist air missions were flown by Russians who had strict instructions to remain over friendly territory; the Soviet Government dared not risk the possibility, with its attendant worldwide publicity, of their pilots being shot down and interrogated. Secondly, the Russians at this time had no stockpile of operational nuclear weapons, nor did they have any nuclear-capable aircraft. Although their first atomic test had been carried out in August 1949, this had involved a device only, and it would be the summer of 1951 before they were in a position to test the prototype of an operational weapon, which produced a yield of about twenty-five kilotons and was codenamed 'Joe 2' by the Americans.

On 29 December 1950 the NKA II Corps launched an attack on the ROK forces holding the line in central Korea. Two days later, on New Year's Eve, the Chinese opened up with mortar and artillery fire along the whole of the Eighth Army's front, and at daybreak the shock troops of the Fourth Field Army opened the offensive in bitter cold, sleet and pitch darkness. The weather conditions were near ideal for the Chinese: as long as they lasted, the troops would be safe from air attack.

But they did not last. During the morning of 1 January the clouds broke, leaving clear skies. Fifth Air Force pilots flying armed reconnaissance near the front line found the roads leading to Seoul congested with long columns of Chinese infantry. From then on, it was a massacre. Between New Year's Day and 5 January 1951 Fifth AF fighter-bombers flew 2,956 sorties. By nightfall on the 5th, the aircrews estimated that they had killed approximately 8,000 communist troops; the Eighth Army, counting the enemy dead on the battlefield, put the total at nearer 15,000. Neither did the air onslaught cease with the onset of darkness. Night attacks were carried out by B-26s of the 3rd Bombardment Wing, the crews seeking out enemy concentrations by the light of flares dropped by C-47s. The latter, nicknamed 'Lightning Bugs', could carry 130 Mk 8 flares of the type used by US Navy maritime patrol aircraft. Igniting at 5,500 feet they turned night into day for about five minutes, giving the B-26s ample time to locate and attack their targets before the enemy troops could disperse. The air attacks, however, were not enough to check the enemy advance. On 2 January the Eighth Army began to break contact, and the following day, with masses of Chinese infantry crossing the ice-covered Han river, the evacuation of Seoul began. On the 4th, with Kimpo airfield under threat, the 4th Fighter Interceptor Wing withdrew its Sabres to Johnson AFB in Japan, and a day later the 18th Fighter

Bomber Wing evacuated Suwon, the Mustangs pulling back to Chinhae.

Meanwhile, in central Korea the US 2nd Infantry Division had been ordered north to Wonju, where the ROK II Corps and the US 1st Marine Division were coming under heavy pressure from the NKA II and V Corps. Air support in this sector was the responsibility of carrier aircraft from the USS *Valley Forge*, *Philippine Sea* and *Leyte*, but on 6 January a return of severe weather brought a halt to all carrier operations for three days. In the meantime, the defenders of Wonju were kept going by the C-47s of the 21st Troop Carrier Group, which landed or airdropped 115 and 460 tons of supplies respectively. However, the enemy drive could not be contained, and by 10 January Wonju was in enemy hands. The Allied forces withdrew to new positions three miles farther south, which they held with the renewed assistance of tactical air support. On the 11th the weather cleared sufficiently to allow Fifth AF to hammer enemy troop columns attempting to outflank the 2nd Division, and the following day ten B-29s of the 98th Group attacked Wonju with 500lb general purpose bombs fused to burst in the air.

At sea, while US Navy aircraft covered the east coast of Korea from their carriers in the Sea of Japan, the British light fleet carrier HMS *Theseus* and her task group patrolled the Yellow Sea off the west coast with her CAG 17 and its complement of twenty-three Sea Furies and twelve Fireflies. After returning from an exercise at Hong Kong, *Theseus* mounted a series of strikes between 6 and 26 December 1950, the aircraft concentrating on roads, bridges, airfields and rolling stock. During this period CAG 17 flew 630 sorties, and anti-submarine patrols were flown by a Firefly fitted with a fifty-five-gallon long-range tank in place of its

Sea Furies and a Firefly ranged on the deck of the British aircraft carrier HMS Theseus *in the depths of a Korean winter.*

radar. It was reported that the small North Korean Navy had two Russian-built submarines, believed to be active in the Yellow Sea, but they were not sighted. A combat air patrol was also maintained during daylight hours and a staggering total of 3,900 interceptions and visual identifications was logged by the Sea Furies. All the aircraft intercepted proved to be Allied types, mainly B-29s, Neptunes and Sunderlands.

Top cover – up to 40,000 feet – for all strikes launched by *Theseus* and subsequent Commonwealth carriers operating off Korea was provided by the Fifth AF, the strikes directed by T-6 or L-4 'Mosquito' aircraft. Armed reconnaissance was the task of No. 810 Squadron's Fireflies, flying at 1,500 feet or less over enemy territory – an increasingly risky business because of intense small arms fire. The information they and other UN reconnaissance aircraft brought back was co-ordinated by the Joint Operations Centre at Taegu, where two US Navy and one Royal Navy liaison officers analysed potential targets for assignment to the carrier aircraft. The high quality of the reconnaissance, resulting in very accurate and damaging air strikes, soon made enemy movements in daylight extremely hazardous. Bridges were among the main objectives.

Following the early strikes, however, reconnaissance showed that the enemy was rebuilding these almost as quickly as the Fleet Air Arm knocked them down, so from then on delayed-action bombs were used to make this task more difficult. Because of the shallow waters off the Korean coast *Theseus* had to stand off at a distance of up to seventy miles, a long haul for an aircraft suffering from battle damage. It was here that the 'plane guard' S-51 helicopters proved their worth: they rescued four ditched pilots and snatched four more from behind enemy lines.

In January and February 1951 aircraft from the *Theseus* were engaged in spotting for Allied naval forces bombarding Inchon. Afterwards, the carrier moved from her station on the west coast into the Sea of Japan, where between 9 and 19 April, in company with the US carrier *Bataan*, her aircraft spotted for warships shelling Wonsan and Songjin. It was the British carrier's final operation in Korean waters, where she had spent a total of six and a half months. During that time her aircraft had made 3,489 operational sorties, dropping ninety-two 1,000lb and 1,474 500lb bombs, launching 7,317 rocket projectiles, and firing over half a million rounds of 20mm ammunition. Her pilots had never

Firefly of HMS Theseus's *air group pictured during an attack on Chinnampo docks.*

encountered any enemy aircraft. Many of the operational sorties had been flown in bad weather, particularly in December and January, when snowstorms often swept across the country without warning. *Theseus* was relieved by another light fleet carrier, HMS *Glory*, whose operations followed the pattern laid down by her predecessor. Throughout her tour, *Theseus* was supplied by the support carrier HMS *Unicorn*, bringing up spares and replacements from Singapore.

As the communist advance swept away UN control of one airfield after another, the crews of Combat Cargo Command found themselves once more working overtime to keep up the flow of supplies to the ground forces. Anything that remotely resembled an airstrip was knocked into shape by the troops. With the help of these improvisations the transport crews flew in 12,486 tons of supplies during the first three weeks of January 1951, as well as evacuating 10,489 casualties. C-46s and C-47s bore the brunt of these operations, although a further 2,000 tons of supplies were airdropped during the same period by C-119s.

By the end of the third week in January it was estimated that the communists had suffered 38,000 casualties, about half of them inflicted by air attack. Not even an apparently bottomless well of manpower could sustain losses of this kind, and on 15 January it was reported that the enemy was pulling back in several sectors to rest and regroup. Had they enjoyed the benefits of air support the communists would undoubtedly have been able to keep up a sustained pressure, but for reasons already explained – but not then appreciated by the Allies – they had decided not to commit their air power to the battle. MiG-15s appeared only once in January, when fifteen of them crossed the Yalu to attack a solitary B-29 near Sinuiju; they broke off the attack after only a minute or so and the bomber got away unharmed. Apart from an abortive attack on a B-26 of the 452nd Wing by a North Korean Yak-9 fighter on 15 January, the only other enemy air activity took the form of several nuisance raids on Allied troops at night by Po-2 biplanes, but the psychological effect of these attacks was far greater than the damage they actually caused.

By the end of January the Allied front was stabilised south of Wonju, and it became apparent that the enemy offensive had petered out. The war that developed now was to be unlike any other conflict in history. It was to become a fearful war of attrition, a war with no clearly defined aims, in which thousands of men on both sides would die for possession of a useless hill or ridge or valley. It was to be a trial of strength between two power blocs which neither side could win, and which neither side dared lose.

Douglas Dakota of No. 30 Sqn, Royal Australian Air Force. RAAF Dakotas were used in the casualty evacuation as well as transport roles.

Successful emergency landing by a Firefly of No. 812 Squadron, HMS Glory, *after sustaining flak damage over Korea.*

Short Sunderland of the RAF Far East Flying Boat Wing at Iwakuni, Japan.

CHAPTER 8
The Communist Air Offensive, January-May 1951

T he American response to the North Korean invasion of the south, and the stalemate that subsequently developed, presented the Soviet leader, Josef Stalin, with a dilemma. Although he had sanctioned the invasion, his support hinged on the concept that the North Koreans would secure a rapid victory before the United Nations, and in particular the United States, could intervene. Stalin, in fact, badly miscalculated the scale and determination of the American intervention, and when the North Koreans failed to secure the anticipated victory he was left with two choices: either to withdraw his support for Kim Il-sung, which was out of the question, or to encourage Chinese involvement in the war with Soviet personnel playing a covert but active part.

By the beginning of 1951 there was a substantial contingent of Soviet aviation personnel in China, ranging from combat pilots through engineers to intelligence officers. The first Russian pilots to see combat over Korea were drawn from the ranks of the

Main Picture: Arming a Thunderjet.
Inset: F-80 pilot and mechanic. (via Robert F. Dorr)

most experienced veterans of World War Two, men who were now instructors at the various fighter leaders' schools and combat training establishments in the Soviet Union. As well as flying in combat, these pilots set about training selected Chinese aircrew to fly the MiG-15 and introduce them to combat. Early experiences against the F-86 Sabre, however, showed that it would be a long time before the Chinese pilots were capable of holding their own against the Americans, if ever, and so the cutting edge of fighter operations remained in the hands of the Russians. Ground attack operations by the CPAF's Ilyushin Il-10 assault aircraft and Tupolev Tu-2 light bombers were a different matter: the Chinese were quite capable of handling these types, and in January 1951 the interrogation of Chinese officers revealed that at least one officer from each Chinese regiment had been through a recent ground/air liaison course, while units equipped with Il-10s were undergoing intensive training. The onus of working out a battle plan for the future participation of communist air power in Korea fell on the shoulders of General Liu Ya-lou, the former Chief of Staff of the Chinese Fourth Army who had been appointed air force C-in-C in 1949. In addition to the numerous operational problems that confronted him, Liu was also engaged in a political battle with his superiors, many of whom feared that direct air support of the Chinese ground forces in Korea might lead to immediate and massive American retaliation, particularly if ground attack operations were carried out

from Manchurian bases. Liu's battlefield support plans, however, did not envisage the use of bases in Manchuria: his reasoning was influenced by technical rather than political considerations. To reach the combat area his piston-engined ground attack aircraft would have to fly 250 miles, and in an environment dominated by UN jet fighters few of them would be likely to get there. Fighter cover would not be available, for the early model MiG-15 had a combat radius of little more than 100 miles. What Liu could do with his MiG-15s was endeavour to establish a definite margin of air superiority over north-western Korea. Once this had been achieved the Chinese could go ahead with the rehabilitation of old airfields and the construction of new ones in the north, turning them into heavily defended bases for future ground attack operations in the vicinity of the 38th Parallel. Runways would be lengthened and strengthened to accommodate jet fighters as well as piston-engined types, and well-camouflaged satellite strips would be built closer to the battle area. The idea was that combat aircraft would be flown into the latter to be fuelled and armed only a matter of hours before the launching of an air strike in the south, after which – if sufficient fuel remained – they would fly to the permanent bases in the North to avoid the possibility of being caught on the ground by Allied fighter bombers.

The first phase of Liu's plan was put into effect late in January 1951, when the MiGs began to operate over the Yalu in larger formations than ever before. On

Dramatic photograph of an F-84 strike on enemy communications in Korea.

Top: F-84E Thunderjet being armed for a mission at Taegu, Korea in 1952. (Martin Bambrick)
Above: F-80 Shooting Star bombed up and ready for a combat mission over Korea. (via Robert F. Dorr)

21 January two formations of MiGs – twelve and sixteen aircraft respectively – crossed the river to attack United Nations aircraft. The first formation trapped four F-80s near Sinuiju and destroyed one of them; the remainder managed to escape. The other sixteen MiGs headed south towards the Chongchon river, where they bounced eight F-84 Thunderjets which were attacking bridge targets. One F-84 went down in flames but Lt-Col William E. Bertram, commanding the 523rd Squadron, evened up the score by shooting a MiG down into the river. Meanwhile, in accordance with the second phase of General Liu's plan, Chinese and North Korean

engineers had begun to repair the airfields at Sinuiju and Pyongyang. Sinuiju was the better placed of the two from the point of view of defence, for it was protected both by the MiG air umbrella from Antung and by heavy anti-aircraft emplacements on both banks of the Yalu. The AA defences at Pyongyang, which was beyond the MiGs' combat radius, were steadily increased until over 100 guns encircled the airfield.

On 20 January General Partridge, who was particularly worried about the heavy defensive screen around Pyongyang, asked Brigadier-General James E. Briggs – who had assumed command of FEAF Bomber

69

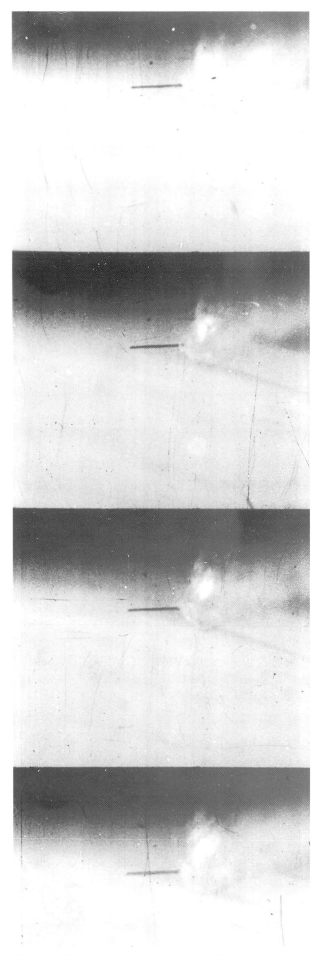

This MiG, like many flown by inexperienced Chinese pilots, made no attempt to take evasive action, continuing to fly straight and level as a Sabre pilot shot it down.

Command from General O'Donnell a few days earlier – to lay on a B-29 strike against the airfield. Briggs agreed, although he stressed that first it would be essential for the Fifth Air Force's fighter-bombers to go in low and fast to knock out the AA batteries. While plans for this raid were being discussed Colonel Ashley B. Packard, commanding the 27th Fighter Escort Wing, came up with a proposal for a heavy attack on Sinuiju airfield by a large force of Thunderjets. The scheme was approved, and on 23 January thirty-three Thunderjets took off from Taegu and headed towards their objective. While twenty-five provided top cover, the other eight made a fast strafing attack on the airfield before climbing hard to join the others as dust clouds across the river betrayed the take-off of MiG-15s. By the time the eight Thunderjets reached altitude the first MiGs were already diving across the river and the Americans turned to meet them, intending to bring the enemy fighters down to below 20,000 feet where the Thunderjet had a tighter turning radius than its swept-wing adversary. The tactics paid dividends: in the first two minutes of combat Lt Jacob Kratt destroyed two MiGs, and before the communists broke off the action two more went down before the guns of Captains Alan McGuire and William W. Slaughter. It was a superb victory for the Thunderjet pilots over aircraft which were superior to their own in most respects.

Half an hour later, forty-six F-80s of the 49th Fighter Bomber Wing attacked Pyongyang and pounded the surrounding flak emplacements with gunfire, bombs and rockets. As they streaked away twenty-one B-29s of the 19th and 307th Bombardment Groups, bombing through the pall of smoke and dust, cratered the newly-repaired runways from end to end. There was sporadic anti-aircraft fire from the few emplacements that had escaped the F-80s' flak suppression attack, but none of the bombers was damaged. Both these attacks had shown that the enemy still had a long way to go before he could hope to challenge UN air superiority with any prospect of success, but a few days later the 27th and 49th Wings withdrew from Taegu to airfields in southern Japan, leaving only detachments behind to service and rearm aircraft on combat missions over Korea. This meant that until further notice Fifth AF would not be able to guarantee jet fighter escort for medium bombers and reconnaissance aircraft operating over the north-western sector of the country.

Because of the urgent need to acquire photographic intelligence, FEAF had once again authorised RB-29 missions over north-western Korea in December 1950 with fighter escort. Now that this was absent the RB-29s' task became extremely hazardous, and to fill the air reconnaissance gap FEAF Bomber Command, on 31 January 1951, took over control of Reconnaissance Detachment A, 84th Bombardment Squadron, which had been operating a pair of North American RB-45C aircraft – the reconnaissance version of America's first operational jet bomber – on trials over Korea for the past three months. The four-jet RB-45C, which had a radar-mapping facility as well as cameras, could operate at 38,000 feet at 0.72M, so it had a far better chance of survival than the RB-29. The RB-45Cs operated over the Yalu from the beginning of the Chinese invasion of Korea, and one of the original pair was shot down by MiG-15s on 12 December 1950 with the loss of its crew. With Bomber Command, the RB-45Cs were assigned to the 91st SRS and continued to provide valuable

F-80s. (via Robert F. Dorr)

intelligence throughout the war. A superb aircraft to fly, the RB-45C was manoeuvrable at altitude and was usually able to outrun pursuing fighters, although there were some narrow escapes. On 9 April 1951, for example, an RB-45C was intercepted by four MiG-15s which continued to attack it until they had used up all their ammunition, amazingly without scoring any hits. Lockheed RF-80s continued to fly the majority of reconnaissance sorties over north-western Korea and were attacked by MiGs on several occasions in February 1951, although all managed to get away. The only decisive air combat of the month occurred on 5 February when Major Arnold Mullins of the 67th Fighter Bomber Squadron, attacking an airstrip near Pyongyang in his Mustang, surprised a Yak-9 with its wheels and flaps down on the approach to land and shot it down in flames.

The lack of a sustained Allied air interdiction campaign meant that the communists were able to carry out repairs to at least ten North Korean airfields virtually unmolested, a fact that seriously alarmed United Nations Command. However, this state of affairs was not to last for long. On 25 January the Eighth Army launched a counter-offensive, codenamed Operation 'Thunderbolt', with the twofold objective of reaching the Han river and destroying as many enemy forces as possible. Suwon and Inchon were quickly recaptured, and in a secondary action, called Operation 'Punch', a

task force of the 25th Division took the strategic position of Hill 440 north of Suwon, on 5 February. When the operation ended on 9 February the United Nations forces counted over 4,200 Chinese dead on the battlefield; the UN lost seventy men killed. By the 10th the UN I Corps – comprising the US 3rd and 25th Divisions, the Turkish Brigade, the 29th British Brigade and the ROK 1st Division – had reached the Han river, retaking Seoul and Kimpo on the way. General Partridge immediately gave orders for aviation engineers to start work on the rehabilitation of Suwon, Kimpo and Seoul airfields, although it was obvious that it would be some time before they were fit for use by jet aircraft. Nevertheless, the engineers reported that Suwon could be made serviceable enough to accept jet fighters in an emergency, and General Partridge was sufficiently encouraged by this news to authorise the return of the 4th Wing's 334th Fighter Interceptor Squadron to Taegu on 22 February.

Towards the end of February Bomber Command, working on the assumption that the Sabres would be able to stage through Suwon and provide escort all the way to the Yalu, launched another interdiction campaign over north-western Korea. In fact the assumption was false: Suwon had taken such a battering during the fighting that it would not be serviceable for weeks to come, and operating out of Taegu the Sabres had just enough range to take them as

Scene on board a Task Force 77 carrier. The Panthers are armed with 5" HVAR modified to carry 6.5" anti-tank aircraft rocket (ATAR) warheads, effective against the T-34 tank. (via Robert F. Dorr)

Stencilled bombs on its fuselage denote the long combat career of this F9F of VMF-311.

far as Pyongyang. Nevertheless, it was decided to go ahead with the interdiction programme, escorting the B-29s with F-80s.

The first mission, on 1 March 1951, was a disaster. The F-80s reached the rendezvous on time, but there was no sign of the B-29s. The fighters orbited, using up precious fuel, and eventually the B-29s – eighteen aircraft of the 98th BG – turned up after being delayed by unexpectedly strong headwinds. By this time the F-80s were critically low on fuel, and were forced to abandon the bombers while still some miles short of the target, a bridge at Kogunyong. As the B-29s began their bombing run they were attacked by nine MiG-15s, and although no bombers were lost ten were damaged, three so severely that they had to make emergency landings in South Korea.

On 10 March, following days and nights of non-stop work by the aviation engineers, Suwon airstrip was declared serviceable enough for use by Sabres, albeit with a certain element of risk. The 334th Squadron accordingly moved up from Taegu, its place at the latter base taken by another squadron of the 4th Wing, the 336th, fresh out of Japan. With minor exceptions the tactics used by the Sabres in their renewed patrols over north-western Korea were the same as those employed during December, the flights arriving in 'MiG Alley' at intervals and quartering the sky ready to converge on any point in the area where the MiGs appeared. Despite this, there were still gaps in the fighter screen. On 12 March, for example, while patrolling Sabres converged on a spot where a formation of MiGs was reported to be assembling north of the Yalu, twelve more MiGs slipped across the river undetected and attacked a flight of four F-80s of the 8th FBG. Luckily the communist pilots appeared to be of low calibre; the Shooting Star pilots claimed four MiGs damaged and saw two more collide while taking evasive action. Five days later, more 8th Group F-80s were again attacked by three MiGs which slipped through the Sabre screen; one MiG and an F-80 were lost in a mid-air collision.

Following a pause after the 98th BG's disastrous mission of 1 March, Bomber Command resumed its attacks on bridge targets south of the Yalu. On 23 March twenty-two B-29s of the 19th and 307th Groups encountered only light AA fire during a successful attack on important rail bridges at Kogunyong and Chongju. The MiGs were airborne at the time but found themselves engaged in a combat with forty-five Sabres of the 4th Wing several miles away, and none got through to intercept the bombers. This attack was followed, on 30 March, by a raid on the bridges at Chongsongjin, Manpojin and Namsan-ni by thirty-six B-29s of the 19th, 98th and 307th Groups, with Sabres of the 4th Wing flying top cover and F-80s of the 8th and 49th Wings providing close escort. The usual cloud of dust over the river signalled the presence of MiGs, but most of them stayed over their own territory and only a few came across to attack B-29s of the 19th Group. One B-29 was badly damaged, but two MiGs were claimed destroyed by the 19th's gunners.

Meanwhile, US Navy and Marine aircraft had been flying almost daily interdiction sorties against targets in the north. On 2 March 1951 the commanding officer of VF-193, Lt-Cdr Clement M. Craig, was carrying out an armed reconnaissance from the USS *Princeton* when he sighted what was clearly an important target: a 600-foot railway bridge spanning a deep canyon south of Kilchu, in north-eastern Korea. The bridge had five concrete piers supporting six steel spans, and there were two tunnels at either end. The bridge was attacked that same day by Skyraiders of VA-195 led by Lt-Cdr Harold G. 'Swede' Carlson, but only minor damage was inflicted on the approaches. On 3 March the Skyraiders dropped one span, followed by another on the 7th, but a week later reconnaissance showed that the bridge was well on the way to being repaired and would be serviceable again within a few days. On 15 March it was attacked with napalm, which set fire to the new wooden structures under the original spans; a third span was destroyed and a fourth badly damaged. The remaining spans were knocked out in an attack on 2 April. These attacks on what became known as 'Carlson's Canyon' were later used as the background to James A. Michener's novel *The Bridges at Toko-ri*.

A batsman brings a Corsair curving towards the round-down of USS Boxer.

During the first week of March 1951 the Marine Air Wing underwent some changes. VMF(N)-542 returned to El Toro, California, to begin conversion to the Douglas F3D-1 Skynight jet night fighter; its F7F-3N Tigercats were allocated to VMF(N)-513, together with a pair of F-82 Twin Mustangs. The unit retained its Corsairs, which continued to operate by day.

On 2 April two F9F-2B Panthers of VF-191, USS *Princeton*, each armed with four 250lb and two 100lb bombs, carried out a strike on a bridge on a railway bridge near Songjin. It was the first time that US Navy jet fighters were used in the fighter-bomber role. Two days later, VMF-312, operating from the USS *Bataan*, suffered an unfortunate loss when its commanding officer, Major D.P. Frame, was killed in action; his

replacement, Major Frank H. Presley, was wounded on 20 April. The next day the squadron flew forty-two sorties over Korea, and one mission produced an unexpected result. Captain Philip C. DeLong, a veteran of World War Two with eleven Japanese aircraft to his credit, was leading a section of two Corsairs on an armed reconnaissance near Chinnampo on the Yellow Sea coast when they were attacked by four Yak-9s. DeLong's aircraft was hit and he took evasive action; meanwhile, his wingman, Lt H. Daigh, engaged the leading enemy fighter and shot it down. In the ensuing fight DeLong destroyed two more Yaks and Daigh scored hits on another, which made its escape.

April 1951 began well for the 4th FIW, its Sabre pilots claiming four MiGs on the 3rd and 4th. On the

A MiG-15 falls victim to the gunners of a B-29 over Korea and the pilot descends under his parachute after ejecting.

6th, after an enforced lull caused by bad weather, B-29s of the 98th and 307th Groups were detailed to attack the railway bridges at Sinuiju and a road bridge at Uiju. The bombers were escorted by forty-eight F-84s of the 27th Wing operating out of Itazuke, and these fought a hot engagement with thirty MiG-15s which attacked the B-29s as they were bombing their targets. The Thunderjet close escort proved so effective that only one MiG got through, but this destroyed a B-29 of the 307th Group. The F-84s claimed one MiG destroyed for no loss to themselves.

It was a different story on 12 April when B-29s of the 19th, 98th and 307th Groups were once again ordered to attack the bridges at Sinuiju, which still refused to collapse despite the battering they had received. Close escort was again provided by the 27th Wing, which sent up thirty-nine aircraft, while the Sabres of the 4th Wing flew top cover. With the target still several minutes' flying time away, the bomber formation was attacked by about forty MiGs whose pilots employed new tactics, diving at high speed through the escorting fighters to make their firing passes at the 19th Group's eight bombers. One B-29 was shot down and five more damaged. The attack was scarcely over when twenty more MiGs attacked the 307th Group's twelve aircraft, destroying one of them and badly damaging another. It later crashed and was destroyed while trying to make an emergency landing at Suwon. A small number of MiGs also attacked the 98th Group, which came through unscathed. On the credit side, the Sabres claimed four MiGs destroyed and six damaged, while the Thunderjet pilots claimed three probably destroyed. The B-29 gunners also claimed ten MiGs destroyed, but in the confusion this was wildly exaggerated; it is doubtful whether any MiGs were shot down by the bombers at all.

For the time being, it was the end of B-29 missions in the Sinuiju area. Bomber Command was now directed to neutralize the North Korean airfields which were being built and which would soon be operational. The

Rocket-armed F9F Panthers of VF-721 crossing the Korean coast. VF-721, an NAS Glenview Reserve unit, operated from USS Boxer *in August 1951.*

B-29 Superfortresses on a mission to North Korea. (via Robert F. Dorr)

attacks began on 17 April, and any threat from the MiGs was kept at bay by the Sabres of the 334th and 336th Squadrons, which were now based side by side at Suwon. To counter the enemy's new tactics the Sabres now operated in flights of six aircraft and timed their arrival in the combat area at closer intervals. This policy apparently took the enemy pilots by surprise, because when thirty-six MiGs crossed the Yalu to attack twelve Sabres on 22 April, no doubt believing they could expect to enjoy numerical superiority for at least ten minutes, they were immediately bounced by a second formation of twelve Sabres coming along behind. Four MiGs were destroyed and four others damaged.

During a week of operations up to 23 April, Bomber Command repeatedly hit nine North Korean bases. The same targets were also attacked by Fifth Air Force fighter bombers and by night-flying B-26s. By the 23rd air reconnaissance showed that the airfields had been sufficiently damaged to render them unusable for several weeks to come, and Bomber Command was ordered back to its more usual task of interdiction.

On 9 May a major attack was carried out against the airfield at Sinuiju, the best-defended target in North Korea. The enemy had thirty-eight aircraft deployed there, all piston-engined types, but concrete revetments had been built around the airfield perimeter and there were indications that these would soon house jet fighters. In the early afternoon of 9 May a maximum-effort operation was launched, with Shooting Stars of the 8th, 49th and 51st Wings, Mustangs of the 18th Wing, and Corsairs of the 1st Marine Air Wing – a total

of 312 aircraft – pounding Sinuiju for forty-five minutes while 4th Wing Sabres, 27th Wing Thunderjets, and Panthers of the Marine Air Wing flew top cover. The Shooting Stars went in first to suppress the flak, and the subsequent attacks destroyed a fuel dump, twenty-six ammunition and supply dumps, 106 buildings, and all the enemy aircraft on the ground. Eighteen MiGs were sighted crossing the Yalu, but most of these avoided combat and the Allied fighter pilots claimed only two damaged. All the Allied aircraft returned safely to base.

The air battles of May 1951 saw the emergence of the first Sabre ace, although not, as has often been erroneously stated, of the first jet ace in history – twenty-two German Me 262 pilots had already claimed that distinction in World War Two. He was Captain James Jabara, a pilot with the 334th FIS. On 7 May, when his squadron was rotated back to Japan, Jabara stayed on at Suwon to fly and fight with its replacement, the 335th FIS. At that time his score stood at four MiGs destroyed. On 20 May a large number of MiGs crossed the Yalu to engage twelve 4th Wing Sabres. Two more flights of Sabres, one of which included Jabara, were quickly summoned to the scene of the action. Jabara got on the tail of one of the enemy fighters and saw his bullets registering strikes on the MiG's wings and fuselage. He followed it down to 10,000 feet and saw the pilot eject, then climbed back to 25,000 feet and within a couple of minutes was fighting with a second MiG, which he set on fire. He had time to watch it spin down in flames before being forced to break hard as a third MiG got on his own tail. He went into a long dive, losing the enemy fighters, and returned to base. His two victories were made all the more noteworthy by the fact that one of his wing tanks had refused to jettison, a circumstance that would have compelled most pilots to abandon the mission immediately. Other Sabre pilots claimed one MiG destroyed, with one probable and five damaged. Jabara himself scored no further victories before the end of his current tour, but he returned to Korea later in the war and increased his score to fifteen.

After the battle of 20 May the MiGs avoided combat for ten days, then on the 31st twelve of them crossed the Yalu to attack two B-29s of the 19th Group heading for Sinuiju. One MiG was destroyed by the B-29 gunners and two more were shot down by a flight of Sabres. The MiGs appeared again the following day, but this time they were more cautious; they waited until the Sabre escort turned for home, short of fuel, before crossing the river to attack four 98th Group B-29s which were bombing a bridge near Sinanju. One bomber was shot down and two more badly damaged, but the B-29 gunners claimed the destruction of a MiG and two more were downed by the pilots of a second Sabre flight which came up from the south.

Although they had failed to establish air superiority over the North, the communists believed that sheer weight of numbers would enable them to overwhelm the Allies during their two major ground offensives of April and May 1951. By mid-April there were some 700,000 communist troops deployed in North Korea, the majority Chinese. Command of the CCF now rested on the shoulders of General Peng Teh-huai, while General Nam Il remained Chief of Staff of the Korean People's Army. Behind both men loomed an all-powerful cadre of Soviet advisers led by Lieutenant-General Vladimir Razuvayez, who held undisputed control of all communist military operations in North Korea. The available communist manpower was organised into 70 divisions, with thirty-six Chinese divisions on a line between the Imjin river and Hwachon reservoir and a further twelve deployed eastwards between the reservoir and the Sea of Japan. To the west of the reservoir four CCF army groups were deployed along a seventy-five-mile front between Hwachon and Munsan. Facing them was a front-line strength of 230,000 United Nations troops under the command of Lieutenant-General James van Fleet, who had succeeded General Ridgway as commander of the Eighth Army on 14 April 1951.

The communist spring offensive began on the night of 22 April, the initial assault following the now familiar pattern of 'human wave' attacks by massed infantry all along the front. The Chinese scored an early success when, striking hard at the weakest part of the Allied line, they cut the ROK 6th Division to pieces, leaving a dangerous gap between the Marine Division on its right flank and the 24th Infantry on the left. It was now clear that the main Chinese objective was to isolate Seoul with an enveloping movement from the north and north-east, and General van Fleet was determined to hold on to the city at all costs.

On 26 April the Chinese offensive was checked in the eastern sector by the 27th Commonwealth Brigade and the attention now switched to the west where six Chinese armies were throwing everything they had into a desperate bid to reach the South Korean capital. The main weight of the offensive here fell on the British 29th Infantry Brigade which held a 12,000-yard front and defended the vital river crossings over the Imjin. The epic stand of the 29th Brigade – and particularly that of the 1st Battalion the Gloucester Regiment on Hill 235 above the hamlet of Solma-ri – has gone down in history. General van Fleet later described it as the most outstanding display of unit bravery in modern warfare. The Brigade held on for three days against overwhelming odds before a general withdrawal was ordered to new positions north of Seoul. This holding action not only saved the left flank of the Eighth Army's I Corps, making possible an orderly withdrawal down the road to Seoul, it also disrupted the entire timetable of the Chinese offensive, robbing it of its momentum. In addition, during three days of savage fighting, the 29th Brigade had destroyed an entire Chinese division.

By 29 April the Eighth Army had established a new defensive line running across the Korean peninsula from Seoul to Sabangu and then on to Taepo-ri on the east coast. That same day the communists made a final attempt to reach Seoul along the Inchon road by ferrying 6,000 assault troops across the Han estuary, but this was broken up by air attack and the troops that managed to reach the opposite bank were mopped up by ROK marines. The next day the CCF began to pull back. Their offensive had cost them at least 70,000 casualties, ten times the loss sustained by the United Nations Command. But the battle was not yet over.

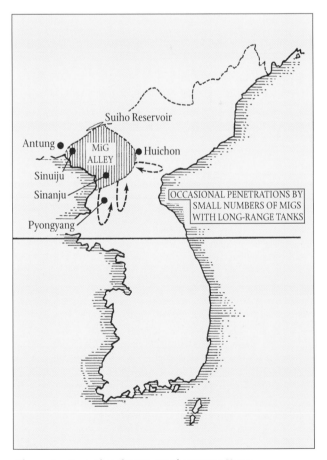

The main air combat theatre, north-western Korea.

CHAPTER 9
The Red Air Offensive -
Final Phase, June-July 1951

F-80 pilot and aircraft. Note the nose art. (via Robert F. Dorr)

Aware that the enemy had so far committed only half his forces to the first spring offensive, General van Fleet lost no time in strengthening his defences to meet a renewed onslaught. Determined to smash the enemy in no-man's-land, he assembled an enormous concentration of firepower and ordered huge minefields to be laid along the entire front. The preparations were completed just in time; on 10 May, air reconnaissance reported that large numbers of Chinese troops were moving south, and soon afterwards Allied Intelligence realised that five Chinese armies were concentrating between Chunchon and Inje. This could mean only one thing: the weight of the enemy offensive would fall on the eastern sector of the front, held mainly by ROK forces.

By the end of the second week in May the communists had deployed twenty Chinese and six North Korean divisions east of Chunchon, and on the night of 15/16 May twelve of the Chinese divisions attacked on a twenty-mile front, routing the ROK 5th and 7th Divisions. The Chinese then swung eastwards to attack the rear of the ROK III Corps, which was

compelled to embark on a headlong fifty-mile retreat down the east coast to avoid becoming encircled. This movement enabled the CCF and NKA to push on rapidly for thirty miles, threatening the right flank of the Marine Division and the 2nd Infantry.

Quickly assessing the situation, General van Fleet decided to allow the enemy advance to continue in this sector while the 3rd Infantry Division and the 187th Airborne Regimental Combat Team made an emergency dash across the peninsula to the assistance of the Marines and the 2nd Infantry. A modified defensive line was quickly established with the help of strong artillery support, and by 19 May it had become obvious that the Chinese offensive was collapsing through lack of logistical support, as van Fleet had anticipated. Further attacks continued until 23 May, then ceased altogether. In the space of a week the enemy had sustained no fewer than 90,000 casualties, many of them victims of the Allied minefields which had been sown with electrically detonated fifty-five-gallon drums filled with napalm and petrol. With the communists now caught on the wrong foot, General van Fleet ordered his forces to strike hard and fast, and in the last two weeks of May they inflicted further casualties on the enemy and took 17,000 prisoners. By the beginning of June the enemy had been driven out of the whole of South Korea with the exception of one sector west of the Imjin and south of the 38th Parallel.

Although the Allied bombing campaign against his airfields had prevented General Liu Ya-lou from implementing his plan to position ground attack aircraft closer to the 38th Parallel, so robbing the communist ground forces of vital air support, he directed work on the airfields to continue, despite the continual threat of air attack, in the hope that the bomb craters could be filled in faster than the Allies could make them, so that at least some of his Il-10 ground attack units could be brought forward to support future offensives. In the meantime, light aircraft flown by North Korean crews and operating from unprepared strips would carry out nightly nuisance raids on UN ground forces and installations. The Soviet Air Force had used similar tactics in World War Two. The first of these nuisance raids took place in the early hours of 14 June 1951 when two Polikarpov Po-2 biplanes took off from Sariwon airstrip. One attacked Suwon, dropping two bombs that narrowly missed the runway, and the other released its bombs on an Eighth Army motor transport park at Inchon, causing splinter damage to several vehicles. On the next night a third raider – identified as an MBR-2 amphibian – made a low-level strafing run over Kimpo airfield, fortunately without hitting anything. The next attack, on the night of 16/17 June, produced spectacular results. On this occasion two Po-2s led by Lieutenant La Woon Yung arrived over Suwon, the crews finding to their surprise that the airfield was brightly lit. La Woon Yung had no difficulty in picking out the 4th Wing's Sabres in their dispersals and dropped his pair of bombs on a flight of 335th Squadron aircraft, destroying one Sabre and damaging eight others, four of them seriously. The other pilot dropped his bombs on the parked vehicles of the 802nd Engineer Aviation Battalion, severely damaging several of them.

By day the MiGs were still active, and on 17 June twenty-five enemy fighters crossed the Yalu to attack two flights of patrolling Sabres. The Sabre pilots shot down one MiG and damaged four others for no loss, but on their return to Suwon the Americans reported that the MiG pilots had shown a higher degree of skill and determination than had previously been encountered. The next day forty MiGs that engaged thirty-two Sabres also displayed a high level of competence, but they nevertheless lost five of their number and claimed only one F-86. There was a third fierce air battle on 19 June, and this time the MiG pilots gained the advantage, destroying a Sabre for no loss to themselves, although the 4th Wing pilots claimed four damaged.

On 20 June General Liu ordered his Ilyushin Il-10 ground attack aircraft into action. Eight of them crossed the Yalu and headed for the island of Sinmi-do, which lay just off the Korean coast about seventy-five miles south-east of Sinuiju and which was being held by a small force of ROK troops. Purely by chance the Ilyushins were sighted by Mustang pilots of the 18th Group carrying out an offensive sweep along the road near Sinmi-do. The Allied pilots called up a second flight of Mustangs and then attacked the Il-10s, destroying two and damaging three more in a matter of

minutes. The enemy pilots had evidently called for reinforcements too, because as the Mustangs continued to harry them six Yak-9 fighters arrived on the scene and were promptly engaged by the second Mustang flight. One Yak was shot down by Lt J.B. Harrison. A dozen MiGs which crossed the Yalu were intercepted by two flights of patrolling Sabres, whose pilots damaged four of them, but one broke through the screen and destroyed a Mustang before both sides broke off the action.

The Mustangs had continued to perform sterling work in Korea during the spring and summer of 1951, and their crews – particularly those of the 18th Fighter Bomber Wing – had brought armed tactical reconnaissance to a fine art. Flying over the same terrain day after day, pairs of Mustang pilots were soon able to pick out small changes and detect more and more camouflaged enemy equipment. In February 1951 alone the 18th Wing destroyed 728 enemy vehicles and damaged 137. Commanded by Colonel Turner C. Rogers, the 18th Wing rapidly earned a reputation as the Fifth Air Force's ace 'truck buster' unit. The secret was thoroughness. Before a day's missions the Wing's intelligence officers analysed the previous night's vehicle sightings and, calculating enemy vehicle movement at fifteen miles per hour on average, designated the areas where the enemy vehicles would have to take cover before dawn. Wherever possible, Mustang squadron operations officers assigned flights the same areas or routes for armed reconnaissance each day. The first morning sortie of two Mustangs swept areas of suspected enemy activity in order to detect any vehicles damaged by night intruders and to force the enemy to camouflage, often hastily. Subsequent flights took small sectors of the assigned area or route and searched them methodically. The Mustangs flew low and slow, thoroughly searching every foot of ground, checking and double checking every building, haystack, ravine, wooded area and side road.

In the standard two-ship flight the leader flew 100 to 300 feet above the terrain, his wingman covering him from a height of about 1,000 feet. The standard truck-hunting armament load for the Mustangs was rockets and 0.50-calibre machine-guns, the former useful for suppressing flak and the latter lethal against soft-skinned vehicles. The 18th Wing pilots usually spent up to two hours in the target area. From May 1951, because of greatly enhanced enemy anti-aircraft defences, they flew at increased power settings and no longer made sorties with less than a complete flight of four aircraft. Losses to anti-aircraft fire were high; in fact, Mustang casualties amounted to about sixty per cent of the total loss of eighty-one aircraft sustained in ground attack operations between the beginning of April and the end of June 1951, and as a result the 18th Wing modified its tactics. Trials flown against friendly flak batteries at Seoul airfield showed that the trailing wingman in the low-level element of an armed reconnaissance flight was the most likely to be hit by AA fire. In the revised tactics the flight leader stayed low down to search for targets of opportunity, the element leader flew at 4,000 feet searching for flak areas, while numbers two and four followed the element leader and kept a lookout for enemy aircraft. In this way three men were covering the single pilot who was carrying out the actual armed reconnaissance.

Considerable assistance in locating concentrations of

F-51D Mustang of No. 2 'Cheetah' Squadron, South African Air Force, which was attached to the USAF's 18th FBG in Korea. (via Robert F. Dorr)

camouflaged enemy vehicles was rendered by the RF-51 tactical reconnaissance Mustangs of the 45th TRS. On the basis of night sightings reported to the Joint Operations Centre, the 45th TRS projected the probable locations where enemy vehicles might be expected to take cover before dawn and then dispatched its RF-51s on so-called 'Circle Ten' missions. These involved intensive visual reconnaissance of a circle ten miles in radius around a suspected location of enemy vehicles. After 15 April 1951, because of the growing volume of ground fire, the 45th TRS began to send out two RF-51s on these missions, one to carry out reconnaissance and the other to watch for flak. By the summer of 1951 the 45th TRS formed part of the 67th Tactical Reconnaissance Wing under the command of Colonel Karl L. Polifka, one of the USAF pioneers in the field of tactical reconnaissance. He was shot down and killed on operations in an RF-51 on 1 July 1951.

Of the original Mustang fighter bomber units operating in Korea, No. 77 Squadron RAAF had now re-equipped with Gloster Meteor F.8 jet fighters. The first USAF Mustang unit to receive new equipment was the 40th Squadron of the 35th Fighter Interceptor Wing, which went to Misawa in Japan late in May 1951 for eventual conversion to Lockheed F-94 Starfires. The 35th Wing's other squadron, the 39th, was attached to the 18th FBW for continued service in Korea in a move designed to centralise Fifth Air Force's remaining Mustang assets. The 35th Wing had also given excellent service in Korea, culminating in a four-day period in late April 1951 when its two Mustang squadrons mounted 400 sorties, straining its pilots and aircraft to

near breaking point. The situation was fast arising when there would not be enough Mustangs to go round in Korea. General Stratemeyer made repeated attempts to replace them with F-84 Thunderjets, but the USAF was reluctant to release more of these for service in Korea in view of the NATO commitment in Europe. In desperation, Stratemeyer asked the USAF to send some equally outmoded F-47 Thunderbolts as replacements for the Mustangs, but that request was turned down too.

The nightly visits by the Po-2 raiders, nicknamed 'Bed Check Charlies', continued to be a thorn in the Allies' flesh throughout the summer of 1951, and steps were taken to combat them. The biplanes, cruising at eighty knots and at low level down the valleys on the approach to their targets, proved incredibly difficult to detect by radar, and when night fighters were sent up to intercept them the Po-2 pilots made full use of their low speed and high manoeuvrability to evade them. However, two Po-2s were intercepted and destroyed during June 1951, the first on the night of the 23rd by Captain Dick Heyman flying a B-26 of the 8th Squadron, and the second on the 30th over the Han river by Captain E.B. Long of Marine Squadron VMF-513, flying an F7F Tigercat. His radar intercept officer (RIO), Warrant Officer R.C. Buckingham, steered him to the black-painted target, which he shot down on his third pass after reducing speed to the absolute safe minimum. It was the Tigercat's first combat victory.

The real answer to the night intruder nuisance was to keep on hitting hard North Korea's airfields by day and night, and it was in opposing attacks of this kind that enemy air activity reached a new peak in the last days

F-51D Mustang at Kimpo, early 1953. (via Robert F. Dorr)

of June 1951. On the 22nd, as F-80 Shooting Stars attacked Sinuiju airfield, Sabres and MiGs clashed overhead in an air battle that ended in the destruction of two MiGs and one F-86. It was a measure of the MiG pilots' new-found confidence that on occasions, their aircraft fitted with wing tanks, they now penetrated almost as far south as the 38th Parallel, either singly or in pairs. They also appeared, at last, to be exploiting the advantages of their aircraft, especially the MiG's ability to outclimb the Sabre and out-manoeuvre the American aircraft at high altitude. During this period, UN pilots noted that the enemy was experimenting with new tactics, including one which Sabre pilots nicknamed the 'yo-yo'. A large formation of MiGs would orbit the battle area at maximum ceiling, with small sections breaking off to make high-speed passes at the UN aircraft before zooming up to altitude again.

The MiG-15 was a high-level interceptor and displayed most of its aerodynamic qualities at altitudes of 20,000 feet or more. Below that, it had dangerous tendencies: on several occasions UN pilots were mystified to see undamaged MiGs go into a spin during a combat manoeuvre and fail to come out of it, their pilots ejecting. Later, when a MiG-15 fell into Allied hands, thanks to the defection of a North Korean pilot, they had their answer. The cockpit of a MiG-15 featured a white line painted down the middle of the instrument panel, and if the aircraft got into a spin pilots were

directed to shove the control column hard up against it. If the aircraft failed to recover after three rotations, the standard procedure was to eject. The MiG also had a number of other unpleasant shortcomings, including a tendency to oscillate – which made it a poor gun platform – and to pitch up without warning. There was no stall warning device, the cockpit pressurisation worked intermittently, and the emergency fuel pump was prone to explode when turned on, tearing off the rear fuselage. The relatively poor performance of the MiG-15 at lower altitudes usually enabled the pilots of slower F-80s and F-84s to hold their own in combat. On 24 June 1951, for example, F-80s of the 51st Wing were attacked by MiG-15s while strafing Sinanju airfield and

claimed four enemy fighters damaged for no hurt to themselves. Two days later, Thunderjets of the 136th Fighter Bomber Wing, newly arrived in the theatre, destroyed one MiG-15 of a formation of six that attacked four B-29s over Yongyu airfield, and drove the rest off.

July 1951 was a bad month for the communist fighter pilots. On the 8th, twenty MiG pilots who crossed the Yalu to attack Mustangs of the 18th Wing strafing an airfield near Kangdong probably thought they had an easy engagement on their hands. Instead, they encountered thirty-five Sabres of the 4th Wing, which shot down three of them. The next day six MiGs which took off to intercept six B-29s over Sinanju lost one of their number to the Superfortress gunners and another to the Sabre escort. On the 11th, a fierce air battle developed south of Sinuiju when thirty MiGs attacked twenty-one F-80s; the fight was joined by thirty-four Sabres, and three MiGs were destroyed. Shortly after midnight on 12 July a Corsair night-fighter of VMF(N)-513 surprised a Po-2 raider and shot it down in flames over Seoul. This success was followed, on 23 September, by another scored by an F7F Tigercat. A Po-2 had attacked Kimpo in the early hours and was intercepted by Major Eugene A. Van Grundy and his RIO, Master Sergeant T.H. Ullom. Van Grundy closed in to 500 feet and destroyed the enemy aircraft with 20mm cannon fire.

Below: Flak damage to an F-80C of the 8th FBW.
Bottom: F-84 Thunderjet of the 136th FBW. (via Robert F. Dorr)

CHAPTER 10

Interdiction – April-November 1951

In the spring of 1951, increased enemy opposition, from heavy AAA as well as from MiGs, compelled FEAF Bomber Command to revise its tactics when attacking bridge targets in north-western Korea. Because of the AAA the bombers were forced up to a bombing altitude of 21,000 feet, and the presence of the MiGs made it dangerous to make more than one bombing run. As a solution, the Command began to attack bridge targets with small formations of three or four aircraft under heavy escort, the bombers armed with 1,000 or 2,000lb bombs. The 19th Group, which had specialised in bridge attacks since the start of the Korean War, achieved some success with 1,000lb Razon and 12,000lb Tarzon radio-guided bombs. These weapons had remotely controlled tail fins which responded to the bombardier's radio signals and permitted guidance to the target with range and azimuth corrections. The 19th Group tested the Razon operationally in the autumn of 1950 and destroyed some fifteen bridges with it, but its overall destructive capacity was not great enough; although it was quite accurate, about four were needed on average to destroy a bridge target.

The Tarzon, similar in concept (apart from its guidance system) to the six-ton Tallboy bombs dropped by the RAF in the latter stages of World War Two, was a much better proposition, but it was the largest bomb used by the USAF up to that time and initial trials proved disappointing: out of ten Tarzons dropped operationally in December 1950, only one scored a direct hit. Results improved with operational experience, and on 13 January 1951 a Tarzon dropped from 15,000 feet by a 19th BG B-29 destroyed a key railway bridge at Kanggye. Three more Tarzon attacks in March, following the delivery of a new consignment of bombs to Okinawa, resulted in the destruction of two more bridges and the damaging of a third. The Tarzon missiles, however, were in very short supply, and most of Bomber Command's interdiction attacks were made with more conventional bombs. Early in March 1951, because of the problem of providing effective fighter escort over north-western Korea, most of these attacks were directed against road, rail and bridge targets well clear of 'MiG Alley', but towards the end of the month, with the 4th Wing's Sabres once again operating at full strength from Korean bases, the B-29s returned to the Yalu to carry out further strikes on the international bridges. The first of these, flown on the 29th, was to have included an attack on the Sinuiju bridges by three Tarzon-armed B-29s of the 19th Group, but the raid was dogged by misfortune from the beginning: one B-29 had to return to base with engine trouble; the second, flown by the 19th Group's commander, Colonel Payne Jennings, came down in the sea with the loss of all its crew; and the third, the only one to reach the Yalu,

missed its target by a considerable margin. Later, it was concluded that the premature explosion of Jennings' Tarzon after jettison may have been responsible for the loss of his aircraft.

By 14 April 1951 Bomber Command's crews had destroyed forty-eight out of sixty assigned bridge targets and twenty-seven out of thirty-nine marshalling yards, but the Command paid heavily for its success: eight B-29s were lost between 15 March and 14 April, four through enemy action, and a further twenty-five were temporarily put out of action with battle damage. As a result General Stratemeyer ordered Bomber Command to cut back its sortie rate to twelve a day, although this was stepped up to eighteen when the communists launched their spring offensive on 22 April 1951.

In May, Bomber Command was directed to destroy marshalling yards and supply and communication centres, leaving the Fifth Air Force, Navy and Marines with the task of interdicting the enemy's road and rail system. From time to time the B-29s were also called in to attack enemy troops assembling for an assault on the UN lines; most of these attacks were made at night and achieved considerable success, as the official history describes:

> On the night of 19 May the X Corps implemented the massive night attacks. At about 1800 hours on 19 May the Corps G-2 reported enemy troops preparing for an attack. Eight B-29s saturated the area with eighty tons of proximity-fuzed 500-pound bombs, and no attack materialized. About 2100 hours, on the night of 20 May, fifteen B-29s attacked enemy troops reported to be assembling against the US 2nd Division . . . the radar-aimed bombs inflicted many casualties and caused the enemy battalion to retreat northward in disorder . . . At about 2000 hours, on the night of 21 May, the X Corps received reports that enemy troops were massing on the roads near Hangye and Chunchon. Eight B-29s hit the former area and five worked the latter zone. The Reds finally attacked, but only with two battalions, which were easily repulsed . . . The Reds committed no reserves and made no major night attacks after 20 May.

On 31 May the UN Command implemented Operation 'Strangle', the object of which was to cut off the main line of resistance (MLR) from the rest of North Korea by means of a concerted air offensive against the enemy's lines of communication in a strip of territory stretching across Korea to a depth of one degree of

A flak burst ripped a large slice of nose from this F-80 Shooting Star during a low-level rail interdiction attack. The pilot, 2nd Lt Colin M. McCrary of Hickory Corners, Michigan, appears understandably happy at his safe return.

latitude above 38°15'N. The road system was split up into eight main routes and all bridges, embankments, choke points, defiles and tunnels were placed on the target list. The three westernmost routes were assigned to the Fifth AF, the 1st Marine Air Wing was allocated the three easternmost, while Task Force 77 was given the two centre routes. Naval air strikes in the vicinity of the MLR, within the framework of Operation Strangle, were carried out by the Marine Air Wing and Task Force 95, the UN Blockading and Escort Force established in September 1950. TF 95 was split into two main elements, Task Group 95.1 – under British command and including most of the Commonwealth naval units – patrolling the west coast, and Task Group 95.2 patrolling the east coast from the MLR to the island of Yang-do. Operating with TG 95.1, the Sea Furies and Fireflies of HMS *Glory*'s 804 and 812 Squadrons were extremely active during 'Strangle'; on one occasion in June the British carrier flew off eighty-four sorties in a single day, setting up a record that was only broken in October by the Australian carrier HMAS *Sydney*.

Glory normally worked in a nine-day operation cycle, flying for four days in which she averaged a fourteen-hour flying day, replenishing for one day, returning for a second four-day period and then handing over to the US carrier *Bataan* before going to Kure or Sasebo in Japan for maintenance, and then returning for another nine-day cycle. By 22 June her air group (CAG 14) had expended some 60,000 rounds of 20mm ammunition, over 1,000 rockets and 180 bombs. During her tour,

which ended on 21 September, she lost two Sea Furies and two Fireflies to enemy action, but all the aircrew with the exception of one Firefly pilot were picked up. As mentioned earlier, *Glory*'s relief, HMAS *Sydney* – with the Sea Furies of 805 and 808 Squadrons and the Fireflies of 817 embarked – broke the light carrier record with eighty-nine sorties on 11 October 1951, but when *Glory* returned for a second tour in January 1952 after a refit in Australia she put the record up to 104 sorties.

The initial results of Operation 'Strangle' were encouraging, but it failed in its primary objective of isolating the MLR. For one thing, the main communist sources of supply, the factories in China and the Soviet Union, were untouched by Allied bombing, and the flow of war materiel continued unchecked; for another, the bombing had the power to disrupt only supply routes and rolling stock, whereas the real heart of the enemy's logistical system, the stockpiles of materiel, were well concealed in caves and tunnels that were virtually immune to air attack. Also, Allied Intelligence had badly underestimated the amazing ingenuity of the North Korean Military Highway Administration and the Railway Recovery Bureau, whose bridging, track and road-laying techniques were so efficient that they were able to keep supplies moving continuously despite the bombing. Lastly, the air interdiction campaign suffered from the outset because it was not co-ordinated with offensive action by UN ground forces. Any advantages gained by comprehensive interdiction in the MLR were

Firefly preparing for launch, with a US Navy S-51 plane guard helicopter hovering watchfully.

consequently not exploited as they might have been.

The ability of the communists to move men and supplies in secrecy at night emphasised the importance of night intruder operations. Since the autumn of 1950 these had been flown in the main by the 3rd Bombardment Wing and the 731st Bombardment Squadron, operating B-26s out of Iwakuni, and Marine Squadron VMF(N)-513, flying Corsairs from Itazuke, Wonsan and Yonpo, but neither aircraft type was really suited to intruder operations. In addition, the 3rd Wing suffered from a shortage of aircraft and from the fact that the steel plank strip at Taegu, through which the B-26s staged on their nocturnal missions, inflicted severe wear on tyres. Despite everything, however, the Wing managed to fly up to forty-eight sorties nightly in April 1951, at the height of the enemy's spring offensive. Most of the B-26 intruder sorties were flown in conjunction with 'Lightning Bug' C-47 flare ships, a flight of which was usually on alert at Taegu; each could carry about 130 US Navy type Mk VIII flares, enough for five hours of target illumination. In the early days the C-47s worked as far north as Sinuiju, but with the stiffening of the enemy anti-aircraft defences in that sector they were later forbidden to go north of latitude 39°30'. Sometimes, as a variation from flare-dropping, the C-47s scattered loads of roofing nails over roads in enemy territory to puncture the tyres of communist vehicles. About thirty vehicles were immobilised in this way and destroyed by B-26s.

From March 1951, since the C-47s could no longer operate far north of the MLR, most of the 3rd Wing's B-26s were adapted to carry Mk VI flares on their rocket rails. Fuzed to ignite at about 3,500 feet, the flares burned long enough to permit two or three strafing passes. Some of the Wing's most successful intruder crews, however, flying B-26Cs with glazed noses, scorned the use of flares altogether, preferring to fix a convoy's position by noting its relation to ground shadows in the few seconds before the enemy switched off their lights, and making a single pass with 100lb M-47 fire bombs and 260lb M-81 fragmentation bombs.

In April 1951 the 3rd Wing claimed to have destroyed sixteen locomotives and 227 vehicles, and in May it claimed five locomotives and 629 vehicles. The effectiveness of one of its strikes, on 8 May 1951, was described in graphic detail by a shot-down American airman who escaped from his captors, and his account is repeated in the official history:

> We came to the place [near Taegwangni] where the B-26 had dropped its load. The place was in an uproar. First we began meeting little carts with wounded on them, then came hand-carried stretchers, and then handmade 'makeshift' stretchers, then men carrying others on their backs, and finally carts pulled by mules or Chinese soldiers with ten to fifteen dead bodies on each cart . . . I would estimate that there were a minimum of 200 wounded and about twelve to fifteen carts with the dead ones stacked solid on them. Probably 225 dead. I don't know how many B-26s had attacked, but it sure was a mess.

At the beginning of June, to assist the 3rd Wing for the duration of Operation 'Strangle', the 452nd Bombardment Wing was moved up to Pusan East airfield (K-9) and soon began night operations with its glazed-nose B-26Cs, benefiting from the 3rd Wing's experience. Between 11 and 20 June the 452nd Wing destroyed 151 enemy vehicles and damaged 224. The 3rd Wing's tally of enemy transport in June stood at 403 vehicles destroyed and 1,048 damaged.

The work of the night intruders continued unabated during July, and although the overall effectiveness of Operation 'Strangle' diminished steadily the B-26s of the 3rd and 452nd Wings continued to register successes. Throughout the month the 3rd Wing operated its aircraft in pairs, one carrying fifty-two flares to illuminate the targets and the other to attack, but although this technique made for more effective attacks it reduced the number of routes that could be covered. Nevertheless, in four weeks the Wing claimed 240 vehicles destroyed and 693 damaged. The 452nd Wing, on the other hand, preferred to send its aircraft

A flak-damaged B-26C of the 3rd BW makes a belly landing at a South Korean airfield.

Douglas B-26 Invaders. The B-26 light bomber served in the night intruder role throughout the war. (John Sidirougogous)

out singly, and its claim for the month was 471 vehicles destroyed and 880 damaged. One of the 452nd's most spectacular successes was achieved shortly before dawn on 14 July when a lone B-26 flown by Captain William L. Ford attacked two convoys in quick succession, destroying thirty-eight trucks and damaging an estimated thirty.

The Marine intruders of VMF(N)-513, flying out of Pusan's K-1 airstrip in their Corsairs and Tigercats against targets closer to the MLR, also made use of C-47 flare ships – or, more correctly, the US Navy variant, the R4D – as they concentrated on their allotted area south of Pyongyang. The undersides of the R4Ds were painted matt black to minimise reflection from the flares and to make the aircraft less visible to ground defences. On 12 June 1951 the R4Ds were joined by a pair of Consolidated PB4Y-2 Privateers of Patrol Squadron VP-772, which were transferred to Pusan from Naval Air Station Atsugi, Japan on an experimental basis; the experiment proved so successful that other Privateers were assigned to this type of work from VP-9 and VP-871. Between 1 April and 30 June 1951, the Marine intruder pilots reported attacks on 11,890 vehicles and claimed 1,420 destroyed, averaging eighteen sorties a night.

The Fifth Air Force's fighter-bombers, meanwhile, continued to take the lion's share of success, particularly in the early months of 1951. In February they claimed the destruction of 1,366 enemy vehicles

(728 of them to the credit of the 18th Wing's Mustangs); in March the total rose to 2,261, and in April it was 2,336. But the Allied fighter-bomber pilots did not have things all their own way. The communists were now defending their convoys with a wide variety of automatic weapons, including Russian 12.7mm machine-guns and 37mm cannon, the latter effective against aircraft from ground level up to 4,500 feet. The Mustangs, with their liquid-cooled engines, were particularly vulnerable to ground fire, and thirty-eight were lost in April, May and June. The tactics developed by the communists to counter the Allied fighter-bomber attacks were varied. Early in 1951 the Chinese began to organise anti-aircraft groups of infantry armed with light automatic weapons and heavy-calibre machine-guns; these groups would be deployed around cleverly devised 'flak traps' such as dummy troops or vehicles. A highly efficient observer network was also set up with sentries trained in aircraft recognition positioned over 300 yards or so along the main supply routes. By the beginning of July 1951 the enemy had 900 anti-aircraft guns, not counting small-arms, defending their supply routes in North Korea, and as the year went by interdiction became a costly business. To give one example, from 22 August to 30 November 1951 aircraft of the USS *Essex*'s Air Group Five were hit 318 times, resulting in the loss of twenty-seven aircraft and eleven pilots.

CHAPTER 11
The Renewed Air War, Autumn 1951

In June 1951, with the action in Korea settling down to a war of attrition and the ground being laid for what would turn out to be an apparently endless and fruitless series of communist-dominated armistice talks, there were clear signs that a new air offensive was building against the United Nations. At this time the first-line strength of the Chinese People's Air Force stood at 1,050 combat aircraft, of which 690 were based in Manchuria, and several new airfields suitable for jet fighter operation were being constructed just across the Yalu in the Antung area. This airfield complex would shortly house some 300 MiG-15s, controlled by a well-equipped operations centre at Antung. Fighter controllers here were either Chinese or North Korean, but they never made a move without the blessing of the Russian advisers who were always in the background. Soviet pilots were still prominent in the fighter units; in the early days, while the Chinese trained up to combat proficiency on the MiG-15, the Russians had flown most of the combat missions, but as Chinese pilots became more experienced the Russians generally assumed the roles of squadron and flight commanders. At a later date, entire Soviet fighter regiments – or rather their personnel – would be attached to Chinese air divisions for a three-month tour of duty.

A careful assessment of the CPAF's order of battle, coupled with the knowledge that experienced Soviet aircrew were serving in Manchuria in considerable numbers, pointed to the possibility that the communists might be planning a series of surprise attacks on Allied air bases in Korea, and possibly in Japan, as a prelude to a new bid for air superiority. On 10 June 1951 General Otto P. Weyland assumed command of the Far East Air Forces, and within a matter of hours, realising the potential seriousness of the situation, he signalled the Pentagon with an urgent request for four jet fighter wings to be sent out to the Far East, one pair to bolster Japan's defences and the other two for deployment to Korea. At the time of the request there were only eighty-nine Sabres in the Far East, including forty-four in Korea, confronting over 400 MiG-15s; Weyland wanted not only more Sabres, but new F-86E models to replace the F-86As with which the 4th FIW was then equipped. In fact, the USAF undertook to replace FEAF's F-86As with F-86Es on a one-for-one exchange basis, but this process was to take many months. The USAF's objection was that it would be impossible to provide Weyland with a complete wing of F-86Es without depleting Air Defense Command, which was under strength and struggling to meet its commitments. The complacency of the immediate post-war years was

F-84s of the 49th FBW taking off from Taegu. This is not a combat sortie; the aircraft are unarmed.

Gloster Meteor Mk 8 A77-15 of No. 77 Squadron RAAF pictured at Kimpo. (via Robert F. Dorr)

having its effect, and it would be some time before the United States' technical prowess could match the Soviet Union's mass production of air superiority fighters.

In the meantime, the best that could be done was to increase the number of F-84 Thunderjets in the Korean theatre, something which General Stratemeyer had strongly advocated before relinquishing command of FEAF, and on 1 June 1951 the 27th Fighter Escort Wing began the process of converting pilots of the 49th and 136th Wings, which had been operating F-80s, to the F-84E. As the F-80 pilots qualified on the new type the 27th Wing's Thunderjets were turned over to the 136th Wing, squadron by squadron, until by the end of August the 27th Wing's personnel were relieved of duty in the Far East. In addition, the USAF authorised the deployment of one F-84 wing – the 116th – to Japan; the seventy-five Thunderjets arrived on 24 July and the Wing settled in at Chitose and Misawa Air Bases. The 116th FBW formed part of the 314th Air Division, which since 8 May 1951 had been established as a separate FEAF command responsible for the air defence of Japan. Also within the Division were the 68th and

339th Fighter Interceptor Squadrons and the 35th Fighter Interceptor Wing, which with the exception of the Mustang-equipped 39th Squadron was transferred to Johnson Air Base on 25 May; the Wing's 40th Squadron went to Misawa for conversion to F-94 Starfires.

The only other unit under Fifth Air Force control to receive new equipment in the first half of 1951 was No. 77 Squadron RAAF, which returned from Korea to Iwakuni at the end of April to re-equip with the Gloster Meteor F.8. Fifteen of these aircraft, together with a pair of Mk 7 trainers, had been shipped out to Japan in February in the aircraft carrier HMS *Warrior*. Twenty more Mk 8s arrived during April, accompanied by four RAF pilots with considerable Meteor experience to assist in the task of conversion: Flight Lieutenants Max Scannell, Frank Easley, Ian 'Joe' Blyth, and Flight Sergeant Lamb. All four volunteered to go to Pusan as soon as they arrived in Japan, rather than hang around at Iwakuni, and saw some operational Mustang flying before returning to Japan with the Squadron. By this time most of the Australian pilots – starting with No. 77 Squadron's CO, Sqn Ldr Richard Cresswell, who had

already done a jet conversion course on F-80s – had been checked out on the Meteor, sandwiching the conversion course between operational commitments as the opportunity arose. The Australians viewed the prospect of going into action in the Meteor with mixed feelings. They had been hoping to get Sabres, and there were some who believed the British fighter to be hopelessly outclassed. Others were reluctant to give up their faithful Mustangs. Also annoying for the Australians was the big security clampdown to which everyone connected with the Meteor was subjected. The reason was one of diplomacy: at this stage Britain did not want to be seen to be too closely associated with the war in Korea. But the Australians viewed it all as an unnecessary nuisance, especially since the Meteors had made the voyage to Korea on the deck of the aircraft carrier, in full view of everyone.

The conversion proceeded fairly smoothly, although there were a number of accidents. The first aircraft casualty occurred on 7 May when a Meteor 8 flown by Sgt Bessel ditched in the sea eight miles south of Iwakuni after running out of fuel. The pilot paddled ashore safely and the aircraft was later salvaged for use

as spares. The first total aircraft loss occurred under curious circumstances on 14 June when Sgt Stoney, making a normal climb-out from Iwakuni, was suddenly shot through the canopy in his ejection seat. As Stoney descended in his parachute, the Meteor spiralled round him several times, frighteningly close, before crashing into a hillside.

Meanwhile, early in May, the Meteor had been tested in mock combat against a Sabre flown down from Johnson Air Base by Flt Lt Daniels, an RAF pilot attached to the 335th FIS. The trials lasted two days, and among the conclusions drawn was that the Sabre outclassed the Meteor in a steep dive or a long straight and level run, while the Meteor was superior in turning, zooming, and in a sustained climb. This seemed to indicate that the Meteor would at least be able to hold its own against the MiG under most combat conditions, and the Australians were now looking forward to taking their jets into action for the first time.

Unfortunately, it was not to prove quite so simple. Acting on American advice, General Robertson, commanding the British Commonwealth forces in Japan, issued orders forbidding the Meteors to be

Capt. Richard S. Becker points to the spot where his bullets hit a MiG-15. Becker, a pilot with the 4th FIW, destroyed five.

deployed to Korea until radio compasses had been installed in them. The first ARN-6 radio compass components arrived in June and installation work began at once. During this frustrating period of delay the Squadron's two Meteor 7s made frequent hops to Kimpo, their rear seats usually occupied by signals officers whose task it was to work out joint communications procedures with their American counterparts. Some of the Squadron's Meteors had still not been fitted with radio compasses when, towards the end of June, authority was finally given for the move to Kimpo to begin, on the understanding that the aircraft without radio compasses could only fly with a cloud base minimum of 1,000–1,500 feet. When the Squadron did move to Kimpo, it was in the interceptor role. There had previously been a lot of uncertainty about how best to employ the Meteors, as they were not cleared for ground attack work and they had serious combat limitations by comparison with the MiG-15, including restricted rearward vision because of the metal fairing at the back of the cockpit, but Sqn Ldr Cresswell had managed to convince senior officers of both the RAAF and Fifth AF that the Meteor could perform favourably as an interceptor if tactics were evolved enabling it to operate in concert with the Sabres.

On 30 June No. 77 Squadron's supporting equipment was flown to Kimpo in seventeen C-119s and seven C-54s, the personnel following in Dakotas of No. 86 (Transport) Squadron RAAF. After Iwakuni, Kimpo was a depressing sight; the summer rains and the continual comings and goings of heavy transports had churned most of the airfield into mud. During most of July No. 77 Squadron was engaged in training and familiarisation flights, and it was not until the 30th that

the Squadron flew its first operational mission: a sweep by sixteen Meteors south of the Yalu. The Meteors flew in finger fours between 30,000 and 35,000 feet, with sixteen Sabres of the 4th FIW 10,000 feet lower down. No contact was made with the enemy. Several more sweeps were flown in the first three weeks of August with the same negative result. During one of them, on the 20th, two Meteors collided during a formation change and crashed north of the Han river. Both pilots – Sgt Mitchell and Flt Sgt Lamb, the latter one of the RAF instructors – were killed.

On four or five occasions during August the Meteors were detailed to escort B-29s and RF-80s to Sinanju, and it was while escorting a flight of Shooting Stars with two sections of four Meteors on the 25th that MiGs were sighted for the first time. Two enemy jets were spotted south of Sinanju and one of the Meteor flights gave chase; the leader, Flt Lt Scannell, opened fire at extreme range but no hits were claimed. The first real test came four days later on the 29th when eight Meteors were detailed to escort B-29s and another eight to carry out a diversionary sweep north of Sinanju. At 1120 the latter flight, led by Squadron Leader Wilson, spotted six MiGs at 40,000 feet over Chongju, 5,000 feet higher than themselves. Keeping the enemy in sight Wilson manoeuvred his formation up-sun, but as he did so two more MiGs appeared a few thousand feet below. Wilson decided to attack and went into a dive followed by his number two, Flying Officer Woodroffe. As the two Meteors levelled out, however, Woodroffe's aircraft suddenly flicked into a spin (an unpleasant tendency of the Meteor 8, caused by the effects of compressibility if the aircraft exceeded 0.8M at altitude) and dropped away; the pilot managed to recover several thousand feet lower down, but now Wilson had no one to cover his tail. As he began his approach to attack, a MiG jumped him out of the sun, unnoticed in the thirty-degree blind spot caused by the dural structure at the rear of the Meteor's cockpit. The first warning Wilson had of the danger was when cannon shells passed over his wing; he immediately put his aircraft into a maximum-rate turn in a bid to shake off his pursuer. He was rescued by Flight Lieutenant Cedric Wilson and Flying Officer Ken Blight, who spotted his predicament and drove the MiG away, but not before cannon shells had shot away Sqn Ldr Wilson's port aileron and punched a three-foot hole in his port wing, puncturing a fuel tank. Despite the damage Wilson reached base safely, touching down at thirty knots above normal landing speed.

Meanwhile, a fierce air battle had developed over Chongju as the other Meteors were hotly engaged by thirty MiGs. The weight of the attack fell on 'Dog' section led by Flt Lt Geoff Thornton; one Meteor was shot down and its pilot, Warrant Officer Don Guthrie, baled out to spend the rest of the war in a PoW camp.

On 1 September 1951, by which time the CPAF order of battle included 525 MiG-15s, the communists judged that the time was ripe to launch their new air offensive. The MiGs began to appear in greater numbers than ever before, as many as ninety crossing the Yalu at one time. They were also better led, better organised and displayed superior tactics, clear evidence that the Russians were in full control. They also employed tactics hitherto untried in Korea: some MiGs attacked in

line astern, others used the Lufbery circle (a defensive circle in which an attacker coming in astern of any aircraft in the circle would come under fire from the one behind) named after WW1 ace Raoul Lufbery, and on one occasion four flights of MiGs made line-abreast head-on attacks in which all sixteen aircraft fired on a single opponent. World War Two veterans of the European theatre had seen similar tactics before; they had been used by Luftwaffe fighter formations attacking American daylight bombers.

During September 1951 the 4th Wing's pilots sighted 1,177 MiG sorties over North Korea and engaged 911 MiGs in combat, usually fighting against odds of three or four to one. Despite this the Americans gave an excellent account of themselves; on 2 September, for example, twenty-two Sabres engaged forty-four MiGs in a thirty-minute air battle between Sinuiju and Pyongyang and destroyed four of them, and on 9 September, in a fight between twenty-eight Sabres and seventy MiGs, Captains Richard S. Becker and Ralph D. Gibson claimed a MiG apiece to become the second and third aces of the Korean conflict. Three F-86s were lost in these clashes.

The Meteors of No. 77 Squadron, on the other hand, continued to fare badly. On 5 September six Meteors, escorting RF-80s at 20,000 feet in the Antung area, were bounced by a dozen MiGs attacking from astern in pairs. During the five-minute battle that followed Warrant Officer W. Michelson was attacked by three MiGs which severely damaged his tail before he succeeded in shaking them off. Three Meteor pilots –

Meteors of No. 77 Squadron RAAF in their revetments at Kimpo. Nearest the camera is Plt Off Ken Murray's aircraft, Black Murray.

Pilots of No. 77 Sqn RAAF at Kimpo.

Blyth, Cannon and Dawson – fired at MiGs, but with no result. There was another skirmish on the 26th when twelve Meteors – once again escorting RF-80s – were attacked by more than thirty MiGs. One of the enemy fighters was cut off from the rest by Flt Lt Thomas, who chased it well to the south of Pyongyang before its superior speed enabled it to escape. Another pilot, Flt Lt Dawson, fired several bursts at a second MiG and saw pieces fly off it, but the ciné film of the combat was over-exposed and this could not be confirmed. In this action Sgt Ernest Armitt's Meteor was hit and damaged, but he returned to base safely. The Thunderjets also had several skirmishes with enemy fighters during September, and in one of these, on the 19th, Captain Kenneth L. Skeen of the 49th Wing destroyed a MiG-15, several more being claimed by B-29 gunners. Allied combat losses for the month were three Sabres, an F-80, an F-84, and a Mustang.

By the end of September enemy fighters were seriously interfering with the activities of Allied fighter-bombers attacking targets in north-western Korea, and General Weyland once again stressed the need to provide an additional Sabre wing, or failing this to convert one of the existing F-80 wings to F-86s. The USAF's response was blunt. Supporting the existing Sabre wing in the Far East was difficult enough, supporting a second was out of the question. As soon as he received this news, General Frank F. Everest – commanding the Fifth Air Force since 1 June 1951 – immediately ordered a halt to all fighter-bomber attacks on targets in the north-west. Instead, the fighter-bombers were to concentrate on a zone between Pyongyang and the Chongchon river.

Necessary though this decision was in the light of the growing communist challenge to Allied air superiority, it had dangerous implications. It meant that the enemy's airfield construction and rehabilitation programme in North Korea – brought to a virtual standstill by comprehensive interdiction attacks during the spring and early summer – could now get under way again, and it soon became apparent that the communists were taking full advantage of the lull in UN fighter-bomber activity. During late September and early October reconnaissance aircraft located three major airfields under construction inside a twenty-mile radius north of the Chongchon. Each of these airfields could be defended by a fighter umbrella from one of the others, and it was clear that the communists planned to use them as a base in an attempt to establish air superiority as far south as Pyongyang. The airfield complex was immediately targeted for a B-29 strike, but before this could take place it was essential that the UN established firm, even if only temporary, command of the sky over north-western Korea. Beginning on 1 October, the 4th Fighter Interceptor Wing accordingly stepped up its counter-air operations with the object of bringing the MiGs to battle and inflicting a severe defeat upon them. The result was to be some of the bitterest fighting in the history of air warfare.

CHAPTER 12

The Martyrdom of the B-29s, October 1951

F9F Panther moving up for launch off Korea. (via Robert F. Dorr)

In the late summer of 1951, while UN fighter-bombers pressed home their attacks on targets close to the Yalu, FEAF Bomber Command had concentrated most of its effort on railway targets. The first attack took place on 25 August when thirty-five B-29s of the 19th, 98th and 307th Bombardment Wings led by Colonel Harris F. Rogner, the deputy commander of Bomber Command, set out for Rashin, an important port and rail complex close to the Soviet border. So far, because of its proximity to Soviet territory, Rashin had been off limits to Bomber Command, but on 1 August General Ridgway had sought and obtained the approval of the Joint Chiefs and President Truman to attack the port in view of the extensive railway facilities there. Such approval had been given only on the understanding that the attack would be carried out under visual bombing conditions, and that it would not be publicised.

Near Songjin the bombers made rendezvous with twenty-three F9F Panthers and McDonnell F2H-2 Banshees from the USS *Essex*. The Banshee, new to the theatre and deployed with VF-172, had carried out its first combat operation – a ground attack sortie over north-eastern Korea – two days earlier, and this was its first escort mission. As the bombers approached the target the Navy fighter pilots kept a watchful eye on the

sky over the Soviet frontier, but no hostile aircraft appeared and the run-in was made without incident. Rashin's marshalling yards were obliterated by 291 tons of bombs, only light flak was encountered, and none of the Allied aircraft was hit.

During the first two weeks of October, in preparation for the planned airfield attacks, the 4th FIW's Sabres intensified their combat patrols, destroying two MiGs on the first day of the month, six on the 2nd, one on the 5th, and nine on the 16th. Two more MiGs were destroyed on 3 October when twelve F-80s of the 8th FBW, led by Colonel James B. Tipton and responding to a call for help from another fighter-bomber formation, took the enemy attackers by surprise. Meanwhile, Brigadier Joe W. Kelly, who had assumed command of FEAF Bomber Command at the end of September 1951, had been working out how best to approach the problem of attacking the three new enemy airfields – which were at Saamcham, Namsi and Taechon – given the probability that the enemy would put every available fighter into the air to defend them. For safety's sake it was envisaged that small numbers of bombers would attack the targets by radar under cover of darkness, the B-29s having been fitted with Shoran short-range navigational radar (comprising two AN/APN-2 ground radar beacons and an AN/APN-3 transceiver in

Sabres of the 4th FIW. (via Robert F. Dorr)

the aircraft), but the first two Shoran raids, in which B-29s of the 307th BW bombed the airfield at Saamcham on the nights of 13 and 14 October, produced disappointing results. Since the rapid destruction of the enemy airfields was a matter of supreme importance there was no alternative but to carry out large-scale daylight attacks, relying on a strong fighter escort to keep the MiGs at bay.

The first of the daylight attacks, carried out on 18 October by nine B-29s of the 19th Group and a similar number from the 98th Wing, met with only limited success. The 98th Wing aircraft, scheduled to bomb Taechon, missed their escorts and had to divert to secondary targets, and only the 19th Group attacked Saamcham as planned. The 98th Wing once again failed to rendezvous with its fighter escort in another attempt to attack Taechon on 21 October, and it was left to the 19th Group to carry out this mission on the following

day. Shortly after the Group's nine B-29s had bombed the target their escort of twenty-four F-84s was scattered by a strong formation of MiGs, and under cover of the diversion three more MiGs dropped down out of a cloud bank and attacked the B-29s with such speed and surprise that their startled gunners failed to return the fire. The fighters scored hits on one bomber that had already been crippled by flak, but its crew managed to keep it airborne until they reached the coast, where they

baled out and were picked up.

There were indications that this interception had been unplanned and that the MiGs had come upon the Allied formation by chance, but it was a different story on 23 October. This time the enemy knew that the B-29s were coming, and the fighters were waiting for them. At 0900 eight B-29s of the 307th BW made rendezvous with fifty-five Thunderjets of the 49th and 136th Wings and set course for the airfield at Namsi. Ahead and above, thirty-four Sabres of the 4th FIW provided distant cover. Suddenly, at 0915, over 100 MiGs swept across the river. Within minutes the Sabres, effectively boxed in, were fighting for their lives. While this battle – in which two MiGs were shot down – was in progress, fifty more MiGs approached the B-29 and Thunderjet formation and circled it at some distance, evidently intent on drawing off the F-84s. The latter, however, refused to take the bait, and after a while the MiGs launched their attack, coming in from all directions. Using their superior speed to good advantage they ripped through the F-84 escort to make several passes at the B-29s as the latter headed towards their target. Two B-29s went down a matter of seconds after they had released their bombs; a third, burning fiercely, staggered towards the coast where its crew baled out – all except the pilot, Captain Thomas L. Shields, who sacrificed his own life to keep the crippled bomber flying until the other crew members got clear. One Thunderjet also failed to return from this mission. Four MiGs were claimed as destroyed, three by B-29 gunners and one by an F-84 pilot. The surviving bombers, all but one with battle damage and most with dead and wounded on board, struggled back to emergency landings in Korea and Japan. It was Bomber Command's blackest day since the war began, and although the 307th Wing's subsequent mission report was full of praise for the efforts of the F-84 escort, it also observed that nothing short of 150 Sabres would have been adequate to protect the bombers.

The next morning eight B-29s of the 98th Wing set out to attack a railway bridge at Sunchon, escorted by ten F-84s and sixteen Meteors of No. 77 Squadron. En route the formation ran into a battle between Sabres and about sixty MiGs, some of which turned to attack the bombers, and a running fight developed. One Meteor, flown by Flying Officer Hamilton-Foster, was badly hit almost immediately and went into a spiral dive as its starboard engine flamed out. The pilot managed to recover and made a successful landing at Kimpo. Behind him the fight still raged as the MiGs chased the B-29s almost as far as Wonsan, inflicting severe damage on one bomber. It ditched in Wonsan harbour and all the crew were picked up. The B-29 gunners claimed one MiG destroyed.

On the morning of Sunday, 27 October, sixteen Meteors and thirty-two Thunderjets were detailed to escort eight 19th Group B-29s in an attack on a rail

bridge near Sinanju. Because of reports that the MiG pilots were reluctant to fight over water, the bombers were routed to the target in such a way that they stayed over the Yellow Sea as long as possible. The trouble started when the formation turned inland towards Sinanju and was engaged by ninety-five MiGs, which quickly overwhelmed the fighter escort. Fortunately the MiG pilots seemed disinclined to press home their attacks, and in a fight lasting ten minutes three kills were claimed by the B-29 gunners. Flying Officer Reading of 77 Squadron severely damaged a MiG, and other hits were claimed by Meteor and Thunderjet pilots. Four B-29s were damaged, one of them seriously.

October 1951 drew to a close with the destruction, during the month, of thirty-two MiGs – twenty-four claimed by Sabres, seven by B-29 gunners, and one by a Thunderjet. But the Allies had suffered too, having lost seven Sabres, two F-84s and an F-80 in air combat. And the battles of October had cost Bomber Command its worst losses of the war. At the beginning of the month the Command had lost only six B-29s in action, but when the month ended five more had been destroyed by

Top: Picketing an F2H Banshee on a TF 77 carrier at sunset. Below: F2H-2 Banshee of USS Essex's *air group.*

flak or fighters and eight others seriously damaged. In one week fifty-five aircrew had been posted dead or missing and twelve others had been wounded. The aircrew losses were particularly serious because by now the B-29 units in the Korean theatre were having to rely heavily on Air Force Reserve personnel who had flown B-29s during World War Two in order to avoid an unacceptable drain on SAC's aircrew resources. The outcome was inevitable: the B-29 force was restricted to night operations. By the end of November 1951 most of the Superfortresses had been fitted with Shoran, and although early Shoran night raids met with only limited success the B-29s soon began to inflict heavy damage on the North Korean airfields. The enemy set up heavy flak batteries along the arcs followed by the bombers on their radar bombing runs, but although several B-29s were damaged, none was lost. As yet, the communists possessed no effective night fighter force; the few night interceptions reported by the B-29 crews were carried out on a hit-or-miss basis by MiG-15s relying on searchlights to illuminate their targets. The only B-29 lost in November was on a leaflet-dropping mission along the Yalu; it was hit by flak but succeeded in reaching the coast, where its crew parachuted to safety.

By the end of October the enemy had begun to move numbers of combat aircraft to airfields south of the Yalu; air reconnaissance revealed twenty-six MiG-15s in revetments at Uiju and about sixty piston-engined aircraft, mostly La-9s, Il-10s and Tupolev Tu-2 twin-engined bombers, at Sinuiju. This was the situation that confronted the US Air Force Chief of Staff General Hoyt S. Vandenberg when he flew to the Far East late in October to make an on-the-spot assessment. After reviewing all available intelligence and conferring with FEAF commanders, he came away convinced that General Weyland was right and that the enemy air threat was more serious than ever before. 'Almost overnight,' he commented later in a press statement, 'Communist China has become one of the major air powers of the world.'

As soon as he returned to the USA, General Vandenberg ordered the redeployment of seventy-five F-86s, with air and ground crews and full supporting equipment, from Air Defense Command to the Korean theatre. General Weyland planned to use these aircraft to re-equip the 51st Fighter Interceptor Wing, returning an equal number of F-80 pilots and ground personnel to the USA in exchange. Transfer of the new batch of Sabres was carried out by sea – the aircraft this time properly waterproofed – between 1 and 9 November. Meanwhile, the whole of the 4th FIW, including the 335th Squadron from Japan, was moved to Kimpo, which it shared with the Meteors of No. 77 Squadron and the RB-26s of the 67th TRW. The arrival of the Sabre reinforcements was eagerly awaited, for in addition to their overwhelming numerical superiority the enemy jet fighter squadrons now had another advantage. Allied pilots reported encounters with what appeared to be a much improved model of the MiG-15 with a far better all-round performance. The aircraft was in fact the MiG-15 *Bis* with an uprated VK-1 turbojet, the latest type to equip Soviet first-line fighter squadrons, and in the hands of a capable pilot it was more than a match for the F-86A.

In the meantime, the pilots of the 4th FIW, now under the command of Colonel Harrison R. Thyng, another World War Two ace, were hard pressed to handle the MiG-15s which appeared over North Korea almost daily in November 1951. Up to eighty MiGs would cross the Yalu in co-ordinated 'trains', known to the Allies as the 'west coast train' and 'central train', and head south at over 35,000 feet to rendezvous over Pyongyang before returning towards Manchuria, detaching flights to attack UN aircraft as the opportunity arose, – the favourite targets being Sabres or fighter bombers on their way home, short of fuel. These tactics meant that no United Nations fighter-bombers or reconnaissance aircraft could operate in the zone betwen Pyongyang and the border without interference from enemy jets, and all reconnaissance flights into this area had to be escorted by Sabres, F-80s, F-84s or Meteors. RF-80 photojets were

Crewmen on the USS Essex *push an F2H Banshee of VF-172 off the flight deck elevator in preparation for a launch.*

Top: An F2H of USS Essex's *air group over the Korean coast.*
Above: RF-80A reconnaissance aircraft at Kimpo. (via Robert F. Dorr)

bounced by MiGs eighteen times during October and November, and although only one was lost several sorties often had to be made before a target was successfully photographed.

On 6 November 1951 the Chinese used their Tu-2 light bombers for the first time in an attack on the island of Taehwa-do in the Yellow Sea, where ROK forces were fighting North Korean marines. Three days later there was an air battle between eight F-80s of the 80th Fighter Bomber Squadron and more than twenty MiGs near Kunu-ri; the Shooting Stars came out on top, shooting down two MiGs for no loss to themselves. On the 18th a flight of 4th Wing Sabres strafed twelve MiGs which were dispersed on Uiju airfield, destroying four of them, and on the 27th another four enemy jet fighters were shot

down in an air battle over the Yalu. One of them was destroyed by Major Richard D. Creighton, making him the fourth jet ace of the Korean War.

Then came 30 November, and the biggest single air combat success so far for the UN pilots. That afternoon thirty-one Sabres of the 4th FIW led by Colonel Benjamin S. Preston sighted a formation of twelve Tu-2 bombers flying in boxes of three, heading for Taehwa-do. The bombers were escorted by sixteen La-9s, and a similar number of MiG-15s, the latter flying top cover. In the battle that ensued the Sabre pilots destroyed eight Tu-2s, three La-9s and one MiG-15. Two American pilots, Major George A. Davis and Major Winton W. Marshall, became aces during the combat; Davis destroyed three of the bombers and the MiG.

CHAPTER 13

The Air Battle Intensifies, December 1951-May 1952

F-80C Guns for Hire *with its pilot. (via Robert F. Dorr)*

While the 4th FIW held the line against growing odds, the 51st FIW had been preparing to convert its two F-80 squadrons to Sabres, and in preparation for the change Colonel Francis S. Gabreski assumed command of the Wing at Suwon on 6 November 1951. Gabreski had destroyed twenty-eight German aircraft while flying P-47 Thunderbolts during World War Two, and he already had two MiGs to his credit in Korea. He was to down a further four and a half MiGs while commanding the 51st FIW, the half MiG shared with another World War Two ace, Major Bill Whisner. On 19 November the 51st FIW transferred its F-80s to the 8th Fighter Bomber Wing, and after a short working-up period flew its first Sabre combat missions on 1 December 1951.

FEAF now had 165 Sabres in the theatre, of which 127 were committed to combat in Korea. The reinforcements came only just in time, for in December the pace of the enemy air offensive showed no sign of slackening and the communist pilots continued to display a high level of aggression. On 1 December, for example, twelve Meteors of No. 77 Squadron RAAF led by Flight Lieutenant Geoff Thornton were carrying out an offensive sweep at 19,000 feet when some fifty MiGs were sighted high above. At that height the Meteor pilots knew they had no hope of holding their own in a turning fight; the odds would be better if they could

draw the MiGs down to their own level, although the Australians were at a great tactical disadvantage. The MiGs saw them and came down in pairs to make a fast diving attack on 'Charlie' flight, which broke on Thornton's command. One pilot, Flying Officer Drummond, left it a little late and was hit in the fuel tanks. His call for help was answered by Flying Officer Bruce Gogerly of 'Able' Flight, who got on the tail of a MiG and shot it down with a long burst of 20mm fire – the Meteor's first confirmed combat victory in Korea. Gogerly was himself subjected to a series of head-on attacks by pairs of MiGs, as were some other pilots; a second MiG was shot down and was subsequently claimed by several pilots, so it was credited to the whole squadron. The jubilation of the Australian pilots, however, was short-lived. On returning to base they found that three Meteors were missing, having been picked off by MiGs. Two of the pilots, Drummond and Sergeant Thomson, were taken prisoner and survived the experience, but the third pilot, Sergeant Ernest Armitt, was killed.

During the next few days the MiGs also shot down two F-80s and an F-84, but to achieve these successes they had to descend to lower altitudes, where they were outclassed by the Sabres. This was well illustrated on 2 and 4 December when the Sabre pilots claimed ten MiGs, five on each day. These combats gave the pilots

101

Captured by the gun camera of an F-86 Sabre, the pilot ejects from a crippled MiG-15 over Korea. The Sabre pilot was Lt Edwin E. 'Buzz' Aldrin, who later became the second man to walk on the moon.

of the 51st FIW first chance to draw blood, two MiGs falling to their guns. On 5 December two more MiGs were shot down by Major George Davis, commanding the 334th FIS, and on 13 December Davis claimed a further four MiGs in a series of air battles that flared up along the Yalu. On that day the 4th Wing's Sabres met 145 MiGs in combat and destroyed thirteen of them. After that, serious encounters became more sporadic; the MiGs continued to appear over North Korea in large numbers, but they stayed at high altitude and showed little inclination to fight. Only three more MiGs were destroyed before the end of December, one by the 4th Wing on the 14th and the others by the 51st Wing on the 15th and 28th.

Despite very strenuous efforts, the communists had again failed to wrest command of the air from the United Nations in the autumn and winter of 1951, and sometime in the middle of December the CPAF/NKAF air command evidently implemented a new operational plan. During the latter part of the month United Nations Command Intelligence reported that the CPAF had moved several air divisions from the Antung airfield complex to bases in China proper, replacing them with fresh units. The 'pincer-and-envelopment' tactics were abandoned; large numbers of MiGs continued to enter North Korean airspace in 'trains', but they generally did so over the Sui-ho reservoir, patrolled unaggressively at altitudes between 35,000 and 42,000 feet as far south as

the Chongchon river, then turned northwards to Antung. Apart from routine maintenance work at Uiju, Sinuiju, Pyongyang and Sariwon, the communists also abandoned serious efforts to build or rehabilitate airfields in North Korea. The only logical explanation for this behaviour was that the enemy had given up hope of attaining air superiority, and were now using Korea exclusively as an air combat training arena. After December 1951 Sabre pilots began to notice a definite pattern to enemy air operations. It appeared that the MiGs operating at very high altitude were flown by inexperienced pilots; as these gained proficiency they came down to lower levels, became more aggressive, and gradually engaged the Sabres using fairly well-planned tactics. When each 'class' reached a peak of operational proficiency it was rotated and a new one came in, repeating the process. In this way the communists – and that meant the Russians for the most part – were seeking to train the maximum number of pilots and to test their equipment and organisation against the principal enemy, the United States Air Force.

To the pilots of the 4th and 51st Wings, the early months of 1952 were times of frustration. They were desperately eager to get to grips with the MiGs, but the MiGs did not seem to want to fight. In one sense perhaps it was just as well, because the unprogrammed conversion of the 51st FIW to Sabres had placed an enormous strain on logistical support, which the USAF had earlier claimed was inadequate to support even one Sabre Wing in combat. Proof of this was in the unserviceability rate for January 1952, when on average forty-five per cent of the Sabres were out of commission, 16.6 per cent for want of spares, and 25.9 per cent because of maintenance problems. With two Sabre Wings now operational, the requirement for external fuel tanks rose by 500 per cent in four months so that supplies of these tanks in the Far East theatre were practically exhausted by January 1952. Throughout that month Sabre pilots flew combat patrols with only one tank. They reduced their patrol times by way of compensation, but even so many pilots barely made it home and had to make dead-stick landings, their fuel exhausted. Emergency supplies were flown by C-124 Globemaster aircraft direct from the contractors in the USA to the combat area, but the Sabre Wings still had to reduce their combat sorties to a minimum in February 1952. The USAF Air Materiel Command launched a crash programme called 'Peter Rabbit', its aim to raise stocks of spares to an acceptable level, and by April 1952 the unserviceability rate due to lack of spares was down to 2.4 per cent.

Another major problem was the provision of trained combat pilots in adequate numbers. Until the autumn of 1951 the line had been held by the 4th Wing's highly qualified career pilots, many of whom had vast combat experience, but as these were rotated at the 100-mission mark they left a huge gap that was only partly filled by an influx of pilots whose previous combat experience had been gained in multi-engined transports and bombers. This meant they had to be converted to the Sabre under conditions that were, to say the least, undesirable. The replacement pilots kept on arriving early in 1952 when aircraft serviceability was at its lowest and there were not enough aircraft to go round. As a result Sabre pilots were able to fly on average only ten combat missions per month, which was not enough to permit them to maintain combat proficiency. The situation improved in March when increased serviceability allowed more combat operations, and the Sabre wings began to receive young pilots fresh from combat training in the United States.

There remained the problem of getting to grips with the high-flying MiGs. This was particularly acute in the case of the 4th Wing which, although it had begun to receive the new model F-86Es, was still equipped mainly with F-86As and which claimed only five MiGs in January 1952. The 51st Wing, equipped entirely with F-86Es, fared better: its pilots claimed twenty-five kills during the month, many of them on the 6th and 25th. On these days the 51st FIW's pilots entered the combat area at 45,000 feet, enabling them to make diving attacks from astern on MiGs that were sighted lower down. The MiGs were now crossing the Yalu in forces of up to 200 aircraft flying at high Mach numbers, up to 0.99M on occasions.

February 1952 saw the loss of Major George Davis, one of the 4th Wing's leading pilots. On the 10th Davis was leading eighteen Sabres on an escort mission to Kunu-ri when he sighted a large number of contrails north-west of the Yalu, heading in his direction. Leaving the main body of the Sabres to defend the fighter bombers he headed for the enemy aircraft, accompanied by his wingman, intent on breaking up the threat before it developed. The two Sabres engaged twelve MiGs and apparently took them completely by surprise. Davis shot down two of them and was pressing home an attack on a third when his aircraft was hit and crashed into a mountainside. He was subsequently awarded a posthumous Medal of Honor. His score at the time of his death stood at fourteen enemy aircraft destroyed, a record that was not beaten until the following year. On 25 February, Major William T. Whisner of the 51st FIW destroyed his fifth MiG to become the Wing's first ace and the seventh of the Korean War. Whisner, who commanded the 25th FIS, already had twenty-one kills in World War Two.

F-86 pilot 1st Lt Martin Bambrick inspects a hole made in the wing of his Sabre by a 37mm shell from a MiG-15. (Martin Bambrick)

Early in March 1952 the MiG pilots suddenly turned aggressive again. Although some sorties continued to cross the Yalu at high altitude and avoid combat, others showed a willingness to fight in elements of two, four and six aircraft lower down. Coming out of Manchuria at 40,000 feet at high Mach, they would make turning sweeps to lower levels in MiG Alley in search of UN fighter bombers before making a high-speed dash for their bases at low level. The MiG pilots had now learned to stay below contrail level wherever possible, so that spotting them in time became something of a problem. In general, the Sabre formations entered the combat area stacked down from 40,000 feet to give themselves a good chance of engaging the MiGs. The tactics worked well: in the eight weeks up to the end of April 1952 the F-86 pilots claimed eighty-three MIGs for the loss of six Sabres. The MiG-15s also shot down two F-84s and an F-80. It was hardly surprising that several Sabre pilots found themselves promoted to the 'ace' category during these two months, with five or more enemy aircraft to their credit. They included Captain Iven C. Kincheloe, who also destroyed four Yak-9s on the ground in two separate strafing attacks on Sinuiju airfield on 22 April and 4 May; Captains Robert H. Moore and Robert J. Love, and Major Bill Wescott. They were joined in May by Captain Robert T. Latshaw, Major Donald E. Adams, Lieutenant James H. Kasler, and Colonel Harrison R. Thyng. James Kasler later increased his score to six. Colonel Harry Thyng, who among other types had flown Spitfires with the 31st Fighter Group in North Africa, already had eleven enemy aircraft to his credit in World War Two. He was perhaps the most diversified of all the American aces, his victories including German, Italian, Japanese and French aircraft – the latter a Dewoitine D.520 of the Vichy French Air Force – as well as Russian-built MiGs.

In May 1952 it appeared that the communist air offensive had again taken a new turn. High-altitude operational training flights over North Korea ceased altogether, and the communist air commitment in general was greatly reduced. United Nations pilots encountered only 620 MiG sorties during the month, and from the wide variety of markings observed on the MiGs it seemed that the aircraft were being drawn from many different air units. The two Sabre Wings flew the Korean War's peak monthly total of 5,190 F-86 sorties in May 1952, shooting down twenty-seven MiGs and five Yak-9s for the loss of five of their own number. The MiGs claimed three F-84s and a Mustang, two of the Thunderjets in the course of an engagement between twelve MiGs and twenty-four F-84s of the 49th FBW over Sonchon on 17 May. Realising that the MiGs were now entering North Korea at altitudes of between 15,000 and 35,000 feet, the Sabres lowered the altitudes of their barrier patrols and provided top cover for fighter bomber strikes in MiG Alley. On 13 May, in a pioneer dive-bombing attack with 1,000lb bombs, Sabres of the 4th Wing knocked out Sinuiju's runway, proving that the F-86 was a suitable aircraft for this type of operation. It underlined the fact that the communists could not hope to garrison their North Korean airfields without first gaining air superiority, and this, in the spring of 1952, they had again failed to achieve.

During these latter weeks it was clear that the communists were making extensive use of radar in carrying out their fighter interceptions. On several occasions Allied fighter bombers were attacked by MiGs which dropped down through a cloud layer, obviously vectored to their targets by radar controllers. Early warning radars had been in place since December 1950 and had been identified by 91st SRW reconnaissance aircraft as being American-manufactured SCR-270 sets, supplied to the Soviet Union under lend-lease during World War Two. They had an effective range of about 150 miles, but were unable to detect an aircraft flying higher than 40,000 feet at a greater range. Another American-built radar, the SCR-584, formed a second component of the system, automatically tracking an intruding aircraft detected by the SCR-270 and directing

Lt James H. Kasler, an ace of the 4th FIW, paints MiG kill symbols on the wall of his quarters at Kimpo. Kasler destroyed six MiGs before being shot down and taken prisoner. (via Robert F. Dorr)

anti-aircraft fire on to it. The ground controlled interception (GCI) radar identified in 1952, however, was of Russian design and was codenamed Token, and it was better than anything that had been deployed previously. The communists lost no time in using it to develop countermeasures against the B-29 night strikes; hitherto, such countermeasures had taken the form of searchlight and anti-aircraft batteries directed by the SCR-584 stations, but by the end of May 1952 the deployment of Token made it possible for the enemy to form at least one specialist night fighter unit using Tupolev Tu-2 light bombers equipped with AI radar. These aircraft assumed the role of master night fighters. Having located the bomber stream they would fly immediately above it and control the final interception phase, the other fighters having been guided to the scene by Token. The B-29s would then be constantly tracked by searchlight batteries, enabling the night fighters to launch their attacks. These tactics produced results. On 10 June 1952, four B-29s of the 19th BW were suddenly illuminated by twenty-four searchlights after being shadowed for some minutes by an unidentified aircraft. A few moments later they were attacked by twelve MiG-15s. One B-29 exploded over the target, a railway bridge at Kwaksan, and another went down somewhere over North Korea. A third was so badly damaged that it barely made an emergency landing at Kimpo. The fourth aircraft used counter-measures to break the searchlights' radar lock and got away unharmed.

In the first half of 1952, with plans for the deployment of most of the Fifth Air Force to Korea well advanced, the possibility of communist air attack on airfields and other UN installations in South Korea was still seen as a major threat. Air defence, and particularly airfield defence, was given high priority. A fairly efficient early warning network had already been set up by the end of 1951, and the overall efficiency was increased still further when, in February 1952, a warning radar station was installed on Cho-do Island off north-western Korea; this enabled Allied air defence operators to keep the enemy fighter airfield complex at Antung under twenty-four-hour surveillance. In addition, UN aircraft were fitted with Mk III IFF (Identification Friend/Foe) equipment, which was later supplanted by the more modern Mk X.

From the beginning of 1952 the Fifth Air Force kept between thirty and forty fighters on dawn and dusk alert as a matter of routine. These included the Meteors of No. 77 Squadron RAF which – following the

disastrous combat of 1 December 1951, which left it with only fourteen serviceable aircraft – had been detailed to carry out area and airfield defence. The Meteor, which had a better rate of climb at low altitude than the Sabre, was considered to be particularly suited to this role. For the Australians it was a period of stagnation and frustration. In the end the Squadron's new CO, Wing Commander Ron Susans, managed to convince the authorities that the Meteors would be far better employed in the ground attack role. The necessary approval was obtained, and on 8 January 1952 Susans led a flight of four Meteors in a cannon attack on a water tower at Chongdan. From then on, ground attack was to be No. 77's main occupation during the remainder of its time with Meteors.

The fears of large-scale enemy air attacks on the Allied air bases proved unfounded, but the nuisance raids by Po-2s continued to keep the night defences on the alert. Four T-6 Texans armed with .30 calibre machine-guns were kept on readiness at Kimpo during the hours of darkness, but they never had any luck; neither did the 68th FIS's Lockheed F-94B Starfires, which replaced the unit's Twin Mustangs in December 1951. Two F-94s were deployed to Suwon, where they were joined in March 1952 by the 319th FIS, whose F-94s were deployed to Korea from McChord AFB, Tacoma, Washington. One F-94 did manage to shoot down a Po-2 by throttling right back and lowering landing gear and flaps to reduce its speed, but it stalled immediately afterwards and spun into the ground, killing its crew. Another F-94 was lost when it collided with a Po-2.

F-86 pilot in front of a 4th FIW sign at Kimpo. (via Robert F. Dorr)

Airman 1st Class Donald Bedenstedd of Carroll, Nebraska, takes a picture of Capt. Ben Fithian (right) and 2nd Lt Sam Lyons, the first F-94 Starfire crew to destroy an enemy aircraft.

Fleet Air Arm Fireflies also joined the battle against the night intruders towards the end of the war in Korea. R.K. Simmons, an observer with No. 810 Squadron on HMS *Ocean,* recalls:

> On 7 July 1953 I was detached with the CO, Lt-Cdr A.W. Bloomer RN, to the 319th FIS at K-13 [Suwon] to determine whether the Firefly V could be used as an interceptor to counter the threat posed by Po-2s which were operating from road strips just short of the front line. These aircraft were flying at night just below the level of the air defence radar, with ladies in the back throwing out 40lb bombs by hand. We were patrolling at night with wheels and flaps down at ninety-five knots, just above the stall.
>
> It was soon found impracticable to operate the Firefly from a jet base, so we were transferred to K-6 [Pyongtaek-ni] with Marine Air Group 12. We had no luck with Po-2s; indeed, the only bogey we had managed to outpace was believed to be a Yak-9.
>
> It is interesting to note that the 319th FIS was supposed to have a complement of twenty-four aircraft. In fact they were reduced to eighteen aircraft after a number of landing accidents. During the time I was with them they managed a maximum serviceability rate of six aircraft, and frequently could put only two aircraft into the sky. The Squadron had a complement of 117 aircrew [i.e. about fifty-eight crews] who were lucky to get a flight once every ten days. With so little flying practice it was no wonder that many aircraft were damaged in landing accidents when weather was marginal.

Late on in the war the Po-2s were joined by other training types, notably Yak-18s. Their heckling missions reached a climax of success on the night of 16/17 June 1953 when they destroyed five million gallons of fuel in a dump at Inchon. Between 30 June

and 16 July Lieutenant Guy P. Bordelon, a pilot with an F4U-5N detachment of VC-3 deployed to K-6 from the USS *Princeton* for anti-intruder operations, destroyed three Yak-18s and two other aircraft (either Lavochkin La-9s or La-11s) in the Seoul area. He was the US Navy's only ace of the Korean War.

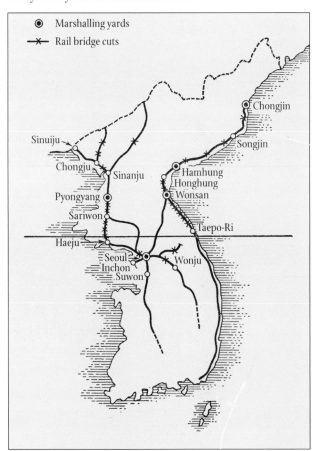

Principal Allied rail interdiction areas.

CHAPTER 14
Railway Interdiction, September 1951-July 1952

Refuelling an F9F Panther on a carrier off Korea. (via Robert F. Dorr)

By mid-August 1951 it was becoming clear to FEAF's target planners that Operation 'Strangle', the offensive designed to paralyse enemy road movements, was not achieving its objectives, and on the 18th of that month the scope of Strangle was extended to include attacks on rail communications. The North Korean railway system, which was in the form of a big letter 'H' with the lines running up the east and west coasts joined laterally by routes running across country, was lightly defended, and experimental attacks carried out so far had shown not only that railway lines were easier to hit than roads, but that it also took the enemy longer to repair them.

The north–south coastal routes were assigned to the Fifth Air Force, each fighter bomber wing being given the daily task of interdicting a selected stretch of track between fifteen and thirty miles in length. Attacks were usually made by between thirty-two and sixty-four aircraft, each carrying two 500lb bombs, with a Sabre escort. Two attack methods were generally favoured by the UN pilots: dive-bombing, or a long, shallow glide approach. The latter made for greater accuracy, although it exposed the attacking aircraft to greater risk from ground fire. Enemy defences were strongest along the lateral route running from Samdong-ni to Kowon,

which was assigned to the air groups of TF 77's three attack carriers, the *Bon Homme Richard*, *Essex*, and *Antietam*. The naval aircraft suffered disproportionately heavy losses during early attacks on this stretch, and as a result switched their main attention to the east coast route, and in particular to twenty-seven rail and road bridges.

Although the rail interdiction campaign in August and September 1951 slowed down the movement of enemy rolling stock and damaged the railways to such an extent that the communists were forced to cannibalise hundreds of miles of track from elsewhere to keep the more important routes open, the bulk of their rail traffic continued to flow. Except where bridges had been destroyed, rail cuts were bypassed with comparative ease: supplies would simply be unloaded from a train on one side of a cut and loaded on another at the other side. Every trick of camouflage was also used to the full in order to conceal the true extent of repair work; for example, FEAF Intelligence believed that Bomber Command had destroyed the bridge at Sunchon, until a night reconnaissance mission by an RB-26 revealed that the enemy were bridging the gaps with movable spans during the night and taking them away again before dawn. Taking everything into consideration, the results achieved hardly seemed to justify the UN aircraft losses, which were substantial. In August 1951 the Fifth Air Force alone lost twenty-six fighter-bombers and had twenty-four damaged; in September the figures were thirty-two lost and 233 damaged; in October thirty-three and 238; and in November twenty-four and 255.

The railway interdiction campaign continued during December 1951, although the further strengthening of enemy defences along the most important routes compelled Fifth AF to direct its fighter-bombers to other, more weakly defended, sectors. The result was an increase in the number of rail cuts and a drop in aircraft losses, although a number of aircraft were damaged when their bombs bounced off the frozen ground and exploded in the air during low-level attacks. FEAF Intelligence, meanwhile, had been seeking a worthwhile railway target for Bomber Command, which had not mounted a major raid since the attack on

B-26s dropped nearly 4,000 500lb bombs on the objective. At the end of it all they had achieved only thirty-three hits and had succeeded in blocking the railway and road for just one week. After that the B-29s were re-assigned to their more usual bridge targets.

Early in March 1952, following recommendations by Colonel Jean H. Dougherty, Fifth Air Force's Director of Intelligence, Operation 'Strangle' gave way to Operation 'Saturate', which instead of targeting railway systems all over North Korea envisaged repeated maximum-effort strikes against short sections of track in the hope of rendering them permanently unusable. Bomber Command, meanwhile, would mount large-scale attacks on selected bridge targets. Bad weather delayed the planned start of the operation, but on 25 March over 300 fighter-bombers dropped 530 1,000lb and eighty-four 500lb bombs on a stretch of track between Chongju and Sinanju. The same target was attacked that night by eight B-26s, which dropped forty-two 500lb bombs, and

A Skyraider of VA-728 about to launch on a strike.

Rashin on 25 August 1951, heralding the start of the railway interdiction offensive. One was found in January 1952 near the village of Wadong on the railway line running laterally across Korea. At this point the railway crossed a main north–south highway in a narrow defile, and Intelligence worked out that if the crossing were to be heavily bombed the enemy would have a very difficult task in getting supplies through the surrounding mountains. During a forty-four-day period, beginning on 6 January, seventy-seven B-29s and 125

the next day 161 fighter-bombers completed the assault with a further 322 1,000lb bombs. Despite this weight of explosive the track was out of action for only five days, yet the attack was considered a success and Operation 'Saturate' was ordered to continue.

Attacks on the Sinanju–Sinuiju line kept it out of action almost continually during April and May 1952, but Fifth AF and TF 77 simply had too few fighter-bombers to permit maximum-effort rail interdiction against multiple targets, and the number of available

Miss Jacque II, the first USAF Thunderjet to complete 1,000 hours, taxies out on her 364th combat mission. This F-84 was a 136th FBW aircraft.

aircraft was falling steadily because of attrition. The Fifth AF's fighter-bomber units, for example, had already lost 243 aircraft, many of them during railway interdiction operations, and a further 290 had sustained serious damage, but only 130 replacement aircraft had been received. Among the worst affected were the 49th and 136th Fighter Bomber Wings, whose authorised establishment of seventy-five Thunderjets each had been reduced to forty-one and thirty-nine respectively. Some of the losses were due to engine failure, a consequence of sustained operations from Taegu's dusty, gritty airstrip. In an attempt to make good at least some of the attrition suffered by the F-84Es, the USAF shipped a number of earlier model F-84Ds to Korea, despite the fact that General Frank Everest had made it clear he did not want them.

While the fighter-bombers continued to attack the North Korean railway system by day, the intruders of the 3rd and 452nd Bombardment Wings were constantly seeking new methods of attacking enemy rolling stock at night. Finding a really satisfactory means of illumination remained a problem, despite the successes achieved with the aid of Navy flares, and in late 1951, by way of an experiment, several of the 3rd Wing's B-26s were fitted with searchlights of the kind used by the US Navy's Goodyear non-rigid patrol airships for surface vessel illumination at night. Once a target had been located and marked with incendiaries, the B-26s were able to make several strafing runs by the light of the eighty-million-candlepower searchlights. The snag was that while the searchlight lit up the target, it also lit up the attacking aircraft and attracted heavy ground fire. After several B-26s were shot down during searchlight-assisted attack runs, the idea was abandoned.

To add to their problems, the 3rd and 452nd Wings,

like most other Fifth Air Force units, were desperately short of aircraft at the beginning of 1952. Many of the replacement aircraft sent out from the United States were useless for operations in the Korean winter because they had the old-type flat-topped cockpit canopies, with escape hatches that were too small to permit aircrew clad in bulky winter clothing and wearing parachutes to get out in an emergency. In addition, many of the replacement crews arriving in the theatre lacked experience and adequate training, and this showed up clearly in a series of poor bombing results early in 1952. By April the attrition suffered by the two B-26 Wings was out of all proportion to the results they were achieving, and it was clear that the old light bomber was approaching the end of its useful life in Korea.

By the end of May 1952 losses suffered by United Nations aircraft in the rail interdiction campaign had reached a new peak, a consequence of denser flak concentrations along all major routes. By the middle of the year the communists had deployed 850 anti-aircraft weapons of all types in defence of their railroads and rail bridges, about half their total arsenal. Despite the increasing flak opposition, however, UN airmen had claimed a total of 20,000 rail cuts throughout the North Korean system since the start of Saturate, and although most of these had been repaired fairly quickly the sustained air pressure had at least disrupted and delayed the enemy's flow of supplies to the battlefront. There is no doubt that the railway interdiction campaign caused the communists to have second thoughts about mounting another major offensive in the spring of 1952. It has been argued that Saturate might have enjoyed far greater success had all air operations been under one controlling authority; as it was, the Fifth Air Force, Navy, and Bomber Command had each

Loading ordnance on the underwing rails of an F9F Panther at sea. (via Robert F. Dorr)

been assigned its own list of targets at the outset of the campaign, and as a consequence attacks had been generally uncoordinated.

While Operations 'Strangle' and 'Saturate' were in progress, there were changes in the order of battle of the US Navy and Marine Corps air units serving in Korea. In October 1951 Marine Attack Squadron 121, the first Marine Reserve squadron to enter the conflict, deployed to the theatre with Douglas AD Skyraiders, and in November began attacks on enemy troop concentrations and bunkers in the Hwachon reservoir area. One Skyraider was shot down, but its pilot, Major Edward B. Harris, was rescued. VMA-121 was to drop more ordnance on the enemy than any other single-engined Navy or Marine Corps squadron in the course of the war. On 15 October the carrier USS *Antietam* brought another Reserve formation, Air Group 15, to Korea. This comprised VF-831 (New York), VF-837 (New York), VF-713 (Denver), VF-653 (Akron), and VA-728 (Glenview), all equipped with Corsairs. Also deployed at this time were detachments of VC-11 with all-weather AD-4W Skyraiders, VC-35 with radar-equipped AD-4NL Skyraiders, and VC-61 with photo-reconnaissance F9F-2P Panthers, all regular US Navy units.

Before the end of October the US Navy had formed its first Air Task Group, ATG-1, for operations in Korea, the idea being to bring together the most experienced squadrons from the regular carrier air groups. Commanded by Commander Charles H. 'Fritz' Crabill Jr, ATG-1 was established on the USS *Valley Forge* and comprised VF-52 and VF-111 with F9F-2 Panthers, VF-453 with F4U-4 Corsairs, VF-194 with AD-2 and AD-3 Skyraiders, VC-3 (Detachment 'George') with F4U-5N Corsairs, VC-11 (Team Seven) with AD-4W Skyraiders, VC-35 (Team Van) with AD-4NL Skyraiders, VC-61 with its F9F-2Ps, and HU-1 (Unit 20) with HO3S-1 helicopters. The Air Task Group mounted its first combat operation on 11 December 1951, attacking railway lines and bridges.

Many US Navy pilots narrowly escaped with their lives during the interdiction campaign. In one instance, a young ensign of VF-51, USS *Essex*, was strafing a target near Wonsan when his Panther was badly hit and began to lose height. At about twenty feet off the ground the aircraft struck a pole and lost three feet off its starboard wing. Despite this, the pilot nursed the crippled aircraft up to 14,000 feet and took stock of his situation. The undercarriage was jammed in the up position, the rockets were hung up, and the radio was knocked out. The only course of action, under the circumstances, was to bale out over friendly territory, which he did. Eighteen years later, on 20 July 1969, that fortunate pilot became the first man to set foot on the moon.

CHAPTER 15
Battlefield Support, 1951-52

O f all the aircraft types operated by the United Nations in Korea, the most hated and feared – if the statements of captured enemy soldiers were to be believed – were the Mosquitoes, the T-6, L-17, L-19 and L-20 tactical control aircraft. The sudden appearance of one of them, popping up briefly from behind some feature of the terrain, was invariably the prelude to an air strike or artillery bombardment, and the communists went to great lengths to shoot them down.

From 25 January 1951 the Mosquitoes operated at maximum effort in support of Operation 'Thunderbolt', the Eighth Army's 'reconnaissance in force' towards the Han river. Throughout the operation the 6147th Tactical Control Group flew from the primitive forward airstrip at Taejon, which permitted its aircraft to patrol the battle area for three hours. In addition to its complement of T-6s the 6147th Group also had at its disposal two C-47s which, orbiting on station about twenty miles behind the front, relayed messages between the airborne controllers, ground attack aircraft and the Tactical Air Control Centre. For direct communications with ground forces, each Mosquito carried an SCR-300 infantry transceiver. Later, when the Group received TG-6G aircraft, re-manufactured and purpose-built for the TAC role, AN/ARC-3, AN/ARC-6 and SCR-522A radios were fitted enabling the crews to communicate over a much wider spectrum. The T-6G was equipped with six underwing rocket racks carrying triple rocket launchers and armed with two 0.30 calibre machine-guns in underwing pods, although the latter reduced the aircraft's speed to an unacceptable degree and were later removed. The 6147th Group had three component squadrons. Two of them, the 6148th and 6149th TCS, were airborne; the third, the 6150th, took care of ground support, which included the tactical air control parties which used radio-equipped jeeps to call in air strikes. Every new Mosquito pilot was required to serve sixty days with one of these ground teams. The two airborne squadrons divided Korea up between them, the 6148th covering the western sector and the 6149th the eastern part. At least one Mosquito was kept airborne over each sector during daylight hours.

Auster and L-19 of No 1913 Flight, RAF, over Korea.

Auster AOP.6 of No 1913 Flight over the rugged Korean terrain.

As the ground war developed into a stalemate the Mosquitoes carried out long-range reconnaissance missions along known enemy supply routes. On one of these, in the summer of 1951, Lt Richard Meade was attacked by a Yak-9 fighter which tried hard to get on his tail. Meade used the T-6's much tighter turning ability to good advantage, however, and it was the Yak that ended up in front. Meade let fly a salvo of smoke rockets at it, whereupon the enemy pilot gave up and flew off to the north.

During the spring of 1951, having observed the effectiveness of the Mosquitoes at first hand, the British Commonwealth Division in Korea made repeated requests for the establishment of its own observation aircraft units. The first of these, No. 1913 Light Liaison Flight, was formed at Middle Wallop in June 1951 with Auster AOP 6 aircraft. These were shipped in crates to Iwakuni, where they were assembled and delivered to airstrips in the Commonwealth Division's area. A second unit, No. 1903 Independent Air Observation Post Flight, arrived in Korea in October 1951. Although Royal Air Force units – the only ones, in fact, to operate from Korean soil – the two flights were manned almost exclusively by Army personnel, and although No. 1913 Flight's main task was liaison, its Austers undertook visual reconnaissance missions from the moment they arrived in Korea, penetrating up to four miles into enemy territory. Pilots normally flew with one ear uncovered so that they could hear the crackle of enemy bullets passing dangerously close and take evasive action. The Flight also possessed one Cessna L-19 on loan from the Eighth Army for use by the GOC 1st Commonwealth Division; the British pilots pronounced the L-19 superior to the Auster in most respects. The principal role of No. 1903 Flight, which as part of No.

656 (Army Co-operation) Squadron had seen service against communist terrorists in Malaya before reaching Korea via Hong Kong, was counter bombardment – in other words, locating enemy gun positions and assisting friendly artillery to engage them. For this dangerous task the Austers' cockpits were armour-plated and the pilots flew solo, carrying parachutes. A daily average of seven sorties was flown, with each pilot putting in about forty-five hours' flying in the course of a good month. Most sorties were flown above 5,000 feet to escape the worst of the small arms fire and light flak, as well as to avoid the trajectories of artillery shells. US Marine Corps units fighting in Korea called on the services of VMO-6, equipped initially with Consolidated OY-1 observation aircraft and, from May 1951, with the Cessna OE-1 (L-19).

The risks run by American and Commonwealth air observation pilots were probably surpassed only by another gallant band of airmen, the crews of the light aircraft and helicopters of the air rescue squadrons, flying deep behind enemy lines to snatch shot-down pilots to safety. On the outbreak of war in Korea there were two search and rescue units at the disposal of FEAF, the 2nd and 3rd Air Rescue Squadrons, the former serving the Thirteenth and Twentieth Air Forces and the latter under the operational control of the Fifth Air Force. Naturally enough, it was the Japan-based 3rd Squadron that was to bear the brunt of air rescue operations in Korea. The Squadron's equipment at the outbreak of hostilities comprised SB-17s and a number of Sikorsky H-5 (S-51) helicopters, but on 28 July 1950 three Grumman SA-16 Albatross amphibians were added to the inventory. Along with the SB-17s, these patrolled the Tsushima Straits between Korea and Japan, ready to go to the assistance of any ditched pilot.

Cessna L-19 Bird Dog was widely used by the US Army in Korea for liaison and observation duties. (via Robert F. Dorr)

On 7 July 1950 the 3rd Squadron sent two L-5 liaison aircraft to carry out 'snatches' from inside enemy territory. Their rescue attempts, however, were hampered by the fact that they were quite unsuited to operating from the sodden paddy fields of the battle area. The situation changed for the better on 22 July with the arrival at Taegu airstrip of the first detachment of H-5s. Within a few days the helicopters were being used to evacuate badly wounded soldiers of the Eighth Army from the mountainous or rice paddy terrain of the front line to hospitals in Miryang and Pusan. These operations were so successful that General Partridge directed the 3rd Squadron to position six of its nine H-5s in Korea. At the same time, General Stratemeyer asked the USAF to allocate twenty-five more H-5s to form a special duties and evacuation unit, and within a fortnight fourteen helicopters were on their way to Korea. By this time Marine Corps Observation Squadron VMO-6 was also operational at the front, and its HO-3 helicopters began operations on 3 August 1950

in support of the 1st Marine Division in the Changwon area, delivering rations and water to troops in mountain positions and evacuating heat-stroke cases. By the end of August 1950 the 3rd Air Rescue Squadron's helicopters had flown eighty-three badly wounded soldiers from the battle area. All of them would almost certainly have died had they been forced to make the journey to a field hospital by ambulance.

The Squadron's operations were now co-ordinated by a Rescue Liaison Office, which had been set up in the United Nations Command Joint Operations Centre on 27 August, and it was while under the control of the Liaison Office that one of the unit's H-5s made history. It happened on the morning of 4 September 1950 when two flights of F-80 Shooting Stars of the 35th Fighter Bomber Squadron crossed the 38th Parallel to attack targets at Hanggandong. During the attack, one of the F-80s was shot down; the pilot, Captain Robert E. Wayne, baled out and landed safely. While two of the F-80s circled the area on the lookout for North Korean

Top: The Grumman SA-16 Albatross was operated by the 3rd Air Rescue Squadron in the ASR role from the first month of the Korean War. (via Robert F. Dorr)
Above: Sikorsky HO3S-1 seen with a Martin PBM Mariner in the background. Mariners patrolled eight separate areas off the Korean and Chinese coasts on missions lasting up to twelve hours; on 31 July 1951 a PBM of Fleet Air Wing Six was attacked by two Chinese MiG-15s, two crew members were killed and two more wounded. (via Robert F. Dorr)

troops, a third climbed and made radio contact with base. Half an hour later, while a flight of F-80s flew combat air patrol overhead to ward off any enemy fighters, Captain Wayne was on his way out of enemy territory in an H-5. It was flown by Lieutenant Paul W. Van Boven who had just become the first ever helicopter pilot to lift a shot-down airman to safety from behind enemy lines.

The H-5 unit, now designated Detachment F and commanded by Captain Oscar N. Tibbetts, moved forward at the end of September 1950 in support of UN forces counter-attacking northwards from the Pusan perimeter, arriving at Seoul during the first week of October. It was from this base that on 10 October the longest helicopter rescue mission so far was flown when an H-5 piloted by Lieutenant David C. McDaniels made a 125-mile flight to Changjon to pick up the wounded pilot of a Sea Fury shot down during a sortie

from HMS *Theseus*. The British pilot was Lieutenant S. Leonard of No. 807 Squadron, who was brought down while making a rocket attack on enemy troops ninety miles behind the lines. The fuselage of his aircraft buckled at the cockpit, trapping him with both legs and one arm broken. He was also knocked unconscious. His flight, and a relief flight, strafed enemy soldiers and prevented them from getting near the crashed Sea Fury. Leonard came to, fired his revolver – with his broken arm – at the nearest enemy, then passed out again. The H-5 arrived after about an hour, carrying a doctor as well as the pilot, and the two men hacked Leonard free while keeping the enemy at bay with bursts from their automatic weapons. The Fleet Air Arm officer received a blood transfusion in the helicopter on the homeward flight, and subsequently made a full recovery. Several more long-range rescue flights were made during November 1950 by H-5s operating from advanced bases

An H-19 of the 3rd Air Rescue Squadron preparing to lift a casualty from the battle zone.

at Kunu-ri and Sinanju. Then came the Chinese invasion, compelling Detachment F to pull its forward elements back to Seoul, and when Seoul was evacuated in its turn the helicopters moved to Airstrip K-37, south of Taegu. By the end of 1950 the H-5s had transported 618 medical cases, compared with fifty-six flown out by the fixed-wing L-5s.

On 15 February 1951 Detachment F was called upon to carry out its most difficult and dangerous task so far, supplying badly needed medical supplies to elements of the US 2nd Division, surrounded by enemy forces in a pocket at Chipyong-ni, some twenty miles east of Seoul. The operation was flown by six H-5s and continued until dark, each helicopter making three sorties into the pocket. On the homeward run they brought out a total of thirty wounded men. The operation resumed at first light the next day, but with only four helicopters; the other two were unserviceable.

The weather grew steadily worse during the morning, with squalls of snow sweeping over the frozen rice fields, and by mid-afternoon the helicopters were battling their way through snowstorms and winds of up to forty knots. They nevertheless succeeded in evacuating a further twenty-two casualties before nightfall. In March 1951 the H-5s rescued six out of seven F-80 pilots of the 35th Fighter Group brought down over enemy territory. By this time the Detachment was badly overworked, its task becoming ever more demanding as the air war over Korea intensified. Apart from rescuing downed aircrew, the helicopters were heavily in demand for casualty evacuation – a major headache, for the H-5 could carry only two passengers in addition to its two-man crew, which often meant several sorties a day into the battle area – as well as a number of other sundry tasks.

The position improved somewhat after 23 March

The Curtiss C-46 Commando was the unsung transport hero of the Korean War. Its reliability was extraordinary.

1951 when two experimental Sikorsky YH-19 (S-55) helicopters arrived in the theatre to be evaluated under combat conditions. Within twenty-four hours they had joined the H-5s in evacuating injured and wounded American paratroops from a dropping zone at Munsan-ni, just south of the 38th Parallel, where the 187th Airborne RCT had been dropped in an attempt to cut off Chinese forces falling back on Kaesong. The drop was part of Operation 'Ripper', the Allied drive north to the Han river, and was the second largest airborne operation of the Korean War with eighty C-119s and fifty-five C-46s of the 314th Group and 437th Wing employed. Before the end of the day the C-119s had dropped 2,011 paratroops and 204 tons of supplies, while 1,436 paratroops and sixteen tons of equipment were dropped by the C-46s. The first helicopters arrived over the DZ only fifteen minutes after the first paratroops had landed, and almost immediately they came under heavy mortar and machine-gun fire. Two H-5s were hit by small-arms fire on the first sortie, but the damage was not serious and they did not have to be withdrawn from the operation. By nightfall on 25 March, after two days of daylight operations, the H-5s and YH-19s had made seventy-seven sorties into the Munsan-ni sector and evacuated 148 paratroops, of whom forty-eight were jump casualties.

In June 1951 the helicopter unit was redesignated Detachment 1, 3rd Air Rescue Squadron, and was split up into four separate flights, one serving the 8055th Mobile Army Surgical Hospital (MASH), another attached to the US 25th Division Command Post close to the centre of the UN battle line, a third earmarked for use by UN truce negotiators, and the fourth on permanent standby at Seoul, once again in UN hands and the Detachment's headquarters. Later in the year two H-5s were moved to the islands of Paengyong-do and Cho-do, from where they made a number of highly effective rescues from Korean waters.

As mentioned earlier, the US Marines had quickly followed the Air Force's lead in establishing a helicopter unit in Korea, and in fact it was the Marines who pioneered the use of the helicopter in the airborne transport role in the theatre. On 30 August 1951 Marine Helicopter Transport Squadron 161 (HMR-161) arrived at Pusan with fifteen Sikorsky HRS-1 (S-55) helicopters

and began operations in support of the 1st Marine Division on 2 September from an auxiliary airstrip, X-83, which it shared with VMO-6. On 13 September HMR-161 carried out the first mass helicopter resupply operation in history. Codenamed Windmill One, this involved the airlifting of one day's supplies, materiel and equipment to the 2nd Battalion, 1st Marines who were engaged in an attack on a strategic ridge called Hill 673 in the mountains near Inje. The operation lasted fourteen hours and was a complete success, the helicopters flying some nine tons of supplies to the Marine units in their positions over 2,000 feet above sea level and bringing out seventy-five casualties. Windmill One was followed by a number of similar operations before the end of 1951: Windmill Two, Summit, Blackbird, Bumble Bee and Farewell. These activities were followed with great interest by General Ridgway, who succeeded General MacArthur as United Nations Commander in Korea in April 1951 and who was impressed by the cargo-carrying performance of the HRS-1 in all kinds of conditions. In November 1951 he asked the Army Department to provide four helicopter transport battalions, each with twenty-eight aircraft. He pointed out that the events of the Korean War so far had proved conclusively that the Army needed helicopters, and recommended that in future each field army should be equipped with ten transport helicopter battalions. The Army Department agreed in principle to this recommendation, but was only willing to approve the assignment of four helicopter battalions to a field army.

For the first five months of the Korean War no helicopters of any kind had served under Army command; patrol, observation and rescue work was carried out by light aircraft, mostly Piper L4s and Stinson L-5s. The pilots of these aircraft, many of which had been flown in World War Two and were rapidly approaching the end of their useful lives, did a magnificent job under incredibly arduous conditions, but their task was hampered by a high unserviceability rate and by the inability of the light aircraft to land where they were most needed. Nevertheless, many Allied pilots owed their lives or their freedom to them. The first Army helicopters did not arrive in Korea until late in December 1950. They were Bell H-13s (Bell 47s), two-seat machines which, although destined for the

Top: Sikorsky HRS-1 helicopter of HMR-161, USMC. (via Robert F. Dorr)
Above: Sikorsky HO3S-1 utility helicopter of Marine Helicopter Squadron VMO-6.

Top: A 6th Transportation Helicopter Company H-19 dropping troops at a forward observation post.
Above: An H-19 of the 3rd Air Rescue Squadron preparing to lift a casualty from the battle zone.

liaison and artillery spotting roles, had a limited casevac capability. Four H-13s equipped the 2nd Army Helicopter Detachment at Seoul and began operations in January 1951 under the command of Captain Albert Seburn. Despite the fact that the H-13 could carry only one casualty, the Detachment had evacuated more than 500 casualties from the battle area by the end of the month, a feat that earned each of the four H-13 pilots the Distinguished Flying Cross. In February 1951 the H-13s were joined by a small number of two-seat Hiller H-23 Ravens, and in the months that followed both types were used increasingly for battlefield surveillance.

By the end of 1951 the helicopters had proved their worth so many times that the arrival of the transport helicopters requested by General Ridgway was eagerly awaited by the Eighth Army. In anticipation of this event, the whole question of the use and deployment of rotary-wing craft in Korea became the subject of heated argument between Army and Air Force. Both factions

were anxious to work out a formula that would avoid duplication of the tasks to be carried out by their respective rotorcraft; air transport within the combat zone, for example, was the Air Force's responsibility, and a much tighter definition of the Army's role in this context was needed. In the end it was agreed that the Army helicopter battalions would be responsible for transporting Army supplies within the combat zone, an area defined as extending up to 100 miles behind the front line, while the Air Force would continue to airlift supplies, equipment and personnel into the combat zone from points outside.

The argument, as things turned out, proved mainly academic because by the time the Army began to receive its promised transport helicopters the war was almost over. It was not until March 1953 that the first Army cargo helicopter unit – the 6th Transportation Helicopter Company, equipped with twelve H-19Cs – arrived in Korea.

118

CHAPTER 16
Air Transport Forces

This USAF C-119 of the 50th TCS, pictured at Clark Field in the Philippines, has been temporarily painted in Armée de l'Air markings for deployment to Indo-China in support of French operations against Viet Minh guerrillas. (via Robert F. Dorr)

In January 1951 the 315th Air Division was activated and assumed operational command or control of all Combat Cargo Command units in the Korean theatre. At the time, these were the 374th Troop Carrier Wing, with two squadrons of Douglas C-54s at Tachikawa and a third – the 21st, with C-47s – at Itazuke; the 61st Troop Carrier Group, with three squadrons of C-54s at Ashiya; the 437th Troop Carrier Wing, with four squadrons of Curtiss C-46s at Brady Air Base, Kyushu; the 314th Troop Carrier Group, with four squadrons of Fairchild C-119s at Ashiya; and No. 13 Flight, Royal Hellenic Air Force, with C-47s at Itazuke. This was to be joined later in the year by a transport detachment of the Royal Thai Air Force. British Commonwealth air transport units operated independently of USAF control. The centralisation of air transport assets under the 315th Air Division went a long way towards ensuring that individual aircraft types serving with the various transport units were utilised to their fullest advantage. The 314th Group's C-119s, which were best suited to airborne operations and dropping large loads, were located close to the main depot of the 187th Airborne Regimental Combat Team,

while the 374th Wing's C-54s, situated near Haneda international airport, were well placed for hauling cargoes over long distances. The C-46s and C-47s, particularly the latter, were suitable for flying cargo into Korea's smaller airstrips, and flights of the 437th Wing and the 21st Squadron were based on airfields near the main supply depots.

The reorganisation, however, went only part of the way towards solving Combat Cargo Command's problems in the Far East. There were, for example, always difficulties in obtaining spare parts, particularly for the C-119s; as a consequence serviceability was always low, and the 314th Wing's four squadrons (ninety-six transports in all) never had enough aircraft available to carry more than sixty per cent of the 187th RCT in a single lift. Combat Cargo Command's most pressing requirement was for a large, modern transport with a very long range and a high load capacity, in other words an aircraft that would perform the same amount of work as two or three of the Command's older types, resulting in an economy of aircraft and crews and reducing congestion on the already badly overcrowded airfields in the Far East. There was one aircraft that

119

Dwarfing other types, a Douglas C-124A Globemaster II takes casualties on board at Ashiya for the long flight back to the USA.

might meet this requirement: the Douglas C-124A Globemaster II, then undergoing service acceptance trials.

At the request of General John P. Henebry, the officer commanding Combat Cargo Command, one of these aircraft was sent out to Japan in September 1951, and in the weeks that followed it made thirteen round trips to Korea, each time carrying about twice the load that could be lifted by a C-54. The USAF was impressed and authorised the re-equipment of two squadrons of the 374th Wing with C-124s starting in May 1952. By the end of July thirteen were in service, six of them used for conversion training and the rest operating a daily shuttle service between Tachikawa and Korea with the 6th Troop Carrier Squadron. Thirteen more C-124s were received in August and September, releasing the 61st Group's two C-54 squadrons for return to the United States.

The service debut of the C-124 in the Korean theatre was not without its problems. Because of the risk of damage to their surfaces, the Fifth Air Force's vital tactical airfields could not be used by the big transports, and they were permitted to land only at Kimpo, Taegu and Suwon. From November 1952 they were also authorised to operate into Seoul municipal airport, following the building of a strengthened runway. Even so the Globemaster's payload had to be restricted to 36,000lb, and utilisation was not high enough to compensate for the loss of the C-54s. Excess cargo still had to be airlifted to Korea by C-46s and C-119s, and all the cargo flown in had to be ferried to the smaller tactical airstrips by C-46s and C-47s. There were

technical problems that had to be overcome, too. In December 1952 several Globemasters developed fuel leaks and the entire fleet had to be grounded while modifications were carried out. Four months of relatively trouble-free operations followed, but in May 1953 two C-124s experienced engine fires in the air, and while an investigation into the cause was in progress a C-124 of the 22nd TCS lost power in one engine on take-off from Tachikawa and crashed, killing all 129 passengers and crew in what was the world's worst air disaster up to that time. The cause was established as generator failure, and the Globemasters were again grounded for several weeks. Modification work was still in progress on some of the fleet when the war ended. In terms of equipment, therefore, Combat Cargo Command finished the war almost exactly as it had begun it, with C-46s, C-47s and C-119s bearing the brunt of airlift operations. In the autumn of 1951 the C-119 fleet in Japan underwent some reorganisation with the transfer of the 403rd Troop Carrier Wing to Ashiya, bringing the number of C-119 squadrons in the theatre to six. One of the 314th Group's four squadrons was returned to the USA, but this was a paper transfer only as its aircraft were distributed among the other units.

The C-119 remained a source of anxiety throughout the conflict. By the middle of 1952 the serviceability situation was so bad that out of a total of seventy-one C-119s available on paper only twenty-eight were fit to fly, and only about half a dozen of these were free from defects. Matters improved a little in July and August when some of the older C-119s were returned to the USA for refurbishing, but even then the average

Overhauling the engine of a 374th Troop Carrier Wing Globemaster. The massive transport aircraft had numerous technical problems.

A 50th TCS C-119 and its crew. (via Robert F. Dorr)

serviceability of the 403rd Wing in the autumn of 1952 was only about sixty per cent. More than half the Wing's aircraft had been operating continuously since 1950, and some of them had little more than scrap value.

Because of undercarriage weaknesses, the C-119s were never allowed to lift more than six tons of cargo. Their propellers, which had hollow steel blades, were another weakness: the blades would develop hairline cracks and then fail in flight. After a C-119 was lost because of propeller malfunctions in March 1953 the fleet was forbidden to carry passengers, but was allowed to go on carrying cargo and paratroops, who presumably would be able to jump to safety if anything went wrong. This state of affairs persisted until May when the 403rd Wing was relieved by the 483rd Wing, equipped with newer C-119s.

Early in 1952 it had been decided to re-equip 437th

Wing's four C-46 squadrons with C-119s at the first opportunity, activating a new transport wing at the same time. When the new 315th Wing was activated at Brady Air Base in June 1952, however, the aircraft handed over to it by the 437th Wing were C-46s, and the Korean War would be over before these magnificent aircraft were at last retired. Time and again the C-46s proved their ability to do almost anything, from paratroop dropping to evacuating casualties from primitive airstrips, and towards the end of 1952, with both the C-119s and C-124s experiencing dire problems, it was the C-46s and C-47s which sustained the airlift. In terms of reliability the C-46 was unsurpassed by any other type – even the C-47 – and the fact that the proposed re-equipment of the C-46 Wing was constantly postponed was the finest tribute that could be paid to an aircraft that had been deemed obsolete as much as four years earlier.

CHAPTER 17
Increasing the Pressure, June 1952-March 1953

Douglas AD-4 Skyraiders approaching the carrier USS Philippine Sea *(CVA-67) off the Korean coast in 1953. (Bill Barron)*

hile the railway interdiction campaign went ahead during the first half of 1952, FEAF planners had been giving consideration to the choice of a worthwhile target system in North Korea. What FEAF badly needed was to find a means of maintaining sustained and damaging air pressure on the enemy, and it was generally agreed that the best way to achieve this was through a series of maximum-effort air strikes on selected strategic targets in the North, preferably those in which China and the Soviet Union had an interest. It was felt that the destruction of such targets might influence the communists into speeding up the laborious peace negotiations that were taking place at Panmunjom.

The problem was that high-value strategic targets were scarce in North Korea. The exception was the country's hydro-electric power system, but until now the Joint Chiefs had been reluctant to approve attacks on the hydro-electric plants. It was not until the spring of 1952, with the armistice talks apparently moving towards total deadlock, that the attitude in Washington began to change and it was admitted that additional military force would be necessary to break the stalemate. Although the hydro-electric plants were now regarded as profitable and justifiable military targets at the highest level, the proposal to attack them led to a sharp difference of opinion between General Weyland,

who favoured the attacks, and General Ridgway, who did not. Ridgway took the view that so long as the Panmunjom talks continued, the use of additional force was fundamentally wrong. He insisted that before any attacks could be made on the hydro-electric plants, such a move would have to be recommended to him via the normal channels, and since the Joint Chiefs would not authorise the attacks until they had Ridgway's recommendation, what would later be called a 'Catch-22' situation developed. The problem was eventually resolved on 28 April when Ridgway was replaced by General Mark Clark as the United Nations Commander in Korea. He had none of Ridgway's reservations, and it was not long before General Weyland had obtained his approval for the attacks to proceed. Four principal plants – Suiho, Fusen, Choshin and Kyosen – were scheduled for attack, and the planners realised that in order to swamp the defences it would be necessary to carry out the whole operation in the space of forty-eight hours. This was a task of such magnitude that it could not possibly be accomplished by FEAF alone; the Navy was therefore called in to help, and by 19 June 1952 a joint Navy–Air Force operations team had worked out plans for a co-ordinated attack.

Everything depended on perfect timing. After discussions between Vice-Admiral J.J. Clark, the new commander of the US Seventh Fleet, and General Glenn

O. Barcus, who had recently succeeded General Everest as commander of the Fifth Air Force, it was agreed that the big plant at Suiho would be the target of a co-ordinated air strike by Fifth AF and TF 77 fighter-bombers. Other Air Force fighter-bombers would make a simultaneous attack on Nos. 3 and 4 plants at Choshin and Fusen, while Naval aircraft would hit Kyosen and Fusen's Nos. 1 and 2 plants. After dark it would be Bomber Command's turn, with a Shoran attack by B-29s on Nos. 1 and 2 plants at Choshin. The Suiho attack was potentially the most dangerous, with 250 MiGs fewer than forty miles away at Antung. It would be the first time since 1950 that aircraft of Task Force 77 had ventured into MiG Alley.

After a delay of several hours caused by bad weather the operation got under way at 1600 on 23 June. The first strike wave, comprising thirty-five Skyraiders and a similar number of Panthers, was launched from the carriers *Boxer*, *Princeton* and *Philippine Sea*. While eighty-four Sabres flew top cover, the Panthers attacked eighty flak emplacements around Suiho, clearing the way for the Skyraiders to hit the generator plant. Within the next hour the plant was also attacked by seventy-

night, but instead its B-29s were ordered to fly radar-directed close support operations at fifteen-minute intervals. It was someone's idea of reminding the communists that this was the second anniversary of the outbreak of hostilities. Choshin and Fusen were again bombed by the Fifth AF on 26 and 27 June. In all, the Navy, Marine and Air Force units flew 1,654 sorties against the hydro-electric plants during the series of strikes. When the attacks ended nine-tenths of the country's hydro-electric system had been laid waste; the lights went out all over the North, and stayed out for a fortnight. The Allies lost only two aircraft, both to ground fire, and in each case the pilot was rescued.

In July 1952, following the success of the hydro-electric plant attacks, FEAF implemented a reorganisation programme designed to meet the requirements of a sustained high-pressure air campaign. The equipment situation was now much better than it had been at the beginning of the year. Thanks to the purchase of sixty additional F-86E Sabres from the Canadair Aircraft Company, which was producing them for the NATO air forces in Europe, FEAF was able to bring both its F-86 Wings up to strength while still

51st FIW crew chief on the flight line at Suwon with F-86Es in the background. (via Robert F. Dorr)

nine F-84s and forty-five F-80s. In all, the attacking aircraft dropped 145 tons of bombs on Suiho, and post-strike reconnaissance showed that the plant had been almost completely destroyed. The feared interception by enemy fighters never happened; early in the attack dust clouds across the Yalu showed that MiGs were taking off, but instead of crossing the river they flew away into Manchuria, possibly in the belief that an attack on their airfields was about to take place.

While the Suiho attack was in progress, Fifth Air Force Mustangs bombed Nos. 3 and 4 plants at Fusen, while Panthers of the 1st Marine Air Wing attacked Choshin's Nos. 3 and 4. A little later, Skyraiders, Corsairs and Panthers from the *Boxer*, *Princeton* and *Bon Homme Richard* attacked Fusen's Nos. 1 and 2 plants and the complex at Kyosen. The onset of darkness prevented further attacks that day, but on the 24th the same targets were again heavily hit. Bomber Command was to have attacked Choshin during the

retaining a fifty per cent reserve. The 51st Fighter Interceptor Wing was brought up to a three-squadron establishment by the transfer of the 39th FIS from the 18th Wing early in June, the 39th being equipped with the new F-86F. There were changes in Bomber Command's organisation, too. In the summer of 1952 the Command's authorised strength was 99 aircraft, a figure set a year earlier. Attrition replacement was now becoming easier, as the conversion of Strategic Air Command Wings in the USA released B-29s for service in the Far East. As part of a process designed to streamline administration and organisation, SAC deactivated all combat group headquarters and made the Combat Wings entirely responsible for squadron operations; accordingly, on 8 July 1952 the complete headquarters of the 98th and 307th Bombardment Wings were transferred to FEAF Bomber Command for an indefinite period of temporary duty.

Another significant step was taken in July when the

F-84G Thunderjet on a combat mission over Korea. The aircraft has a refuelling probe extending forwards from both wingtip tanks. (Martin Bambrick)

Joint Chiefs of Staff authorised the USAF to maintain an SAC fighter escort Wing on a rotational tour of duty in Japan, and for the first time fighter aircraft crossed the Pacific using flight refuelling. The unit involved was the 31st Fighter Escort Wing commanded by Colonel David C. Schilling, and the operation was codenamed Fox Peter One. Schilling led fifty-eight F-84Gs from Turner AFB, Georgia to Misawa and Chitose Air Bases, Japan. On the first leg of the flight, from Turner to Travis AFB, California, the fighters were refuelled by KB-29 tankers of the 2nd and 91st Air Refueling Squadrons; the second refuelling, on the Travis–Hawaii leg, was carried out by the 2nd, 91st and 93rd ARS. From Hawaii, the fighters island-hopped to Japan via Midway, Wake, Eniwetok, Guam and Iwo Jima. The operation, which involved a flight of 10,919 miles, took ten days to complete. A similar operation, Fox Peter Two, was mounted in October 1952 when seventy-five F-84Gs of the 27th Fighter Escort Wing under the command of Colonel Don Blakeslee made a 7,800-mile flight from Bergstrom AFB in Texas to Misawa, releasing the 31st Wing for return to the USA at the end of its ninety-day rotational tour. The rotation of the F-84 fighter escort wings to Japan also meant that the Misawa-based 116th Fighter Bomber Wing could now be released for service in Korea. The 116th was one of the two Air National Guard Thunderjet units called up for active service, the other being the 126th Wing. Since ANG units could only remain in Federal service for a specified period, both wings were relieved from combat duty in July 1952, their personnel and equipment allocated to the newly activated 474th and 58th Fighter Bomber Wings. The 474th was the first of the new Wings to go into action, staging its F-84s through Kunsan airfield (K-8) from 10 July.

By September 1952 all the Fifth Air Force's Thunderjet units were once again up to full strength. The stop-gap F-84Ds, which had been a continual source of trouble since their arrival in Korea, began to be phased out in August and replaced by the F-84G, production of which had finally caught up with the requirements of both the USAF and NATO air forces. The Fifth Air Force's light bomber units also underwent some reorganisation during the summer of 1952, the 452nd Bombardment Wing being deactivated and replaced by the 17th Wing. By September both the 3rd and 17th Bombardment Wings were up to full strength, which in itself indicated that there would be no replacement for the B-26 in the foreseeable future.

Early in July 1952 the United Nations Command implemented Operation 'Pressure Pump', which involved a series of maximum-effort air strikes on thirty high-value targets in the North Korean capital, Pyongyang. For several days beforehand UN aircraft dropped leaflets over the city warning the population of the impending attacks. These began at 1000 on 11 July with strikes by combined air units from Air Group 19 (USS *Princeton*), Air Group 7 (USS *Bon Homme Richard*), Nos. 802 and 825 Squadrons (HMS *Ocean*), Fifth AF Thunderjets, ROK Mustangs, and Meteors of No. 77 Squadron RAAF. The attacks were repeated at 1400 and 1800 by the Fifth AF and Fleet Air Arm, and after dark eight targets in the city were hit by B-29s. In all, 1,254 sorties were flown during the day; three of the assigned targets were totally destroyed and most of the remainder badly damaged. Allied losses were a Panther, a Corsair, and a Thunderjet. Pyongyang Radio, which was badly hit, was off the air for two days; when it began broadcasting again it announced that 1,500 buildings had been destroyed and that 7,000 innocent civilians had been killed or injured. Surprisingly, there was no reaction to this claim from the communist delegation at Panmunjom.

On the nights of 19/20 and 21/22 July forty-four B-29s bombed the power plant at Chosin, and on the last night of the month sixty-three Shoran-directed B-29s attacked the Oriental Light Metals plant near Sinuiju. This was the largest medium bomber strike against a single target during the Korean War, and post-strike reconnaissance showed that the objective had been ninety per cent destroyed. The bomber stream received a number of firing passes from enemy fighters, but a thin undercast confused the searchlights and the bombers escaped damage. An important cement plant at Sungho-ri, a lead and zinc mill at Sindok, tungsten mines at Kiju, and a chemical plant at In-hung-ni were attacked by the Fifth AF and TF 77 in the course of the month, and a B-29 attack was made on a munitions plant at Nakwon.

On 29 August Pyongyang was subjected to further heavy attacks, and on this occasion, in addition to military objectives, public buildings were on the target

Grumman F6FK Hellcats were used in Korea as pilotless drones carrying an explosive charge. They were guided to their targets by radio link from a 'mother' aircraft. (Bill Barron)

list. The three strikes, carried out at 0930, 1330 and 1730, were flown by Fifth AF Thunderjets, ROK Mustangs, Marine Panthers and Corsairs, and Banshees, Panthers and Corsairs from the carriers *Boxer* and *Essex*. Flak suppression was carried out by Thunderjets of the 474th and Mustangs of the 8th Fighter Bomber Wings, while Sabres and Meteors patrolled to the north along the line of the Chongchon river. The UN aircraft flew over 1,400 sorties, and photo-reconnaissance the next day showed that the raids had been highly successful.

During August, an unusual unit called Guided Missile Unit 90 deployed on USS *Boxer*. Equipped with AD Skyraiders and F6F-5K drones, each drone armed with a single 2,000lb bomb. It flew its first mission on 28 August, when the pilot of the Skyraider parent aircraft guided the Hellcat down by TV command to an impact on the Hungnam bridge. The latter was completely destroyed, and five more bridge attacks were carried out by GMU 90 before the end of 1952.

On 1 September 1952 Task Force 77 launched its biggest air strike of the war when twenty-nine aircraft from the USS *Essex*, sixty-three from *Princeton*, and fifty-two from *Boxer* attacked the Aoji oil refinery in north-eastern Korea and left it a blazing ruin. This success was marred by a tragic accident ten days later when six F9F-4 Panthers of VMF-115 were returning to Pohang (K-3) after a combat mission over North Korea. Diverted to Taegu (K-2) because of bad weather, they were preparing to make an instrument let-down when they crashed into a 3,000-foot mountain peak some twenty-five miles south-east of K-2. There were no survivors.

Because of the growing danger from enemy defences, FEAF Bomber Command's operations were now restricted to nights when there was substantial cloud cover in the target areas. This was predicted when thirty B-29s set out to bomb the power plant at Suiho on the night of 12/13 September 1952, but when the bombers reached the objective they found the skies clear. Six more B-29s orbited to the east of Suiho, jamming the enemy radars with electronic countermeasures, but the enemy put up a very concentrated box barrage and

F4U-5 Corsairs overflying their carrier, the USS Boxer.

several of the attacking bombers were damaged. A few bombers were illuminated by searchlights, and one 307th Wing aircraft was shot down by night fighters. The other B-29s destroyed the target with 2,000lb bombs.

In this and other attacks, B-26 light bombers were used in the flak and searchlight suppression role, with some success. In a raid on the Namsan-ni chemical plant on 30 September/1 October, however, the B-29s themselves assumed the flak suppression role; the three leading aircraft suppressed the defences with air-bursting fragmentation bombs and then orbited nearby, jamming with chaff and ECM, while forty-five more B-29s arrived one by one and walked their bombs across the plant, which was effectively destroyed. The B-29s also operated in the flak suppression role on 8 October when ten aircraft of the 98th Wing escorted by USN Banshees plastered Kowon with 500lb proximity-fuzed bombs in a daylight formation attack. The defence suppression was so effective that only one AA gun fired at US Navy jets when they attacked the rail junction there a few minutes later.

The B-29s' night bombing campaign revealed a serious deficiency in reconnaissance techniques and equipment. The 91st Strategic Reconnaissance Squadron's RB-45Cs, although equipped for radar mapping, could not be used for night photography because they buffeted too badly when the forward bomb bay was opened for flash photography. The problem was that Bomber Command needed bomb damage assessment photography as quickly as possible after an attack, so that if necessary the target could be attacked again before the enemy had time to strengthen his defences, and this required night reconnaissance. The 91st SRS therefore converted its RB-29s to night photography, but the problems mounted when these aircraft were sent out on operations. For safety reasons, and also to receive accurate Shoran directions, they had to fly at altitudes of over 20,000 feet; from such heights the standard M-46 photoflash bomb did not provide adequate illumination, and the camera equipment could not secure photographs of sufficiently large scale for accurate interpretation. The situation improved somewhat with the arrival of more powerful M-120 photoflash bombs in July 1952, but no new camera equipment was forthcoming and results remained undependable.

A further threat to Bomber Command's night operations over north-west Korea developed in December 1952 when FEAF Intelligence received strong indications that two Russian night fighter squadrons had been deployed to the Antung airfield complex and were already in operation. Between 18 November 1952 and 31 January 1953 the communist air defences achieved notable successes at night, destroying five B-29s and damaging three more so badly that they had to be withdrawn from service. In the words of the official history:

Nevertheless, Bomber Command was to lose no more B-29s to enemy action after January 1953. This was due to a number of countermeasures as well as to natural causes, such as the raising of the contrail-forming level with the onset of spring; attacks were arranged on an irregular basis; attack altitudes were varied as much as Shoran direction allowed; the bomber stream was compressed so that attacking aircraft passed through the target area in the minimum time; contrail-forming altitudes were avoided, and heavily defended targets were attacked as far as possible in the dark of the moon.

Another solution to the enemy night fighter problem was to provide bomber support, using night intruders to penetrate deep into enemy territory. Since June 1952 VMF(N)-513 had been making four F7F Tigercats available for bomber support each night, the fighters preceding the bomber stream by about five minutes in the run-up to the target area. They proved ineffective against the enemy's MiG-15s, and it was not until VMF(N)-513 re-equipped with twelve Douglas F3D-2N Skynights early in November 1952 that matters began to improve. On the night of 3 November, during the Skynight's second bomber support mission, Major William T. Stratton Jr was brought to within visual range of a target by his radar operator, Master Sergeant Hans Hoglind. Stratton put three bursts of cannon fire into it and it went down in flames. The enemy aircraft was identified as a Yak-15 (Russia's first jet fighter), which is unlikely; it was more probably a piston-engined Yak-9 or a Yak-3, from which the Yak-15 was developed. Five nights later another Skynight crew destroyed an enemy aircraft, believed to have been a MiG-15, near Sonchon. Later in November, General Hoyt S. Vandenberg, the US Air Force Chief of Staff, personally authorised the removal of the restrictions that had hitherto prevented the 319th Fighter Interceptor Squadron's F-94 Starfires from operating over enemy territory for fear that their modern fire control system might fall into enemy hands. From then on flights of four to six F-94s flew barrier patrols about thirty miles ahead of the bomber stream while the Skynights took up position 2,000 to 3,000 feet above the bombers. These new tactics quickly produced results, the Skynights scoring two new kills in moonlight conditions, one each on the nights of 28 and 31 January

On the night of 18/19 November 1952 the Reds revealed new tactics when they shot down a 98th Wing B-29 coming off its supply-centre target at Sonchon. Riding above the B-29, a Red spotter dropped flares every time the bomber changed direction. The flares allowed searchlights to lock on the bomber, and four Red fighter passes riddled the bomber, forcing its crew to abandon ship over Cho-do. On the night of 30/31 December, when a full moon was at its zenith and contrails were streaming at bombing altitudes, Red searchlights coned three 19th Group B-29s which were attacking an ore-processing plant near the Yalu at Choak-tong. A conventional airplane called signals from above the bombers, and Red fighters shot down one B-29 and damaged two others so badly that their crews were forced down at Suwon. Bomber Command blamed the moonlight and the contrails for the losses, but in the dark of the moon on the night of 10/11 January 1953 a 307th Wing B-29 was coned by searchlights, hit by flak, and shot down by fighters over Anju's marshalling yards. The position of this bomber was apparently betrayed by light contrails.

On the night of 12 January Red fighters intercepted and shot down a lone 91st Reconnaissance Squadron RB-29 which was distributing leaflets along the Yalu. On 28/29 January enemy fighters apparently silhouetted a 19th Group B-29 against a full moon over Kimpodong and needed no other illumination to shoot it down. Moonlight again betrayed 307th Wing B-29s when they bombed the Unjong-ni supply area on the night of 30/31 January. Some ten Red fighters prosecuted attacks which so badly damaged a B-29 that it barely made an emergency landing in South Korea. The total number of Red interceptions was not great. Bomber Command reported only twenty non-firing and twenty-three firing passes made against its aircraft in January 1953. But the Red night interceptions were becoming extremely effective. Darkness was no longer affording the old B-29s the protection they needed to attack targets in North Korea . . .

An F3D Skynight of VMF(N)-513 over Korea. The Skynight intruders took the night war to the enemy.

1953. On the night of 30 January Captain Ben Fithian and Lieutenant Sam R. Lyons scored the F-94's first kill in Korea, shooting down an La-9. Between them the Skynights and Starfires destroyed fifteen enemy aircraft in the first half of 1953. It was a relatively small contribution in terms of enemy aircraft destroyed, but it helped the war-weary B-29s to survive those last months of conflict in Korea.

Another factor that helped them survive was electronic countermeasures, the development of which was accelerated by FEAF after June 1952. Data on enemy radars and electronic systems collected by the 'ferret' RB-29s of the 91st SRS was collated, evaluated and disseminated by a special section of the 548th Reconnaissance Technical Squadron. Despite the use of old equipment and partly trained operators, Bomber Command's ECM programme produced results. Between 1 January and 27 July 1953, in the course of 534 B-29 sorties, 114 aircraft were illuminated by searchlights, and in at least eighty-seven cases the searchlight lock was broken by the use of ECM. Had ECM not been available Bomber Command's losses would almost certainly have been triple what they were.

In March 1953 the B-29 force was committed to Operation 'Spring Thaw', the objectives of which were to disrupt the enemy's supply lines, destroy some of his transport, and force him to consume supplies which were stored in forward areas. Bomber Command's contribution to this operation mainly involved bridge attacks, but – as had always been the case previously – the enemy showed a near miraculous ability to repair bridges almost as quickly as they were knocked down. The training level of the B-29 crews had now reached a new peak, and this was reflected in the operational record for May 1953. In that month, forces of between seven and nine B-29s attacked forty-four targets and effected an average of 69.3 per cent destruction on each of them, virtually doubling the achievement of four or five months earlier.

In February 1953 Fifth AF fighter-bombers joined Bomber Command in attacks on selected industrial targets. On 15 February, for example, twenty-two Thunderjets of the 474th FBW, each carrying two 1,000lb semi-armour-piercing (SAP) bombs, hit the Suiho hydro-electric plant, which was thought to be partly operational again. Attacking at low level while eighty-two Sabres beat off a force of thirty MiGs that made an unsuccessful attempt to intercept, the Thunderjets destroyed the generator building. None of the American aircraft was damaged. This was followed, on 15 March, by an attack with sixteen Thunderjets on industrial areas in Chongjin.

Meanwhile, on the edge of the stratosphere, the air superiority war between Sabre and MiG raged unabated.

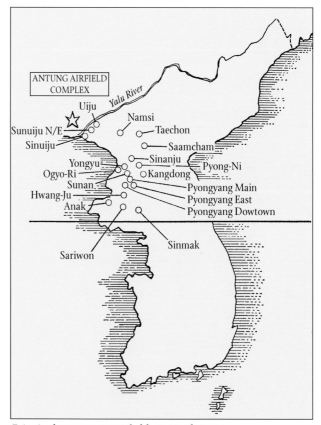

Principal communist airfields in North Korea.

CHAPTER 18
The Air Superiority Battle,
June 1952 - April 1953

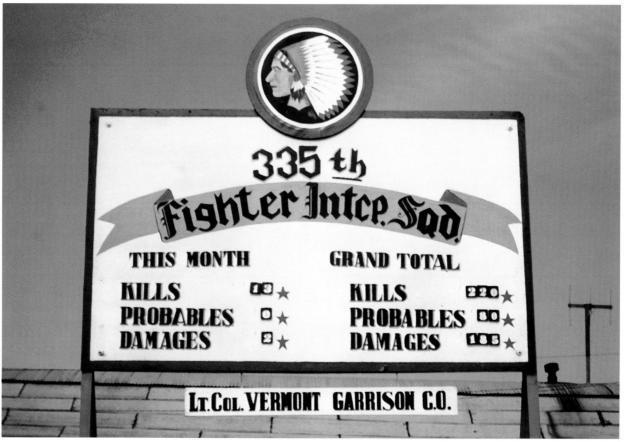

The 335th FIS (4th FIW) scoreboard at Kimpo. (via Robert F. Dorr)

In the summer of 1952 United Nations Command Intelligence once again established that a number of alarming developments had taken place north of the Yalu. By the middle of the year the strength of the communist air forces in Manchuria stood at 1,800 aircraft, of which 1,000 were jet types. There was also another potential threat: Soviet air strength in the Far East, following substantial reinforcement, had risen to over 5,300 aircraft. Not the least disturbing news was that the Chinese People's Air Force had taken delivery of about 100 Ilyushin Il-28 jet bombers, most of which were based in Manchuria. The communists were also hard at work on a new airfield complex across the Yalu in the summer of 1952, and had set up about twenty-five radar stations that were able to provide coverage of air space up to and even beyond the 38th Parallel. There were also a dozen GCI stations, mostly situated in the west coast area, which gave effective fighter control in all weathers over a seventy-mile radius.

From the beginning of June 1952 the communists showed a hitherto absent ability to co-ordinate all their air defence measures in a new challenge to Allied air superiority over north-western Korea. Night-fighters were active against B-29 sorties, while the MiG pilots were displaying much greater tactical proficiency in their daylight battles with the Sabres. This did not prevent the Sabre pilots from claiming twenty MiGs destroyed for the loss of three of their own number in June. One Sabre pilot, 2nd Lt James F. Low of the 4th Wing, joined the ranks of the jet aces during the month by destroying his fifth enemy aircraft – a notable achievement, as he had graduated from flying school only six months earlier.

The MiGs were up in strength on 4 July, when fifty of them crossed the Yalu to intercept Allied fighter-bombers attacking targets at Sakchu. All the fighter-bombers escaped but the MiGs lost thirteen of their number in a fight with the Sabre escort, two F-86s also being lost. Six more MiGs were added to the Sabres' score before the month was out, making a total of nineteen. Four Sabres failed to return from the July engagements. United Nations pilots destroyed thirty-five MiGs in air combat during August, six of them shot down in a fight between thirty-five Sabres and fifty-two MiGs on the 6th. Two Sabres were lost. Yet another ace was added to the list: Captain Clifford D. Jolley, who shot down his fifth MiG on the 8th.

The early part of the month was notable for several deep-penetration missions by the enemy, the MiGs using their superior numbers to slip past the Sabre barrier and rove as far south as Haeju in search of Allied fighter bombers. During one such mission, on 9 August, eight of them encountered the Sea Furies and Fireflies of HMS *Ocean*'s 802 and 825 Squadrons. *Ocean* was the only carrier to experience serious air opposition off the west coast. Already, on 27 July, four of 825 Squadron's Fireflies had been attacked by a pair of MiGs and two damaged, and soon afterwards four Sea Furies were attacked by four MiGs which caused no damage. The encounter of 9 August, however, turned into a full-blown air battle. It was described by Lieutenant Peter Carmichael, the flight leader, who recorded:

'The encounter that my flight had with the MiGs took place at 0600 hours. My No. 2, Sub-Lt Carl Haines, said, "MiGs five o'clock." I did not see them at first and my No. 4, Sub-Lt 'Smoo' Ellis, gave a break. We all turned towards the MiGs. Two went for my Nos. 3 and 4, Lt Pete Davies and Sub-Lt Ellis. They were seen to get good hits on one, who broke away with smoke coming from him.'

Carmichael also got in a good burst at a MiG, which went down and crashed. His report continues:

'Though I have been credited with shooting down the [Royal Navy's] first MiG, I feel that it was more of a flight effort than an individual one, because the one that crashed behind me was fired at by all of my flight. My Nos. 3 and 4 then had another attack on them and got hits on this one. He broke away and the rest of the MiGs broke off the engagement and escorted him away. The impression we got was that these MiG pilots were very inexperienced and did not use their aircraft to any advantage at all. I think it was the next day that we had another engagement with eight MiGs and we were very lucky to get away with it. I reckon they must have sent the instructors down! These pilots put their aircraft to the best use and we managed to ease our way to some cloud that was about twenty miles away. One MiG got on my tail and my No. 3 fired at him and he broke away. The only MiG who made a mistake was one who made a head-on attack on my Nos. 3 and 4 and was hit by them and seen to go away with a lot of smoke and flame coming from him.'

During these two skirmishes the pilots of 802 Squadron claimed the destruction of two MiG-15s, with three more damaged. To Lieutenant 'Hoagy' Carmichael fell the honour of becoming the first piston-engined pilot to shoot down an enemy jet in the Korean War. It was a formidable testimony to the Sea Fury's ruggedness and its excellent dogfighting characteristics.

Contacts between MiGs and US Navy or USMC piston-engined fighters were also very rare, but when they occurred the Americans more than held their own.

Sea Furies of No 814 Squadron await their turn to be launched from HMS Glory *for a strike against targets in northwestern Korea.*

F-86E Sabres of the 51st Fighter Interceptor Wing at Suwon in 1953. (Bill Rogers)

When MiGs penetrated the Sabre barrier to harass Marine close support aircraft in the autumn of 1952, MAG-12 pilots developed tactics that exploited their Corsairs' best advantages to get them out of trouble. In one incident two F4U-4B Corsairs of VMA-312 were approaching their target, a troop concentration on the Taedong river, when two MiGs were sighted. The MiGs attacked and the two American pilots went into a defensive weave. One of the MiGs went into a slow climbing turn immediately in front of the Corsair flown by Captain Jesse Folmar, who gave it a five-second burst of 20mm. The MiG began smoking and the pilot ejected, his flying suit on fire. At this point four more MiGs appeared and the Corsair pilots broke off the action. Folmar's aircraft was attacked and badly damaged; he baled out over the sea and was picked up by an SA-16. His was the only Corsair MiG kill of the war.

September 1952 turned out to be the most hectic month yet. The MiG pilots showed aggressive intentions right from the start when, on the 1st, several of them penetrated as far as Haeju to attack Allied fighter-bombers. Once again, however, the communist pilots threw away their advantage with poor gunnery and teamwork, and only succeeded in damaging one Mustang. On the 4th the sky over the Yalu was criss-crossed with contrails throughout the day as Sabres and MiGs fought seventeen separate battles that resulted in the destruction of thirteen MiGs and four F-86s. One of the MiGs was shot down by Major Frederick C. Blesse of the 4th Wing; it was his fifth enemy aircraft, and before the end of the month he would have three more to his credit. On the 9th no fewer than 175 MiGs crossed the river to intercept Thunderjets which were attacking the North Korean Military Academy at Sakchu, a frequent target since early in August. The Sabre barrier was not strong enough to cope with all of them and some broke through to shoot down one fighter-bomber. Two more Thunderjets and six Sabres were destroyed in air combat during the rest of the month, but the UN pilots claimed a record total of sixty-three MiGs. On 21 September Captain Robinson Risner of the 4th FIW destroyed his fifth MiG near Sinuiju to become the Korean War's twentieth jet ace.

Their heavy losses in September made the communist pilots more cautious during the following month. Most of the work was done by the *honchos*, the nickname – which means 'boss' in Japanese – bestowed upon the enemy's experienced instructors by the UN aircrews. While the big MiG formations stayed safely upstairs at 40,000 feet or more, these experienced flight and squadron commanders would dive down to attack targets of opportunity, tactics they had used before. Alternatively, formations of twelve or twenty-four MiGs, all flown by experienced pilots, would seek out

131

four-Sabre flights and attempt to box them in. To counter these tactics both Sabre wings began to use flights of six or eight aircraft, with the higher-powered F-86Fs operating at 40,000 feet plus and the F-86Es working lower down. The new arrangements worked well and the communists were only able to claim four Sabres and one Thunderjet destroyed for the loss of twenty-seven MiGs. The MiGs, however, also destroyed two of Task Force 77's Skyraiders in the Wonsan area.

Meanwhile, the Allies had no intention of relaxing their air pressure operations, but selecting new target systems for a continuing air offensive presented problems. With most worthwhile fixed target systems in the North already shattered, the only way of hitting the enemy hard now was to lure his troops and equipment out into the open, and then turn the fighter-bombers loose. To achieve this, General Clark and his commanders planned an ingenious hoax. They allowed

Armourers calibrating the 0.50" guns of a 49th BG F-84 at Taegu.

At the end of September 1952, despite the sustained Allied air pressure, the communist negotiators at Panmunjom still showed no sign of weakening, although intelligence sources indicated that both China and the Soviet Union were seeking a means of bringing the war to an end without suffering serious loss of face. This time peace talks had become deadlocked over the issue of repatriating prisoners of war; since thousands of Chinese and North Korean prisoners had no wish to return to their homelands at the end of hostilities the United Nations negotiators were pressing for repatriation on a voluntary basis, but the communists were insisting on the return of all PoWs. When they still remained intractable on this point early in October, the United Nations Command delegates recessed and indicated that they would be prepared to resume negotiations only when the communists had something constructive to offer in the way of new proposals.

the news to leak out that the Allies were planning a large-scale amphibious assault on the coastal village of Kojo, north of Wonsan, in conjunction with a ground offensive by the Eighth Army and an airdrop by the 187th RCT. For a week before the supposed assault was due to begin, FEAF aircraft pounded enemy supply and communications lines in the coastal areas, while an armada of C-46s and C-119s deployed to Taegu. The air operations during this period provided the best example so far of inter-Service co-operation, with Banshees escorting B-29s and Sabres escorting Navy and Marine attack aircraft. Carrying out its part of the hoax to the letter, the US Navy assembled the biggest naval armada since World War Two – Joint Amphibious Task Force Seven – and sent it on its way up the Korean coast towards Kojo. On the night of 14 October the Eighth Army launched a two-battalion thrust into enemy territory – to all appearances a reconnaissance in force heralding a major attack – and the following morning Task Force Seven sent a wave of landing craft towards the beaches. At the same time thirty-two C-119s headed north to Chorwon, as though to make a paradrop. Both air and seaborne forces, however, turned away short of their objectives, the C-119s landing at Taegu and the naval craft returning to the Task Force.

Enemy reaction to the hoax had not been as marked as General Clark and his staff had hoped, but it produced enough movements to present tactical air with a host of targets. Between 9 and 19 October, in an operation called 'Red Cow', the Fifth AF's fighter-bombers and light bombers flew 3,729 sorties, hitting 360 targets of all types, while Bomber Command attacked a further forty-three. During the same period, and continuing into November, aircraft of TF 77 flew over 3,000 sorties in the course of Operation 'Cherokee' against similar targets. The name Cherokee was chosen in honour of Vice-Admiral Joseph J. 'Jocko' Clark, who was a full-blooded Cherokee. He had commanded TF 77 briefly in 1951 and was now Commander, US Seventh Fleet.

The biggest black spot in the operation was the Eighth Army's limited offensive, which had been designed to capture two objectives, Triangle Hill and Sniper Ridge, north of Kumhwa. Both were taken, but only at the expense of heavy casualties, and the United Nations troops holding them were subjected to continual and heavy infantry attacks. In support of the UN forces the Fifth AF and Marine Air Wing flew over 3,500 sorties, but despite this Triangle Hill was recaptured by the communists early in November. The force on Sniper Ridge managed to hold out with air support, which was often delivered through intense automatic weapons fire. During one attack, on 22 November, Major Charles J. Loring of the 8th Wing's 80th Fighter Bomber Squadron deliberately crashed his F-80 into an enemy gun position after he was hit by flak. He was later awarded a posthumous Medal of Honor.

Although November 1952 was a fairly quiet month as far as air combat was concerned, the communist fighter units encountered during previous weeks apparently having been withdrawn for a rest and replaced by new ones whose time was taken up mostly with operational training, the Sabre pilots nevertheless managed to increase their total score by twenty-eight MiGs for the loss of four F-86s. The month saw three new Sabre aces: Colonel Royal N. Baker and Captain Leonard W. Lilley, both of the 4th Wing, and Captain Cecil G. Foster of the 51st Wing.

On 18 November 1952 three F9F-5 Panther pilots of VF-781, a reserve squadron aboard USS *Oriskany*, covering an air strike on the frontier town of Hoeryong, sighted a formation of MiGs circling in the distance over Russian territory. Several MiGs, which bore Soviet Air Force markings, suddenly broke away and attacked the Panthers. In the ensuing engagement two MiGs were shot down and a third, on fire, was seen disappearing into a cloud. Lt E.R. Williams and Lt (JG) J.D. Middleton were each credited with a kill, while the damaged MiG was credited to Lt (JG) D.M. Rowlands. For fear of international repercussions the Navy kept quiet about the incident and it was not made public until some years after the war.

The MiGs enjoyed an increased success rate in December, but it had little to do with the fighting ability of individual pilots. About the middle of the month the

F-80 pilots being decorated for actions in Korea. (via Robert F. Dorr)

communists suddenly re-adopted tactics similar to those they had practised earlier in the war: a formation of MiGs would bypass the Sabre screen and head south to the Chongchon river, where they would lie in wait for Sabres going home short of fuel. A number of Sabre pilots found themselves trapped in this way, and at least four had to eject when their fuel ran out. Apart from that, only two Sabres were destroyed in air combat during the month, while UN pilots claimed twenty-eight MiGs. Both Sabre Wings were now operating a mixture of F-86Es and F-86Fs, the latter having arrived in June. The first batch was assigned to the 39th Squadron of the 18th Fighter Interceptor Wing, which was immediately transferred to the 51st Wing to bring it up to a three-squadron establishment.

The MiGs made extensive use of the revised tactics in

victories were scored by high-flying F-86F pilots who were lucky enough to engage the enemy novices. Two 51st Wing pilots, Captain Dolphin D. Overton III and Captain Harold E. Fischer, became aces during the month, Overton destroying five MiGs in just four missions. On the last day of the month, a Tu-2 bomber – the first encountered for over a year – was shot down by Lt Raymond J. Kinsey of the 4th FIW.

In January 1953 the 18th Fighter Bomber Wing, which included No. 2 Squadron, South African Air Force, began its long-awaited conversion from Mustangs to F-86Fs at Osan-ni airfield. The first three Sabres arrived on 28 January, the day after Mustang operations ceased, and conversion training began on 3 February. On 25 February the 18th FBW flew its first mission with Sabres, four F-86Fs accompanying a

F-86E Sabre of the 51st FIW. (via Robert F. Dorr)

January 1953, but homeward-bound Sabres were generally able to keep out of trouble by flying a curve over the Yellow Sea. Early in the month, UN Sabre pilots reported that although most of the MiGs – presumably still engaged in one of their habitual training cycles – still remained at over 40,000 feet, some of the MiG pilots they were meeting showed a degree of skill that matched their own. The enemy fighters, which were camouflaged pale blue underneath with copper-coloured upper surfaces, bore the plain red star of the Soviet Air Force; their pilots showed every willingness to fight and used every trick in the book. On several occasions Sabre pilots caught a glimpse of their opponents' features; even disguised by oxygen masks and helmets they were plainly Caucasian, not Asian. For example, one Sabre pilot, pulling up close to a stricken MiG, observed that its pilot had a ruddy complexion and light red, bushy eyebrows. The Russians, it seemed, were still keen to learn what they could from the battles over Korea while the war lasted.

The United Nations claimed thirty-seven kills for the loss of one Sabre during January, but most of the

fighter sweep to the Yalu. However, Colonel Frank S. Perego, the wing commander, was not satisfied with the progress that many of the former Mustang pilots were making, so he reassigned them to other Fifth Air Force duties. The deficiency was made good by the arrival of trained replacement pilots from the United States, and the Wing's three squadrons – No. 2 SAAF, the 12th, and the 67th – were up to their task by early April.

It had been originally intended that the 8th FBW was to convert to Sabres after the 18th Wing, but delays in the arrival of F-86s meant that both Wings underwent conversion at about the same time. The 8th FBW, converting from F-80C Shooting Stars, experienced fewer transitional problems than the 18th FBW, and re-equipment of the 35th and 36th Squadrons was completed by early April. The 80th Squadron continued operations with its F-80s until 30 April, when it too equipped with Sabres. The 8th FBW flew its first F-86 mission on 7 April when four Sabres joined a Yalu sweep. It was the 8th FBW, in fact, that flew the first F-86F fighter-bomber mission, on 13 April, and on 14 April the 18th Wing also made its fighter-

F-86F Sabre of No. 2 'Cheetah' Sqn SAAF after the unit and other squadrons of the 18th FBG converted from Mustangs early in 1953. (via Robert F. Dorr)

bomber debut with the new type. Except for the addition of bomb shackles, a modification to its gun-bomb-rocket sight, and special 200-gallon drop tanks, the F-86F was no different from the interceptor, and any fears that it would not adequately fill its new role were soon dismissed. After a month of combat operations, General Weyland predicted that the F-86F would be an excellent fighter-bomber. 'I consider it a particularly desirable improvement in our tactical force,' he said, 'because of its versatility in accomplishing the three phases of the tactical air force mission: that of gaining and maintaining air superiority, interdiction, and close air support.' After four months in combat the Fifth Air Force described the F-86F as the most suitable fighter-bomber employed in Korea. It displayed a superior ability to survive, was a stable gun and bomb platform, had no airfield or operating problems not peculiar to other jets, and possessed satisfactory stability when carrying external ordnance at high altitudes. When fitted with 200-gallon external tanks, the F-86F could carry two 1,000lb bombs to a radius of action of 360 nautical miles.

On the air superiority front, February 1953 saw the start of a friendly tussle for the position of top jet ace before the Korean hostilities ended. Major James Jabara, with six MiGs to his credit during his earlier tour with the 4th Wing, was back in Korea, and his score was already beginning to climb. The target was fourteen enemy aircraft destroyed, which was the score achieved by the late George Davis before his death in action the year before. Jabara was coming up fast, but so were a number of other pilots, and one in particular stood out among them. Captain Joseph McConnell had been turned down for pilot training during World War Two, and had flown a couple of tours as a navigator on B-24s. It was only after the war that he was accepted as a pilot, finally emerging as one of the first batch of Shooting

Star pilots in February 1948. When the Korean War broke out McConnell was in Alaska; he immediately applied for combat duty, but instead of being transferred to Korea he was sent to George AFB in California. It was not until the autumn of 1952 that he eventually got his wish and joined the 51st FIW at Kimpo. He destroyed his first MiG on 14 January 1953. Just over a month later, by which time he was a flight commander with the 51st Wing's 16th Squadron, his score had risen to five and he was racing almost neck-and-neck with Captain Manuel J. Fernandez of the 4th Wing. Fernandez downed four more MiGs in March, bringing his score to ten, while McConnell accounted for three more, making a total of eight. Three other pilots also became aces during the month: one was Major James P. Hagerstrom of the 18th FBW, and the others were Colonel James Johnson and Lt-Col George L. Jones, both of the 4th Wing.

The MiG pilots proved particularly aggressive during March 1953, penetrating as far as Chinnampo equipped with wing tanks and descending to altitudes as low as 17,000 feet to join combat, but the Sabres once again came out on top and claimed thirty-four MiGs for the loss of two F-86s. March was also the month when the Meteors of No. 77 Squadron RAAF met MiGs for the last time. It happened on the 27th, when Sergeants John Hale and David Irlam spotted three enemy jets while on patrol over Sinmak, south-east of Pyongyang, and immediately went in to the attack. One MiG broke away, but the others turned and made passes at the Meteors. Hale jettisoned his ventral fuel tank and fired two air-to-ground rockets at the oncoming MiGs, which took evasive action; one of them tried to get on the Meteor's tail, but overshot and presented Hale with the chance he was waiting for. 'For a second,' the Australian pilot said, 'he was flying parallel to me, about fifty yards ahead. I could see the pilot clearly and swung behind him and hammered at him with my cannon. Strips of metal began to peel off the MiG and it rolled on to its back and headed straight down from about 10,000 feet. Black smoke was pouring out, but I didn't see him crash. Now there were more MiGs, and two came at me with guns blazing. Again I managed to S-turn on to their tails. The Meteor was flying like a bomb. They tried to climb away, and as I blasted one I saw bright flashes near the wing root and white smoke poured out. Then my guns stopped firing. There was no more ammunition and I had to turn for home.' Two more Meteors came up and the MiGs broke off the action. It was probably just as well; when the Meteor pilots returned to base they found that Irlam's aircraft had 112 holes in it.

In March 1953 the 4th FIW played host to a project called Gun Val, in which eight F-86F Sabres armed with 20mm cannon in place of their .50-calibre machine-guns were sent to Korea for combat evaluation. The cannon showed promise for the future, but the trials showed that the installation was not yet ready to be cleared for combat. Much thought was also given during this period to improving the Sabre's overall combat performance; one scheme, tested in the autumn of 1952 and rejected by the Fifth Air Force, involved fitting the Sabre with externally-attached solid fuel rockets which were supposed to give the fighter an extra turn of speed when overtaking a MiG. The real boost to the performance of the F-86F came with the installation of solid wing leading edges, which were tested by the Air Research and Development Command. While manoeuvring at high altitude, Sabre pilots had been unable to use the maximum permissible rate of turn without encountering transonic buffeting and risking pulling out the leading edge slats. Considering this problem, North American test pilot George Welch suggested removal of the slats and extension of the wing leading edges. The new wing leading edge increased chord by six inches at the root and three inches at the tip, and consequently became known as the 6-3 leading edge. The absence of the beneficial effect of the slats on the airflow at low speeds was partly compensated for by the use of small wing fences at approximately seventy per cent span, but the modification raised the stalling speed and produced a yaw-and-roll effect before the stall, making a faster landing approach necessary. Nevertheless, these penalties were considered to be far outweighed by the operational advantages accruing from the wing modification, all-round performance being improved and a sustained 1.5G turn at M0.92 at 30,000 feet now being attainable.

Fifty sets of the new leading edges were shipped to Korea for the modification of F-86Fs, the programme being kept under strict security wraps. The improvement was immediately apparent. The modified F-86F could out-turn the MiG-15 in high-altitude combat, and the lower drag from the smoother aerodynamic shape resulted in slightly higher level flight speeds at all altitudes. The changes were at once incorporated on the production lines and more conversion kits were shipped to Korea. The Sabre was now equipped to outfly and outfight the MiG-15 from the edge of the stratosphere to treetop level. In the words of General Glenn O. Barcus, the Fifth Air Force's Commander, it was time to turn the tigers loose.

Panorama of Kimpo airfield, with C-119 and F-86s. (via Robert F. Dorr)

CHAPTER 19
Last Battles,
April-July 1953

F-86F Sabre of the 335th FIS, 4th FIW, at Kimpo in 1953. (via Robert F. Dorr)

On 26 April 1953 hopes for a speedy end to the Korean War were raised when armistice talks resumed at Panmunjom, only to be dashed once more when the communists again rejected the UN proposals outright. Then, in May, after some tough bargaining, the communists agreed to a UN suggestion that representatives of neutral nations should have custody of all prisoners-of-war pending their repatriation, but there was still no agreement on what was to become of those who did not wish to be repatriated. With yet another breakdown of the talks seemingly inevitable, General Clark recommended to the Joint Chiefs that air pressure operations against North Korea be maintained, and that if necessary the UN should be prepared to launch a limited land offensive, and possibly an amphibious assault, in the autumn of 1953. At the same time US Secretary of State John Foster Dulles dropped strong hints that authority

might be given for a UN air offensive against China's Manchurian bases.

FEAF's target planners now resurrected a scheme, first recommended in October 1952, that involved intense attacks on North Korea's irrigation dams, some of the country's most vulnerable strategic objectives. Twenty of these dams, situated near important supply routes, provided seventy-five per cent of the water necessary for North Korea's rice production. The rice harvest was concentrated mainly in two provinces, Hwanghae and South Pyongyang, and most of the production went to feed the communist armies. By knocking out all twenty dams, FEAF calculated that a year's supply of rice would be destroyed in the ensuing floods. Moreover, the deluge would inundate roads, railways and supply dumps and compel the North Koreans to import vast quantities of rice from China; this would impose an intolerable burden on the Chinese

F-84 Thunderjets taking off from Taegu with the help of JATO. Each aircraft is carrying a pair of 500lb bombs.

economy, which in 1953 was already strained to breaking point. From the psychological point of view it would be better if the dams were destroyed over a period of time, rather than in one blow; in this way, it was hoped that the civilian population would blame the communists for prolonging the war.

As the RAF had learned in World War Two, dams – and particularly earth dams – were very difficult targets to destroy. The US Navy had made a successful attack on the dam at Hwachon in May 1951 during the communist spring offensive using aerial torpedoes for the first and only time in Korea. On that occasion, five Skyraiders of VA-195 and three of VC-35 from the USS *Princeton* launched eight torpedoes at the flood gates; two failed to detonate, but the others destroyed the gates and released the waters of the Hwachon reservoir into the Fukhan and Han rivers, preventing communist forces from making an easy crossing.

The 1953 series of dam raids, however, were to be made with conventional bombs, so the first attack was to be in the nature of an experiment to see if the idea

revealed a scene of total destruction. At some time during the night the pressure of water in the reservoir had caused the dam to collapse, sending a mighty flood down the Potong valley. Five square miles of rice crops had been swept away, together with 700 buildings; Sunan airfield was under water, and five miles of railway line, together with a two-mile stretch of the adjacent north–south highway, had been destroyed or damaged. In this one attack the F-84s had inflicted more damage on the enemy's transport system than they had done in several weeks of interdiction work.

Encouraged by this success, General Weyland immediately authorised attacks on two more dams, at Chasan and Kuwonga, and in the afternoon of 15 May thirty-six Thunderjets of the 58th FBW attacked the Chasan dam. The bomb-aiming, however, was poor; no direct hits were registered, and it was not until five 1,000lb bombs were placed squarely on the target by a second Thunderjet strike the next day that the structure crumbled and the waters burst through to inundate a large area of rice and destroy a half-mile stretch of a

AD Skyraider of the Marine Air Wing at Kimpo. (via Robert F. Dorr)

would work and to develop techniques for future missions. The target was the Toksan dam, a 2,300-foot earth and stone structure on the Potong river twenty miles north of Pyongyang. The dam was attacked in the afternoon of 13 May by fifty-nine Thunderjets of the 58th FBW armed with 1,000lb bombs, and the result seemed disappointing: apart from a slight crumbling of the structure, the dam still stood. The next morning, however, photographs brought back by an RF-80

nearby railway line. The Kuwonga dam was assigned to Bomber Command, and was attacked on the night of 21/22 May by seven B-29s which dropped fifty-six 2,000lb bombs on it using Shoran. Four direct hits were scored on the crest, but the dam held; the enemy, anticipating the raid, had reduced the water level in the reservoir, relieving a substantial amount of pressure on the structure. During a second attack on 29/30 May the B-29s again scored five direct hits with 2,000lb bombs on the dam, but even then the structure failed to crumble. Nevertheless, the damage caused was sufficient to require extensive repairs, and before these could be carried out the reservoir had to be drained completely, which meant that the rice fields in the area were deprived of their vital water supply and the crop suffered as a consequence.

Meanwhile, there were indications that the communists were planning an offensive against UN forces in western Korea, and on the night of 19/20 May fourteen B-29s mounted an attack on a barracks at Unsan-dong, west of Sinanju, destroying 117 buildings. The expected offensive developed on 28 May against

Force 77 also threw everything it had into the battle. Navy and Marine Skyraider squadrons had by this time developed a formidable night attack capability – on 3 May 1953, for example, three AD-4N Skyraiders of VC-35 from the USS *Valley Forge* had completely destroyed the Chosin power station in a flare-illuminated night raid, and now they put their skills to good use supporting Marine infantry units that were coming under attack along the MLR. Many radar-directed strikes were carried out during this phase by the Skyraiders of VMA-121 and VMF-311, the Corsairs of VMA-212 and VMF-323 also providing effective ground support. For seven days Naval airmen flew

Ground crew pose in front of a 51st FIW F-86 Sabre. (via Robert F. Dorr)

the US I Corps, but this proved to be a feint, the main attack falling on the ROK II Corps in the Kumsong area on 10 June. Two nights earlier Bomber Command had again attacked the enemy's rear areas, destroying 250 buildings in the Unhyang-po supply depot twenty miles south-east of Sinuiju.

For three nights after the start of the enemy offensive Bomber Command made Shoran-directed attacks on supplies and communications, while the Fifth Air Force operated intensively during the day. On 12 June, with the ROK defence showing signs of breaking, Task

virtually non-stop from the carriers *Lake Champlain*, *Philippine Sea*, *Princeton* and *Boxer* in the USN's biggest close support effort of the war. On one day alone, 15 June, the carrier pilots flew 532 combat sorties, while the Marines and the Fleet Air Arm flew another 478. Maximum-effort close support operations continued until 19 June, when the Allied front stabilised.

Meanwhile, in April, as part of General Barcus's plan to bring the MiGs to battle, Fifth Air Force aircraft had been waging a propaganda war, dropping leaflets over enemy troop concentrations. The leaflets posed a simple question: where was the communist air force? There was no apparent reaction in April; 1,622 MiG sorties were sighted, but few of the enemy fighters crossed the Yalu to make sporadic attacks, in the process of which the Sabre pilots destroyed twenty-seven for the loss of four of their own. One of the latter was Captain Harold E. Fischer, a 51st FIW ace, whose score then stood at ten MiGs. He was taken prisoner. Joseph McConnell's Sabre was also badly hit during a fight on 12 April, but he ejected and was rescued by an H-5 helicopter of the 3rd ARS. He was back in action within twenty-four hours, shooting down his ninth

promised: 'We will be back every time you broadcast filthy lies about the Fifth Air Force.'

The attack represented the utmost loss of face to the enemy air forces, but their anticipated reaction was thwarted by bad weather that persisted for a week. From then on the MiGs were very much in evidence, but now there was a difference. For the past few months, many of the MiGs encountered had carried the plain red star insignia of Soviet Russia, but now they bore the markings of either Communist China or North Korea. It has been suggested that the Russians decided to pull out their fighter contingents following a United Nations offer of a $100,000 reward to any communist

Gloster Meteor F Mk 8s of No. 77 Squadron RAAF at Kimpo Air Base near Seoul, 1953. (via Robert F. Dorr)

MiG, and he got his tenth on 24 April. He was now level with Captain Fernandez, but the latter crept ahead once more on 27 April when he shot down his eleventh enemy fighter.

As leaflet drops had produced no tangible result, FEAF now planned to prod the enemy into responding by mounting a spectacular attack on Pyongyang Radio on 1 May, communism's red letter day. Unknown to higher command, General Barcus had been flying combat missions with the 51st FIW for the past two months, and on 1 May he flew as airborne commander for the Pyongyang Radio attack. While the 4th and 51st Wings flew screening and covering operations, F-86F Sabres of the 8th and 18th FBWs passed over Pyongyang as though heading out for a Yalu patrol, then suddenly let down to bomb the radio station and its power supply. The attack took the defences completely by surprise and only one Sabre was damaged by AA fire. Circling over Pyongyang and using a radio frequency which the communists were known to monitor, General Barcus identified himself and

pilot who defected and brought a MiG-15 along with him, but it is far more likely that an agreement had already been reached between the Soviet Union and China to bring the Korean hostilities to an end, given a reasonable face-saving period, and that the Russians, having learned all they wanted to learn from nearly three years of air combat, saw little point in involving themselves further. They had, after all, had ample opportunity to examine nearly every type of Allied aircraft involved in the war, many of them having come down virtually intact in communist-held territory.

Whatever the facts, the enemy pilots who now faced the United Nations were no longer *honchos*. They were keen and aggressive enough, but they were inexperienced and they suffered accordingly. The mission of the Fifth Air Force's Sabre wings was now to seek and destroy rather than to screen and protect, and they modified their tactics accordingly. The Sabres now used up to ninety-eight per cent of their power while awaiting combat; the higher speeds reduced the time they could stay on patrol, but it made catching MiGs

51st FIW F-86s. (via Robert F. Dorr)

easier, and if a MiG attacked, its rate of closure was slower. Between 8 and 31 May Sabre pilots sighted 1,507 MiGs, engaged 537 of them, and destroyed fifty-six for the loss of only one F-86. In seven instances the MiGs went into inadvertent spins in combat manoeuvres above 35,000 feet, and in most cases their pilots were seen to eject. In other cases the enemy pilots baled out as soon as a Sabre opened fire.

The Fifth Air Force's fighter pilots threw everything into the MiG hunt in May 1953. Veteran aces added to their scores and a new ace was created. On 10 May Captain Fernandez destroyed a MiG and shared in the destruction of another. With a score of fourteen and a half his lead seemed assured, but by 18 May Joseph McConnell had shot down six more MiGs to bring his personal score to sixteen, a jet combat record that remains unbroken. Fernandez never had a chance to get his revenge, for both pilots were relieved of combat duty on 19 May. Sadly, McConnell was killed on 24 August 1954 while testing a new F-86H Sabre. May 1953 saw the return to combat of Major James Jabara, the original Korean jet ace, whose score stood at seven enemy aircraft destroyed. On the 26th Jabara shot down his eighth and ninth MiGs; just over a month later he was to become a triple jet ace by destroying his fifteenth enemy aircraft, moving into second place behind McConnell. The new ace of the May air battles was Lt-Col George I. Ruddell, commanding the 51st Wing's 39th Squadron.

While the battle raged in the air and on the ground, the ROK Government took action that threatened to sabotage the armistice talks for good. The South Koreans had indicated firmly that they would oppose any armistice that left Korea divided, and dropped strong hints that they would even be prepared to withdraw their forces from United Nations Command and launch a unilateral offensive against the communists. Matters came to a head on 18 June, when President Syngman Rhee – who was opposed to talks of any kind with the enemy – ordered the release of 25,000 anti-communist North Korean prisoners from camps all over the South. These were the men over whose fate both sides had been digging in their toes for the past few months at Panmunjom. It was time for rapid action. In an emergency middle-of-the-night meeting, Secretary of State Dulles and Dwight D. Eisenhower, America's new President, agreed that if the communists reacted to Rhee's move by launching an all-out offensive, possibly supported by Il-28 jet bomber attacks on Japanese bases, the United States would carry the war to mainland China. Lists of targets beyond the Yalu had already been drawn up, and there was

Short Sunderland of the RAF Far East Flying Boat Wing at Oppama, Japan, 1953. (via Robert F. Dorr)

F-86F Sabre of the 8th FBW and a C-119 of the 50th TCS pictured at Kimpo AB just after the end of the Korean War.
(via Robert F. Dorr)

now a stockpile of atomic weapons on Okinawa ready for use by Strategic Air Command if the need arose.

In Korea, the Allied commanders worked hard to strengthen their defences in readiness for a possible major enemy offensive. By 25 June the 315th Air Division, despite the fact that all its Globemasters were grounded with technical troubles at the time, had airlifted the entire 187th Airborne RCT to Korea, with full supporting equipment. During the next few days, operating in very bad weather, the Division's fleet of C-46s, C-54s and C-119s also carried the 24th Division's 19th and 34th RCTs to the war front.

It was as though both sides knew, in June 1953, that the great battle for air supremacy over north-western Korea was drawing to a close. Sabres and MiGs engaged one another in a series of furious combats that resulted in the destruction of seventy-seven enemy fighters, with a further eleven probably destroyed and forty-one damaged. There were no Allied losses. To the Sabre pilots, it seemed that the enemy was really scraping the barrel; often, when an F-86 got on a MiG's tail, the enemy pilot took no evasive action at all, but merely crouched as low as possible in the cockpit and held a steady course while the F-86's fire chopped his aircraft to pieces, relying on the thick armour plate at the rear of the cockpit to keep the bullets from him until he ejected. Sixteen of the Sabres' kills were claimed on the last day of the month, a new record. The June battles saw the emergence of five more aces: Lt-Col Vermont Garrison, Captain Lonnie R. Moore and Captain Ralph

S. Parr of the 4th Wing, and Col Robert P. Baldwin and Lt Henry Buttelman of the 51st.

The bad weather that blanketed much of Korea late in June was a severe hindrance to the UN Command in assembling information on the communists' intentions. It was not until 12 July, when a break in the weather permitted the RF-80s to fly a number of sorties, that Allied Intelligence learned that large enemy troop concentrations, supported by a substantial amount of anti-aircraft artillery, had assembled opposite the sectors held by the US IX Corps and the ROK II Corps.

Meanwhile, the Allied air forces had been devoting much of their effort to keeping North Korea's airfields out of action. One clause of the proposed armistice agreement, approved by both sides, placed a ban on the introduction of any additional troops or equipment into Korea while the armistice was in force, and it was clear from the enemy's frenzied airfield construction activities that they were trying to get as many air bases as possible serviceable so that they could infiltrate jet aircraft into them before the armistice was signed. General Weyland had no intentions of allowing this to happen, and early in May 1953 thirty-five North Korean airfields, all suitable for jet fighter operation, were listed for attack. By 23 June, following intensive operations by Bomber Command, Fifth AF and TF 77, thirty-four of the target airfields had been neutralised. The exception was Hoeryong, close to the Soviet border. Then bad weather brought a temporary halt to air operations, except those flown by Bomber Command

Lt Paul A. Hayek, USS Boxer, *examines the effect of a 37mm shell hit on his Panther.*

with the aid of Shoran, and on the nights of 4 and 9 July B-29s attacked Pyongyang Main, Namsi, and Taechon with 500lb bombs. Up to this time Bomber Command had been using 100lb bombs in airfield attacks, but it was now recognised that 500lb ordnance would penetrate deeper into soggy ground and produce a bigger crater which the enemy would find harder to repair. Despite the B-29 night strikes, when the weather cleared photojet sorties revealed that the enemy had repaired some of the airfields with amazing speed. At Uiju, which had grass landing strips, over forty MiG-15s had been flown in and were dispersed around the airfield. Twenty-one piston-engined aircraft were also sighted at Sinuiju, and the concrete runway at Namsi had been repaired.

On 18 July both Uiju and Sinuiju were attacked by F-86F fighter bombers of the 8th and 18th Wings, and there were several follow-on attacks during the next five days. The attacks destroyed twenty-one MiGs at Uiju and six other aircraft at Sinuiju; the surviving aircraft at the latter base were evacuated to Manchuria. On the night of 21/22 July eighteen B-29s blanketed Uiju's dispersal areas with fragmentation bombs and incendiary clusters, and during the next few nights Bomber Command also carried out attacks on Sinuiju, Namsi, Taechon, Pyong-ni, Pyongyang and Saamcham. By 27 July all North Korean airfields were once again listed as unserviceable by FEAF Intelligence; what Intelligence did not know was that the communists, taking advantage of the cloak of bad weather at the beginning of the month, had flown no fewer than 200 MiG-15s and piston-engined combat aircraft into Uiju and had dispersed them in the countryside adjoining the highway running between Uiju and Sinuiju. Immediately after the armistice came into effect, these aircraft would form the basis of a reconstituted North Korean Air Force.

The Sabres, meanwhile, claimed thirty-two MiG-15s in July. On the 11th Major John F. Bolt, a USMC pilot flying Sabres with the 51st FIW, shot down his fifth and sixth MiGs to become the only Marine Corps ace of the Korean War; on the 15th James Jabara scored his fifteenth and final victory; and on the 19th and 20th two more 4th FIW pilots, Captain Clyde A. Curtin and Major Stephen L. Bettinger, also became jet aces. Bettinger was in fact the thirty-ninth and last jet ace of the war, but it was several months before his status could be confirmed. After destroying his fifth MiG he was himself shot down and captured, and for fear of reprisals the UN kept his victories secret until he was repatriated in October. One other Sabre was also lost on that day.

With the armistice in sight, the communists launched their offensive on the night of 13/14 July 1953, with a strong drive down the valley of the Pukhan directed against the ROK II Corps, which was forced to retreat. The United Nations Command, however, was quick to react, and for a week beginning on 14 July the full weight of tactical air power was unleashed on the enemy. By 20 July the Allied line was stable once more and the enemy had suffered 72,000 casualties – the equivalent of nine divisions – to gain just three miles of ground along an eight-mile front. It had been a bloody and totally unnecessary end to the land war in Korea.

The air war, however, was not yet over. At 1700 on 22 July three Sabres of the 51st FIW led by Lt Sam P. Young entered MiG Alley at 35,000 feet on an offensive patrol. Young felt somewhat depressed; in thirty-four combat missions he had yet to fire his guns in anger, and it was beginning to look as though he would never get his chance. But on this July afternoon his run of bad luck came to an end. Ahead and below, four MiGs crossed his path at right angles. Young dived down, lined up his Sabre carefully, and shot down the number four MiG with a long burst of fire. It was the last MiG to be destroyed in combat over Korea.

On 19 July, as their offensive petered out, the communists had at last indicated that they were prepared to sign an armistice. President Syngman Rhee's government, following a mixture of threats and promises of mutual aid from the United States, also agreed to the terms thrashed out at Panmunjom. The armistice was finally signed at 1000 on 27 July 1953, and was to come into effect at 2201 hours that same day.

The air war was still not over. The last day of hostilities found four carriers of TF 77 – USS *Lake Champlain*, *Boxer*, *Philippine Sea* and *Princeton* – operating off the east coast, while the USS *Bairoko* patrolled the west coast; together they launched 649 sorties in support of Allied ground forces. The 1st Marine Air Wing also operated until the end; Banshees of VMJ-1 photographed North Korean airfields and railways, while strikes were flown by the F9F Panthers of VMF-115 and VMF-311 in support of Marine outposts. The last Marine combat mission was flown by Captain William I. Armagost of VMF-311, who bombed an enemy supply dump at about 1835. Earlier in the day, at 1030, Thunderjets of the 49th and 58th Wings made three attacks on airfields in the north, while the 4th, 8th and 51st Wings redeployed half their Sabre force to satellite airfields just in case the communists launched a last-minute, face-saving air attack. About a dozen MiGs were sighted by 4th FIW pilots escorting fighter bombers on an airfield strike near Chunggangjin, but they flew away across the Yalu and were not seen again. Soon afterwards, Captain Ralph S. Parr of the 4th FIW sighted a twin-engined aircraft on an easterly heading and went after it with his wingman. It was a twin-engined Ilyushin Il-12 transport, a type not previously encountered in Korea. Whether the pilot had decided to take a short cut across the narrow salient of Korean territory jutting into Manchuria at this point, or whether he was flying supplies to one of the North Korean airfields, will never be known. Parr made two firing passes and the Il-12 crashed in flames. It was the last communist aircraft to be destroyed in the Korean War, and Captain Parr's tenth victory.

After dark, two 98th BW B-29s, supported by two 91st SRS RB-29s, flew from Japan to drop psychological warfare leaflets over North Korea. It was Bomber Command's last combat mission in the theatre. At 2136 a B-26 of the 3rd Bombardment Wing's 8th Squadron – the same squadron that had flown the UN's first bombing mission against a North Korean target three years earlier – flew its last sortie, dropping its bombs on enemy troops near the front line. A few minutes later an RB-26 of the 67th TRW flew southwards through the dark after a final reconnaissance sortie over the North. All other UN aircraft were now south of the 38th Parallel, or more than three miles from the Korean coast.

It was exactly 2200 as the RB-26 crossed the Parallel. All along the front, the guns were silent.

146

CHAPTER 20

Conclusions

US Army H-19C transporting wounded Allied prisoners-of-war at the 121st Evacuation Hospital near Seoul during Operation 'Big Switch', the repatriation of the PoWs after the armistice. (via Robert F. Dorr)

The armistice of 27 June 1953 brought to an end one of the bloodiest, dirtiest conflicts in modern history. It had lasted for a little over three years, during which casualty figures had reached appalling proportions. South Korea had suffered 300,000 military casualties – killed, wounded and missing; American casualties were 142,000, and those of the other UN Allies 17,000. British Commonwealth losses were over 7,000. Chinese and North Korean casualties were estimated by the UN Command to be as high as two million, while the civilian casualties in both North and South Korea were in the order of a million and a quarter.

It was a war that had been started by naked, armed aggression, and was ended by politicians; a war of wholesale and often pointless slaughter as thousands died for the possession of an insignificant hill. It was a conflict of alien mentalities that time and again overturned tactics and strategy which, over the years, had been carefully formulated to combat potential enemies who might be expected to make their moves according to accepted military doctrine. The enemy in Korea was different. His strategy was often totally illogical from the military point of view yet, with hindsight, frighteningly logical in that it always formed the key to some psychological jigsaw puzzle. He was incredibly resilient; he could be fought to a standstill, yet not even overwhelming firepower could inflict a decisive defeat upon him, a fact that the Americans found hard to accept given their earlier experiences against the Japanese. The difference, of course, was that Japan's supply lines, and the sources of her supplies, were clearly defined. Almost from the beginning her sea communications were under constant and crippling attack by Allied submarines, and from the moment the Japanese Home Islands came within striking distance of American heavy bombers – and, later, carrier-borne aircraft – her war effort was doomed. The war in Korea presented an entirely different set of problems in that the principal communist supply bases were immune to attack of any kind because of the restrictions imposed by the Pentagon.

Insofar as the use of air power is concerned, any real appraisal of its contribution to the UN effort in the Korean War tends to be confused by the overwhelming victory of the United Nations fighter pilots over the communist air forces. An overall assessment, however, reveals that Allied air power, apart from blunting the impetus of the communist offensives, never played a decisive part at any time of the conflict; in fact, the ingenuity of FEAF in devising new methods of knocking out enemy targets was outweighed by the communists' ingenuity in patching them up again. Moreover, the results that were achieved must be weighed against the fact that in three years of war the Americans lost the equivalent of twenty combat wings – in other words, roughly a quarter of the USAF's total first-line strength as it stood in June 1950.

Whether air power *might* have been a decisive factor is a different matter; whether far more impressive results might have been achieved had the full weight of the Allied air forces been unleashed on targets in Manchuria is a matter for conjecture. The one thing that does seem certain is that right from the outset, the Allied strategists underestimated China's reaction to the threat of nuclear attack. In fact it was not until the spring of 1953, when the Americans made it clear they were prepared to extend the war into China, using nuclear weapons if necessary, that they fully realised the power of the atomic bomb as a political weapon in forcing the communists to conclude an armistice. Later, Admiral C. Turner Joy, C-in-C Naval Forces Far East, wrote that, 'The threat of atomic bombs was posed. Defeat for Red China became a possibility. In understandable prudence they took the only step open to them to remove the growing threat of a holocaust. It was as simple as that. It had always been as simple as that.'

But it was not as simple as that. The real factor that persuaded China to review her stance at the negotiating table was the death, on 5 March 1953, of Soviet Premier Josef Stalin, an event rapidly followed by a full reappraisal of Soviet policy towards the Korean conflict and the withdrawal of Russian combat units and advisers from Manchuria. Faced with the swift withdrawal of Soviet support for the continuation of the war – and that included the elimination of any possibility that the Russians might be persuaded to carry out retaliatory nuclear attacks on UN targets – the Chinese and North Korean negotiators immediately began to make concessions at Panmunjom.

Any analysis of the causes of the Korean War leads to the inescapable conclusion that the communists would not have risked aggression had it not been for the dangerously weak state of the Allied forces in the Far East. In Europe, the Berlin Blockade of 1948–9 had helped to bring the West to its senses, and the newly formed Atlantic Alliance was quickly forming a defensive barrier against Soviet expansion in Europe, but that barrier was only created at the expense of defence assets elsewhere, particularly the Far East. Before June 1950, few US politicians realised how ill-equipped the United States armed forces had become in the five years since the end of World War Two. The lessons of the Korean War, revealing as they did many deficiencies, gave rise to a whole range of new military and strategic policies, not least of which was the birth of the deterrent – the threat of massive nuclear retaliation which has remained the West's biggest single insurance against global war ever since. The lessons learned in combat formed the basis of a new military technology out of which were borne the awesome weapons systems of the 1960s.

The Korean War had a dramatic effect on the organisation and equipment of both the USAF and the Soviet Air Force. Strategic Air Command, which had already begun re-equipping some of its B-29 medium bomber Wings with the improved B-50 when hostilities broke out, now quickly phased out the rest of its B-29 bombers, converting some to the flight refuelling tanker role, and by the end of 1954 they had been entirely replaced by the Boeing B-47 Stratojet. In 1955 the heavy bomber Wings, then equipped with the huge Convair B-36, began to re-equip with the Boeing B-52 Stratofortress. To facilitate rapid deployment, and to extend the range of the SAC bomber force, the SAC tanker fleet was also greatly expanded, with orders placed for KC-135 jet tankers to replace the Command's existing KB-50s and KC-97s, both of which had superseded the KB-29s. By the beginning of 1957 Strategic Air Command's strength had grown to eleven heavy bomber wings, twenty-eight medium bomber wings, and five strategic reconnaissance Wings, supported by forty flight refuelling squadrons.

The Russians, meanwhile, had viewed the losses sustained by the USAF's B-29s over Korea with concern; their sole strategic bomber, the Tupolev Tu-4 Bull, had been copied from B-29s that had come down on Soviet territory after raids on Japan in World War Two. Late in 1952 the Tupolev design bureau began work on a strategic jet bomber that was to emerge as the Tu-16 Badger, which was roughly the equivalent of the B-47, and during the next two years two strategic heavy bombers, the Myasishchev Mya-4 Bison and the Tupolev Tu-95 Bear, also made their appearance. Although the Russians had three modern strategic bomber types in service by the late 1950s, it is extremely unlikely that the Soviet Strategic Air Force, the Dalnaya Aviatsiya (DA), could have used them to inflict unacceptable damage on the United States during this period. They had no flight refuelling capability (it was first fitted in a version of the Bear in the early 1960s) and geography was not in their favour: their forward bases on the northern coast along the Arctic Ocean and on the Arctic islands of Severnaya Zemlya, Novaya Zemlya and Franz Josef Land were more than offset by US bases ringing the Soviet Union. Also, the strategic bombers in the DA's fleet never matched those in SAC's in numerical terms. The Russians, in fact, were doing little more than responding to American advances in strategic weapons, and it was not until the 1960s that they attempted to jump ahead by placing their reliance on intercontinental ballistic missiles (ICBMs) rather than on manned bombers.

Great changes also swept through the USAF Tactical Air Command as a result of the Korean War. Before the end of 1953 TAC's remaining F-51 and F-80 units had equipped with F-86F fighter bombers, followed by the nuclear-capable F-86H. The long-suffering B-26s had to soldier on for a while longer, but by the middle of 1954 these units had begun to receive the Martin B-57 Canberra, which in turn gave way to the F-100 Super Sabre from 1957. Also in 1954 TAC began to receive swept-wing F-84F Thunderstreaks to replace its Thunderjets, many of which were assigned to European NATO air forces. Later, from the same Republic Aviation stable, came the F-105 Thunderchief, TAC's first true weapons system. The Russians, always tactically minded, fielded the Sukhoi Su-7 Fitter, which replaced ground attack versions of the MiG-15 and MiG-17 – neither of which was suited to the role – from 1956. The Fitter, which was also widely exported, became the standard Soviet tactical support fighter-bomber, and remained so for two decades in a number of developed versions. On both sides of the Iron Curtain three years of jet combat experience over the Yalu was woven into the designs of new air interceptors. In the United States, the agile brain of Lockheed's Clarence Johnson and his design team gave birth to the revolutionary F-104 Starfighter, while Russia's answer was the MiG-21. All-weather fighters, too, assumed high priority: in 1955 the USAF received the first examples of the Convair F-102 Delta Dagger, the outcome of a USAF requirement dating back to 1950, and in the following year Soviet air defence squadrons received the Yakovlev Yak-25 Flashlight.

One major problem that had manifested itself in Korea was strategic reconnaissance. The Americans solved it by developing two types of aircraft: the RB-57, a greatly modified high-altitude version of the Canberra, and the purpose-built Lockheed U-2. But it was in two other areas that the Korean War probably had its greatest impact. The first was in the tactical transport field. Korea had shown the need for a transport aircraft with a large load-carrying capacity that could operate from rough airstrips, and again it was Lockheed that came up with the answer in the C-130 Hercules, the most versatile transport aircraft ever designed. The second involved the multi-role combat aircraft, and

here it was the US Navy that provided the lead. The Korean War had proved beyond all doubt that the fast attack carrier was still the most vital unit in modern naval warfare; at the same time, the deficiencies of the Navy's standard jet types – the F9F Panther and the F2H Banshee – over Korea had aroused serious misgivings, and propeller-driven attack types could no longer hope to survive in a hostile fighter environment. These shortcomings gave rise to a US Navy requirement for an aircraft that could take over the task of the Skyraider, carry a substantial weapons load – including nuclear weapons – at a speed twice that of the conventional aircraft, and stand in as an interceptor when the need arose. The result was the remarkable Douglas A-4 Skyhawk, which was rolled out of Douglas's El Segundo factory only nineteen months after its inception and which flew for the first time in June 1954. At the same time, work went ahead on what was to become the world's first multi-role supersonic combat aircraft – the McDonnell F-4 Phantom.

But the real lesson of the Korean War was this. If you want to kill a snake, you must cut off its head, and in terms of military air power that means destroying an enemy's capacity to wage war by a sustained air offensive against his centres of war production and supply. That was never possible in Korea, where the relevant industries were elsewhere. Nor was it possible in Vietnam, where exactly the same was true fifteen years later.

Yellow stripes painted on this US Army Sikorsky H-19C, hovering over a vessel in Inchon harbour in 1953, indicate that it is being used to fly missions in the truce zone at Panmunjom. (via Robert F. Dorr)

APPENDIX 1

Air Aces of The Korean War

Name & Rank	Unit	A/c	Score	Remarks	Name & Rank	Unit	A/c	Score	Remarks
McConnell, Capt. Joseph	51st FIW	F-86	16	KIFA 25.8.54	Gabreski, Col Francis S.	4th/51st FIWs	F-86	6½	+ 28 Ger in WW2
Jabara, Lt-Col James	4th FIW	F-86	15	+3½ Ger in WW2	Adams, Maj. Donald E.	51st FIW	F-86	6½	KIFA 1952
Fernandez, Capt. Manuel J	4th FIW	F-86	14½		Jones, Col George L.	4th/51st FIWs	F-86	6½	
Davis, Lt-Col George A.	4th FIW	F-86	14	KIA 10.2.52 Post MoH. 7 Jap WW2	Love, Capt. Robert J.	4th FIW	F-86	6	
Baker, Col Royal N.	4th FIW	F-86	13	+ 3½ Ger in WW2	Bolt, Lt-Col John F. (USMC)	51st FIW (Att)	F-86	6	+ 6 Jap WW2
Blesse, Maj. Frederick C.	4th FIW	F-86	10		Kasler, Lt James H.	4th FIW	F-86	6	
Fischer, Capt. Harold E.	51st FIW	F-86	10	PoW 7.4.53	Whisner, Maj. William T.	51st FIW	F-86	5½	+ 5½ Ger in WW2
Johnson, Col James K.	4th FIW	F-86	10	+ 1 Ger WW2	Baldwin, Col Robert P.	51st FIW	F-86	5	
Garrison, Lt-Col Vermont	4th FIW	F-86	10	+ 7 Ger WW2	Becker, Capt. Richard S.	4th FIW	F-86	5	
Moore, Maj. Lonnie R.	4th FIW	F-86	10	KIFA 10.1.56	Bettinger, Maj. Stephen L.	4th FIW	F-86	5	+ 1 Ger WW2
Parr, Capt. Ralph S.	4th FIW	F-86	10		Bordelon, Lt Guy P. (USN)	VC-3	F4U-5N	5	Po-2s; only USN ace of Korean War
Low, Lt James F.	4th FIW	F-86	9		Creighton, Lt-Col Richard D.	4th FIW	F-86	5	+ 2 Ger WW2
Foster, Lt Cecil G.	51st FIW	F-86	9		Curtin, Capt. Clyde A.	4th FIW	F-86	5	
Hagerstrom, Lt-Col James P.	51st FIW	F-86	8½	+ 6 Jap WW2	Gibson, Capt Ralph D.	4th FIW	F-86	5	
Risner, Maj. Robinson	4th FIW	F-86	8		Kincheloe, Capt. Iven C.	51st FIW	F-86	5	
Ruddell, Col George I.	51st FIW	F-86	8		Latshaw, Capt. Robert T.	4th FIW	F-86	5	
Jolley, Capt. Clifford D.	4th Fiw	F-86	7		Moore, Capt. Robert H.	51st FIW	F-86	5	
Lilley, Capt. Leonard W.	4th FIW	F-86	7		Overton, Capt. Dolphin D.	51st FIW	F-86	5	
Buttelmann, Lt Henry	51st FIW	F-86	7		Thyng, Col Harrison R.	4th FIW	F-86	5	+ 6 Ger and Jap WW2
Marshall, Lt-Col Winton W.	4th FIW	F-86	6½	4½ MiGs, 1 Tu-2, 1 La-9	Wescott, Maj. William H.	51st FIW	F-86	5	

APPENDIX II

Some Other Notable Air Combat Victories

(ALL KILLS MiG-15s UNLESS OTHERWISE STATED)

Name & Rank	Unit	A/C	Score	Remarks
Colman, Lt Philip E.	4th FIW	F-86	4	+ 5 Jap in CBI Theatre in WW2
Mitchell, Lt-Col John W.	51st FIW	F-86	4	+ 11 Jap in WW2
Mattson, Capt. Conrad E.	4th FIW	F-86	4	+ 1 Jap in WW2
Preston, Col Benjamin S.	4th FIW	F-86	4	
Price, Lt-Col Harold L.	51st FIW	F-86	4	
Samways, Lt-Col William T.	8th FBG	F-80	4	
Heller, Maj. Edwin L.	51st FIW	F-86	3½	+ 5½ Ger in WW2
Mahurin, Col Walker M.	51st FIW	F-86	3½	+ 21 Ger in WW2
Arnell, Maj. Zane S.	4th FIW	F-86	3	
Chandler, Maj. Van E.	51st FIW	F-86	3	+ 5 Ger in WW2
Glenn, Maj. John H.	51st FIW (Att)	F9F	3	Future US astronaut
Glover, Flg Off Ernest A.	4th FIW (RCAF)	F-86 (Att)	3	
Harris, Maj. Elmer W.	51st FIW	F-86	3	+ 3 Yak-9s on ground
Kratt, Lt Jacob	27th FEW	F-84	3	2 MiGs, 1 Yak-9
Raebel, Lt-Col James B.	4th FIW	F-86	3	
Kelly, Lt-Col Albert S.	51st FIW	F-86	2½	
Brueland, Maj. Lowell K.	51st FIW	F-86	2	+ 12½ Ger WW2
DeLong, Capt. Philip (USMC)	VMF-312	F4U-4	2	Yak-9s
Eagleston, Lt-Col Glenn T.	4th FIW	F-86	2	+ 18½ Ger WW2
Fox, Lt Orrin R.	80th FBS	F-51	2	Both Yak-9s
Hulse, Sqn Ldr Graham S	4th FIW (RAF) (Att)	F-86	2	
McElroy, Lt-Col Carroll B.	4th FIW	F-86	2	

Name & Rank	Unit	A/C	Score	Remarks
Meyer, Col John C.	4th FIW	F-86	2+	24 Ger in WW2
Wayne, Lt Robert E.	35th FBS	F-80	2	Both Il-10s
Amen, Lt-Cdr W.T.	VF-111	F9F	1	First Navy pilot to shoot down a jet aircraft
Andre, Lt John W. (USMC)	VMF(N)-513	F4U-5N	1	Yak-9 (night) + 4 Jap in WW2
Bertram, Lt-Col William E.	523rd FES	F-84	1	First F-84 kill
Best, Lt-Col Jack R.	51st FIW	F-86	1	
Brown, Lt Russell J.	51st FIW	F-80	1	First MiG-15 shot down
Burns, Lt Richard J.	35th FBS	F-80	1	Yak-9
Carmichael, Lt Peter (RN)	802 Sqn	Sea Fury	1	First piston engined a/c to destroy a MiG-15
Chandler, Capt. Kenneth D.	4th FIW	F-86	1	+ 4 MiGs on ground
Daigh, Lt H.	VMF-312	F4U-4	1	Yak-9
Dewald, Lt Robert H.	35th FBS	F-80	1	Il-10
Dickinson, Flg Off R.T.F. (RAF)	4th FIW (Att)	F-86	1	
Emmert, Maj. Benjamin H.	4th FIW	F-86	1	+ 6 Ger in WW2
Fithian, Capt. Ben L. and Lyons, Lt Sam R. (RIO)	319th FIS	F-94	1	La-9 (night) First F-94 kill
Folmar, Capt. Jesse (USMC)	VMA-312	F4U-4B	1	Only Corsair MiG kill
Gogerly, Flg Off Bruce (RAAF)	77 Sqn	Meteor Mk 8	1	
Granville-White, Flt Lt J.H. (RAF)	51st FIW	F-86 (Att)	1	
Hale, Sgt John (RAAF)	77 Sqn	Meteor Mk 8	1	(+1 damaged)
Harrison, Lt J.B.	18th FBG	F-51	1	Yak-9

Some Other Notable Air Combat Victories

(ALL KILLS MiG-15s UNLESS OTHERWISE STATED)

Name & Rank	Unit	A/C	Score	Remarks
Heyman, Capt. Richard	8th BS	B-26	1	Yak-9
Hinton, Lt-Col Bruce H.	4th FIW	F-86	1	First Sabre pilot to shoot down MiG-15
Hockerey, Capt. John J.	51st FIW	F-86	1	+ 7 Ger in WW2
Hovde, Maj. William J.	4th FIW	F-86	1	+ 10½ Ger in WW2
Hudson, Lt William G.	68th FS (AW)	F-82	1	Yak-9
Keyes, Lt-Col Ralph E.	51st FIW	F-86	1	
Kinsey, Lt Raymond J.	4th FIW	F-86	1	Tu-2
La France, Flt Lt Claude A. (RCAF)	4th FIW	F-86 (Att)	1	
Lamb, Lt William E. (USN)	VF-111	F-9F	1	+ 5 Jap in WW2
LaVene, Cpl Harry J.	31st SRS	RB-29 (Gunner)	1	First MiG-15 kill by B-29 gunner
Levesque, Flt Lt J.A.O. (RCAF)	51st FIW (Att)	F-86	1	
Lindsay, Sqn Ldr James D. (RCAF)	51st FIW (Att)	F-86	1	
Little, Maj. James W. (RIO)	339th FS (AW)	F-82	1	Yak-9; also 5 E/A WW2
Long, Capt. Edwin B. (USMC) and WO Buckingham, R.C. (RIO)	VMF (N) 513	F7F	1	Po-2; first F7F Tigercat kill
Lovell, Flt Lt J.H.J. (RAF)	4th FIW (Att)	F-86	1	
McGuire, Capt. Allen	27th FEW	F-84	1	
McKay, Sqn Ldr John (RCAF)	4th FIW (Att)	F-86	1	
Marsh, Lt Roy W.	8th FBW	F-80	1	Il-10
Martin, Col Maurice L.	18th FBW	F-86	1	
Mickley, S/Sgt Nyle S.	3rd BG	B-26 (Gunner)	1	Yak-9; first E/A shot down by air gunner in Korea (29.6.50)
Middleton, Lt (JG) J.D. (USN)	VF-781	F9F-5	1	SovAF-MiG-15
Moran, Lt Charles B.	8th FIW	F-82	1	Yak-9
Mullins, Maj. Arnold	67th FBS	F-51	1	Yak-9
Norris, Lt William T.	8th FBW	F-80	1	La-7
Plog, Lt L.H. (USN)	VF-51	F9F	1	Yak-9: first USN kill in Korea
Sandlin, Lt Harry T.	80th FBS	F-51	1	Yak-9
Schillereff, Capt. Raymond E.	35th FBS	F-80	1	Il-10
Schirra, Lt Walter (USN)	136th FBW (Att)	F-84	1	Later US astronaut
Simmonds, Flg Off W. (RAAF)	77 Sqn	Meteor Mk 8	1	
Skeen, Capt. Kenneth L.	49th FBG	F-84	1	
Slaughter, Capt. William W.	27th FEW	F-84	1	
Stratton, Maj. William T. and Hoglind, M/Sgt Hans (USMC)	VMF(N)-513	F3D-2N	1	First Sky-night kill. Listed Yak-15, but probably Yak-9
Thomas, Lt John B.	36th FBS	F-80	1	Yak-9
Van Grundy, Maj E.A.	VMF(N)-513	F7F-3N	1	Po-2
Visscher, Lt Herman W.	51st FIW	F-86	1	+ 5 E/A in WW2
Williams, Lt E.R. (USN)	VF-781	F9F-5	1	SovAF MiG-15
Wurster, Lt Charles A.	36th FBS	F-80	1	Yak-9
Young, Lt Sam P.	51st FIW	F-86	1	Last MiG destroyed in Korea

APPENDIX III
Orders of Battle

FEAF ORDER OF BATTLE, 1 JULY 1950

Fifth Air Force (Japan)

Base	Units	Equipment
Ashiya	8th FBS	F-80C
	3rd ARS 'D' Flt	SB-17, L-5, H-5
Itazuke	8th FBG:	
	35th FBS	F-80C
	36th FBS	F-80C
	80th FBS	F-80C
	9th FBS	F-80C
	4th FAWS	F-82
	68th FAWS	F-82
	339th FAWS	F-82
Iwakuni	3rd BG:	
	8th BS	B-26
	13th BS	B-26
	No. 77 Sqn RAAF	F-51 (Att Fifth AF)
Johnson	3rd ARS 'A' Flt	SB-17
Misawa	49th FBG:	
	7th FBS	F-80C
Tachikawa	374th TCG:	
	6th TCS	C-54
	21st TCS	C-54
	22nd TCS	C-54
Yokota	35th FIG:	
	39th FIS	F-80C
	40th FIS	F-80C
	41st FIS	F-80C
	8th TRS	RF-80A
	512nd WRS	WB-29
	339th FAWS	F-82
	3rd ARS 'D' Flt	SB-17, L-5, H-5

Thirteenth Air Force

Clark (Luzon)	18th FBG	F-80C

Twentieth Air Force

Andersen (Guam)	19th BG	B-29
Kadena (Okinawa)	31st SRS	RB-29 (SAC unit)
Naha (Okinawa)	4th FAWS	F-82
	(2 Flts)	

FIFTH AIR FORCE ORDER OF BATTLE, 31 DECEMBER 1950

Chinhae (K-10)	18th FBG:	
	12th FBS	F-51
	67th FBS	F-51
	No. 2 Sqn SAAF	F-51
Kimpo (K-14)	51st FIG:	
	16th FIS	F-80C
	25th FIS	F-80C
	336th FIS	F-86A
Pusan East (K-9)	35th FIG:	
	39th FIS	F-51
	40th FIS	F-51
	No. 77 Sqn RAAF	F-51
	VMF-311	F-9F
Seoul (K-16)	6147th TacCon Sqn	T-6
Taegu (K-2)	49th FBG:	
	7th FBS	F-80C
	8th FBS	F-80C
	9th FBS	F-80C
	543rd Tac Spt Gp:	
	8th TRS	RF-80A
	45th TRS	RF-51
	162nd TRS	RB-26
	6166th AWRS	RB-26
Itami	1st Marine Air Wing:	
	VMF-312	F4U
	VMF-214	F4U
Itazuke	27th FEG:	
	522nd FES	F-84E
	523rd FES	F-84E
	524th FES	F-84E
	68th FAWS	F-82
	4th FAWS (1 Flt)	F-82
	8th FBG:	
	35th FBS	F-80C
	36th FBS	F-80C
	80th FBS	F-80C
	VMF(N)-513	F4U-5N, F7F-3N
	VMF(N)-542	F4U-5N
Iwakuni	3rd BW(L):	
	8th BS	B-26
	13th BS	B-26
	731st BS	B-26

Orders of Battle

Johnson	4th FIG:	
	334th FIS	F-86A
	335th FIS	F-86A
Miho	452nd BW(L):	
	728th BS	B-26
	729th BS	B-26
	730th BS	B-26

FIFTH AIR FORCE ORDER OF BATTLE, 1 JUNE 1952

K-2 (Taegu)	HQ Fifth AF (Rear)	
	49th FBW	F-84
	136th FBW	F-84
	6149th Hospital Group	
	9th Stat Savs Flt	
	417th Eng Avn Brig	
	6151st Air Base Sqn	
K-3 (Pohang)	1st MAW	F-4U, F-9F, F-7F
K-4	6146th Air Base Sqn	
	HQ ROK Air Force	
K-6	MAG 12	F4U, F9F, AD-4
K-8 (Kusan)	3rd BW (L)	B-26
K-9 (Pusan East)	17th BW (L)	B-26
	930th Eng Avn Gp	
K-10 (Chinhae)	18th FBW (Rear)	F-51
	No. 2 Sqn SAAF	F-51
K-13 (Suwon)	8th FBW	F-80
	51st FIW	F-86
	319th FIS	F-94
	934th Eng Avn Gp	
K-14 (Kimpo)	4th FIW	F-86
	67th TRW	RB-26, RF-51, RF-80
	No. 77 Squadron RAAF	Meteor Mk 8
K-16 (Seoul)	HQ Fifth AF (Forward)	
	6167th Ops Sqn	
	5th Mtr Trans Av Sqn	
	931 Eng Avn Gp	
	1st Epidemiological Flt	

	1st Shoran Beacon Sqn	
	5th Comm Gp	
	10th Liaison Sqn	
	30 AWS WB-26	
	44th Sig Avn Const Bn	
	502nd Tac Con Gp	
	1818th AACS Gp	
	6154th Air Base Gp	
	6167th Air Base Gp	
K-18 (Kangnung)	6152nd Air Base Gp	
K-47 (Chunchon)	6147th Tac Con Gp T-6	
Itazuke	8th, 49th, 136th FBWs, 67th TRW (Detachments)	
Miho	3rd, 17th BWs and 67th TRW (Detachments)	
Tsuiki	4th and 51st FIWs (Detachments)	

UN AIR FORCES ORDER OF BATTLE, 31 JULY 1953

K-1 (Pusan)	17th BW(L) Det 1	B-26
	6152nd Air Base Sqn	
	366th Eng Avn Battn	
K-2 (Taegu)	58th FBW	F-84
	1818th AACS Gp	
	6156th Air Base Sqn	
	6157th Air Base Sqn	
K-3 (Pohang)	1st MAW	F4U, F2H, F9F, AD2
K-5 (Pyongtaek)	MAG 12	F4U, AD2
	1st Shoran Bcn Sqn	
K-8 (Kusan)	3rd BW(L)	B-26
	49th FBW	F-84
K-10 (Chinhae)	7th Air Depot Wing	
K-13 (Suwon)	8th FBW	F-86F
	51st FIW	F-86F
	319th FIS	F-94
	VMF(N)-513	F3D
K-14 (Kimpo)	4th FIW	F-86F
	67th TRW	RF-80, RB-26, RF-86
	No. 77 Sqn RAAF	Meteor 8
	6166th AWR	RB-26

APPENDIX III
Orders of Battle

K-16 (Seoul)	6167th Ops Sqn	
	6167th Air Base Gp	
	6154th Air Base Gp	
	30th AWS	
	10th Liaison Sqn	L-5, L-19, L-20
	(Serving 5th AF HQ)	
K-18 (Kangnung)	ROK Air Force (Combat Wing)	F-51
K-37 (Taegu West)	930th Eng.Avn Gp	
K-46 (Hoengsong)	6155th Air Base Group	
K-47 (Chunchon)	6147th TacCon Gp	T-6
K-55 (Osan)	18th FBW	F-86F
	No. 2 Sqn SAAF	F-86F
	934th Eng.Avn Gp	

NAVAL AIR FORCES

US Aircraft Carriers Operationally Involved

Antietam (CV-36)
Badoeng Strait (CVE-116)
Bataan (CVL-29)
Bairoko (CVE-115)
Bon Homme Richard (CV-31)
Boxer (CV-21)
Essex (CV-9)
Kearsarge (CV-33)
Lake Champlain (CV-38)
Leyte (CV-32)
Oriskany (CV-34)
Philippine Sea (CV-47)
Princeton (CV-37)
Sicily (CVE-118)
Valley Forge (CV-45)

Note: Carriers were redesignated from CV to CVA (attack carrier) and CVB (large aircraft carrier) on 1 October 1952.

US Naval Air Units in the Korean War

Unit	Aircraft	Remarks
HU-1	HO3S-1	Air-sea rescue
VA-35	AD-3	
VA-55	AD-4	
VA-65	AD-4	
VA-75	AD-4	
VA-115	AD-4	
VA-195	AD-4	
VA-702	AD-2/4	Reserve Sqn (Dallas)
VA-728	AD-4	Reserve Sqn (Glenview)
VA-923	AD-3	Reserve Sqn (St Louis)
VC-3	AD-3N/F4U-5N	
VC-4	F4U-5N	
VC-6	F4U-5N	
VC-11	AD-4W	
VC-12	AD-4W	
VC-33	AD-4B	
VC-35	AD-4B/AD-4NL	
VC-61	F9F-2P	Photo reconnaissance
VF-11	F2H-2	
VF-22	F2H-2	
VF-24	F9F-5	
VF-31	F2H-2	
VF-32	F4U-4	
VF-51	F9F-3	
VF-52	F9F-3	
VF-53	F4U-4	
VF-54	F4U-4	
VF-62	F2H-2	
VF-63	F4U-4	
VF-64	F4U-4	
VF-72	F9F-2	
VF-91	F9F-2	
VF-111	F9F-2	
VF-112	F9F-2	
VF-113	F9F-2	
VF-114	F4U-4B	
VF-172	F2H-2	
VF-191	F9F-2	
VF-192	F4U-4	
VF-193	F4U-4	
VF-194	AD-2/3	
VF-653	F4U-4	Reserve Sqn (Akron)
VF-713	F4U-4	Reserve Sqn (Denver)
VF-721	F9F-2	Reserve Sqn (Glenview)
VF-781	F9F-2	Reserve Sqn (Los Alamitos)
VF-783	F4U-4	Reserve Sqn (Los Alamitos)
VF-791	F4U-4	Reserve Sqn (Memphis)
VF-821	F9F-2	Reserve Sqn
VF-831	F9F-2	Reserve Sqn (New York)
VF-837	F9F-2	Reserve Sqn (New York)
VF-884	F4U-4	Reserve Sqn (Olathe)
VP-6	P2V-2	
VP-9	PB4Y-2	
VP-42	PBM-5	
VP-47	PBM-5	
VP-772	PB4Y-2	Reserve Sqn (Los Alamitos)

APPENDIX III
Orders of Battle

VP-871	PB4Y-2	
VU-3	F6F5K	Radio-guided drone unit

US Marine Corps Air Units in the Korean War

Hedron-1	F4U-4B, TBM-3	Headquarters Sqn
Hedron-12	F4U-5P	Headquarters Sqn
HMR-161	HRS-1	Transport Helicopter Sqn
VMA-121	AD-3	Reserve Sqn: 'Wolf Raiders'
VMC-1	AD-2Q	ECM Sqn
VMF-115	F9F-2	
VMF-212	F4U-4B	'Devilcats'
VMF-214	F4U-4B	
VMF-311	F9F-2B	First USMC all-jet Sqn
VMF-312	F4U-4	'Checkerboards'
VMF-323	F4U-4B	'Deathrattlers'
VMF-332	F4U-4B	
VMF(N)-513	F4U-5N, F7F-3N F3D-2	
VMF(N)-542	F7F-3N,F3D-2	
VMJ-1	F2H-2P	Photo reconnaissance
VMO-6	HO3S-1, OY-2, OE-1, HTL-4	
VMR-152	R5D	Transport/airborne command

Note: USMC VMF squadrons were later redesignated VMA.

British Commonwealth Air Units in the Korean War

Unit	Aircraft	Remarks
No. 2 'Cheetah' Sqn SAAF	F-51, F-86F	Attached 18th FBW, Fifth AF
No. 30 Transport Unit RAAF	Dakota	Part of No. 91 (Composite) Wing, Iwakuni
No. 36 Sqn RAAF	Dakota	No. 91 (Composite) Wing, Iwakuni
No. 77 Sqn RAAF	F-51, Meteor Mks 7 and 8	
No. 88 Sqn RAF	Sunderland	Far East Flying Boat Wing
No. 209 Sqn RAF	Sunderland	Far East Flying Boat Wing
No. 391 Base Sqn RAAF		No. 91 (Composite) Wing
No. 426 Sqn RCAF	North Star (C-54)	Carried out airlift in support of Commonwealth Div throughout war
No. 800 Sqn, FAA	Seafire 47	HMS *Triumph*
No. 801 Sqn, FAA	Sea Fury	HMS *Glory*
No. 802 Sqn, FAA	Sea Fury	HMS *Ocean*
No. 804 Sqn, FAA	Sea Fury	HMS *Glory*
No. 805 Sqn, FAA	Sea Fury	HMAS *Sydney*
No. 807 Sqn, FAA	Sea Fury	HMS *Theseus*
No. 808 Sqn, FAA	Sea Fury	HMAS *Sydney*
No. 810 Sqn, FAA	Firefly 5	HMS *Theseus*
No. 812 Sqn, FAA	Firefly 5	HMS *Glory*
No. 817 Sqn, FAA	Firefly 5	HMAS *Sydney*
No. 820 Sqn, FAA	Firefly 5	HMS *Glory*
No. 825 Sqn, FAA	Firefly 5	HMS *Ocean*
No. 827 Sqn, FAA	Firefly FR1	HMS *Triumph*
No. 1903 AOP Flt	Auster AOP 6	
No. 1913 Light Liaison Flt	Auster AOP 6, L-19	

APPENDIX IV
Statistics

FAR EAST AIR FORCES

Sorties Flown:

Interdiction	192,581
Close support	57,665
Counterair	66,997
Air supply	181,659
Miscellaneous	222,078
Total	720,980

Bombs Dropped (Tons)	386,037
Napalm Dropped (Tons)	32,357
Rocket Rounds Fired	313,600
Smoke Rockets	55,797
MG Ammunition rounds	166,853,100

Air Combat Losses:

F-86 Sabres	78
Others	61
Total	139

Casualties:

	Killed	Wounded	PoW (Repatriated)
Air Operations	1,144	306	214
Ground Operations	36	62	6
Totals:	1,180	368	220

Note: The above statistics include those for No. 2 Sqn SAAF, serving as an integrated unit of the 18th FBW.

US NAVY AND MARINES

Total sorties flown	167,552	Navy
	107,303	Marines
Bombs Dropped (Tons)	120,000	Navy
	82,000	Marines
Rocket Rounds fired	272,000	Navy and Marines

Aircraft Losses (Navy and Marines):

Air Combat	4
Ground Fire	537
Other causes	642
Total	1,183

BRITISH COMMONWEALTH

Royal Navy:

Sorties Flown	22,000
Aircrew Killed	22

No. 77 Sqn RAAF:

Sorties Flown	18,872
Aircrew Killed	42

Total Aircraft Losses, RN/RAAF/SAAF   152

DAMAGE INFLICTED ON ENEMY AIR FORCES, 1950–53

FEAF Claims:

	Destroyed	Possibly Destroyed	Damaged
In the air	900	168	973
On the ground	53	25	36

US Navy Claims:

In the air	16	(including 4 destroyed by Navy pilots flying Sabres)
On the ground	36	

USMC Claims:

In the air	35	(including 15 destroyed by USMC pilots in Sabres)

No 77 Sqn RAAF Claims:
6 (3 while flying F-51s)

Fleet Air Arm Claims:
2

Total E/A destroyed: 1,050

F-86 SABRE 'KILLS' BY AIRCRAFT TYPES

Ilyushin Il-10	1
Lavochkin La-9	6
MiG-15	792
Tupolev Tu-2	9
Others	2

COMMUNIST MATERIEL LOSSES TO UN AIR ATTACK, 1952–3

Tanks	1,327
Vehicles	82,920
Locomotives	963
Railway Cars	10,407
Bridges	1,153
Buildings	118,231
Tunnels	65
Gun Positions	8,663
Bunkers	8,839
Oil Storage Tanks	16
Rail Cuts	28,621

Estimated number of enemy troops killed by air attack:
184,808.